GENERALS IN THE WHITE HOUSE

GENERALS
IN THE
WHITE HOUSE

By
DOROTHY BURNE GOEBEL
and
JULIUS GOEBEL, JR.

Essay Index Reprint Series

BOOKS FOR LIBRARIES PRESS
FREEPORT, NEW YORK

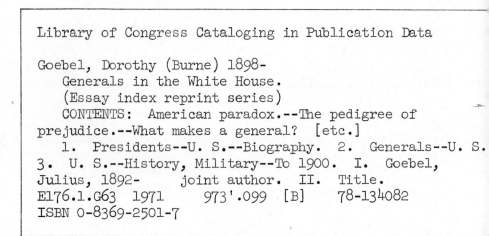
Library of Congress Cataloging in Publication Data

Goebel, Dorothy (Burne) 1898-
  Generals in the White House.
  (Essay index reprint series)
  CONTENTS: American paradox.--The pedigree of
prejudice.--What makes a general? [etc.]
  1. Presidents--U. S.--Biography. 2. Generals--U. S.
3. U. S.--History, Military--To 1900. I. Goebel,
Julius, 1892-   joint author. II. Title.
E176.1.G63 1971   973'.099 [B]   78-134082
ISBN 0-8369-2501-7

PRINTED IN THE UNITED STATES OF AMERICA
BY
NEW WORLD BOOK MANUFACTURING CO., INC.
HALLANDALE, FLORIDA 33009

Acknowledgments

———◄◆►———

THE AUTHORS express their thanks to the New–York Historical Society for permission to use its manuscript and broadside collections, and to quote therefrom. Grateful acknowledgment is likewise made to the following authors, publishers, and authors' representatives, for permission to use the selections indicated:

American Philosophical Society—for some quotations from *Memoirs,* Volume XIV, edited by Albert T. Volwiler.

D. Appleton-Century Company—for quotations from *Campaigning With Grant,* by General Horace Porter.

The Atlantic Monthly Press—for quotations from *Meade's Headquarters 1863–65: Letters of Colonel Theodore Lyman,* edited by George R. Agassiz.

W. H. Bixby—for a selection from his father's book, *Letters of Zachary Taylor,* by William K. Bixby.

Thomas Y. Crowell Company—for quotations from *General Grant's Letters to a Friend 1861–1880,* edited by James Grant Wilson.

Dodd, Mead & Company, Inc.—for selections from *Letters of Mrs. James G. Blaine,* edited by Harriet S. Blaine Beale.

Henry Holt and Company, Inc.—for brief excerpts from *Uncle Joe Cannon, The Story of a Pioneer American,* by L. White Busbey.

Houghton Mifflin Company—for selections from *Diary of Gideon Welles,* edited by John T. Morse, Jr., and from *Congressional Government,* by Woodrow Wilson.

Indiana Magazine of History—for eight lines of verse from that publication.

The Ohio State Archaeological and Historical Society—for selections from *Diary and Letters of Rutherford B. Hayes,* edited by Charles Richard Williams.

Brigadier General John McA. Palmer—for a document in his book *Washington, Lincoln, Wilson—Three War Statesmen.*

Charles Scribner's Sons—for quotations from *Grant and Lee,* by Major General J. F. C. Fuller.

Yale University Press—for quotations from *Life and Letters of James Abram Garfield,* by T. C. Smith.

Contents

List of Maps

GENERALS IN THE WHITE HOUSE

American Paradox

AMERICANS HAVE ALWAYS HAD political misgivings about the man on horseback, yet on many an occasion they have sunk these doubts to make presidents of men who had led others in gallant feats of arms. Of the thirty-two men who have occupied the White House, nine had been generals, four others had held lesser military rank. Our politics have been jeweled with many an inconsistency. There is none which sparkles more brilliantly than this, for it betokens the very human propensity of following the dictate of the heart, despite some sober shaking of the head.

This paradox in our political behavior is a mere offshoot of another paradox more basic and more striking. Devoted as a people to peace more piously than any other upon the globe, we nevertheless have been embroiled in war from the moment of colonization. We are a nation born in war. Since the peace of 1783 we have engaged in five major foreign wars, with some incidental affrays in China and Central America. For four years a disastrous civil war raged within our borders; and for more than a century after independence a running combat of varying intensity was waged with the native Indians.

None of this at any time served to alter the conception of ourselves as devoted to peace. It is a conception which possesses both reality and validity. We have been occupied in warfare but have not permitted ourselves to become consistently preoccupied with war. The currents of opposition in every war may be taken as an exemplification of this. Except for the conflict with Spain, every war in which we have been engaged has been to some degree regarded as a nuisance interfering with the normal pursuits of man. Our wars have been endured because the vestiges of Roundhead fervor still stir in our blood. Said Cromwell, planning the New Model Army, "Let us chuse men warm with regard for their religion, men who shall think it an high degree of impiety to fly before the wicked and profane, to forsake the cause of heaven and prefer safety to truth." The cause of heaven in America has been the cause of liberty, and we have preferred it to safety.

The American feeling about war—and feeling it is—has been reflected in our attitude toward the profession of arms. In the face of a recurrent entanglement in warfare we have nevertheless maintained a posture of great reserve toward the maintenance of a military establishment. When the Republic was founded the decision was made to rest our trust upon the militia, and as an added safeguard authority over it was partitioned between Union and states. A diminutive force of regulars was established by Act of Congress in 1790, but this was done with reluctance and as a necessary provision for a border constabulary. The prevailing fear and distrust of a standing army was too intense for anything more pretentious to be acceptable. Regulars were to be tolerated, but neither affection nor money was to be lavished upon them.

Our history as an independent nation begins thus with a prejudice against a standing army and a predilection for the citizen soldier. Upon this our military policy has been built, and from this policy in action have emerged our military leaders. To them American political parties have repeatedly turned for presidential timber, balancing factors of current availability against the potency of an ingrained suspicion of warriors. The prejudices which underlie our military policy therefore have had potentialities not limited to what has been expressed in laws regulating the size and control of our armed forces. Like the belief in democracy or the "American way," these prejudices have exerted a general political influence and one usually unpredictable. The careers of the generals who have become President cannot be understood without first considering how these notions came into being. This we shall now do.

II

The Pedigree of Prejudice

THE ROOTS OF our military prejudices lie deep in the cold sub-soil of colonial experience—that earth in which so many of our institutions have grown. The seed was sown during the first century of settlement when in England the long-sustained struggle between King and Parliament over army maintenance and control made the soldier's coat the badge of arbitrary authority and the militia the symbol of representative government. The plant was soon enough to spring to life in the New World. It was to flourish forever green because of what was remembranced in the Declaration of Independence:

He has kept among us, in times of peace, Standing Armies, without the Consent of our legislatures.

He has affected to render the Military independent of and superior to the civil power.

Penned as an indictment of George III, these passages, with others that tell of measures intolerable to free men, have stood as warnings of oppression and endure as an everlasting memento of grievance.

The first settlers began their conquest of the American soil in reliance upon their own military power. Trainbands and militia they instituted in imitation of what they had known in England. The obligation of military service was made general. It is true that in the royal colonies a handful of regular soldiers was maintained, but until the French and Indian War (1754–63), the provincial militias were the chief instrument of defense against the savages and against the Frenchmen in Canada.

The decision to eliminate France from the American continent was the signal for the first considerable importation of British regulars to the colonies. They were destined to remain for nearly thirty years. With their advent, trouble began. It began in little ways: troubles about billeting, troubles about requisitions, troubles about brawls, troubles about the police powers of local magistrates. It was enhanced by the obvious contempt of the professional soldiers for the provincial militiamen and their officers. General Wolfe, the conqueror of Quebec, wrote to Sir George Sackville: "The Americans are in general the dirtiest, most contemptible cowardly dogs you can conceive. There is no depending upon 'em in action." On their part the Americans who had been led to the slaughter at Ticonderoga by the incompetent General Abercromby and to the shambles by the booby Braddock might properly wonder about the dependability of the command itself.

Supreme command in the colonies was the perquisite of royal governors and of British generals when designated thereto. The provincial could ordinarily covet no better than a colonelcy in the militia, a rank which conveyed the least of prestige in the eyes of Europeans. The undoubted social luster of the British officers stationed in the American plantations combined with the snobbishness of the profession of arms to produce a feeling of mutual disesteem. Endless and ludicrous quarrels were precipitated by a royal order of 1754 which denied rank to all provincial field officers when serving with similar officers appointed by the Crown, and which settled that all captains and inferior officers in the regulars should outrank provincial officers of the same grade. The colonials who had gone out to fight were resentful. The New England troops on Lake Champlain came close to mutiny, and the protest prepared in 1757 by Washington for the officers of the Virginia Regiment indicates the scope of irritation elsewhere. The words, "We cannot conceive that because we are American we should therefor be deprived of the Benefits common to British subjects," are premonitory of a growing sentiment dangerous to the Crown. Many months later, some amelioration of the situation was effected by William Pitt. But drastic leveling was too much to expect once

General Forbes had written Pitt that his provincial officers "are an extream bad Collection of broken Innkeepers, Horse Jockeys & Indian traders," and that "the Men under them are a direct copy of their Officers."

The frictions of war might have been forgotten in the elation of victory except for the fateful decision to keep the colonies garrisoned and to exact payment for this protection from colonists themselves. In other words, a standing army was to be maintained for which Americans would have to pay taxes. In the conflict over the execution of this policy, revolution was bred. The political struggles over the stamp tax, the tea tax, and the "Intolerable Acts" are familiar. Less so, the continuation of earlier irritations. At headquarters in New York the gaudy officers coin the contemptuous word "mohairs" for the civilian gentlemen. Major Henry Pullen assaults a civilian and suffers the humiliation of an indictment and conviction. The crowning touch is supplied by General Thomas Gage, commander in chief of the British forces. In 1768 he undertook to execute, even as against Governor Sir Henry Moore, orders which he had received respecting precedence of rank. Moore, himself colonial born, objected. The military then arranged a ball at which the issue was forced and which created such "hate and animosities in the minds of His Majesty's subjects here" that the incident had to be taken up with the home authorities.

The transfer of troops to Boston in the fall of 1768, the collisions which culminated first in the Boston Massacre (1770) and finally in the arrival of Gage himself to enforce the isolation of Massachusetts as directed by the Port Bill (1774) filled the colonial cup to the brim. Not many places in America had heard the tramp of well-drilled feet, but the wrathful words of the Declaration of Independence after Lexington, Concord, and Bunker Hill expressed the repugnance for professional armies that was common to all free men.

The opening of hostilities in the Revolution and the dire necessity of relying upon our own military resources did not produce a change of heart regarding a military establishment. The rebelling colonies were little more than a league of states, with the Continental Congress functioning as a distracted moderator. In consequence the supply of soldiers depended largely upon the good intentions of each state, and this in turn was affected by the immediacy of danger. The legislation that looked to the creation of a Continental Army was not of a character to assure more than a framework. About a stout-hearted few the army continually swelled or contracted as enlistments ran out and as militia came and went. Hence Washington's effort to develop a disciplined and cohesive instrument with striking power was a nearly impossible design. The maximum achievement was the creation of state "lines." A United States Army in the sense of a unified organization beyond the control of states was never possible, for the outcry against standing armies was loud even in the hours of most need, and the doctrinaires who sat in committees of safety and state legislatures were no less insistent that the military be utterly subordinate to the civil authority. In the dolorous journals of the Continental Congress, the chatter and quavering over the military arm were incessant. There have been few spectacles more laughable than the debate on this subject while the delegates were lurking in York with only the ragged remnants of the Continentals between them and the British legions at Philadelphia.

If Washington did not succeed in the matter of the army itself, he nevertheless accomplished much in realizing his second purpose—a competent corps of officers. When he arrived to take command of the militiamen at Cambridge in 1775 he was appalled. The men, he wrote, "regarded their officers no more than broomsticks." In the new state militia, as in the colonial, commissioned status was achieved in a variety of ways. Some states, like Massachusetts, provided that officers be elected by their companies; others, like New York, commissioned first by the Provincial Congress and later by the governor. In 1775 general officers in the Continental Army were commissioned by Congress; those lower in rank were to be nominated by the provincial congresses and commissioned by the commander in chief.

The officer problem was never satisfactorily solved as to all ranks, but from the start Washington sought to build a corps of officers upon which he could rely. Not the least of his initial troubles can be traced to the prevailing prejudice and the ineffective democratic preventive against an officer class. Complaining to R. H. Lee about the stupidity of the Massachusetts officers and the difficulty of getting them to execute orders, Washington remarks: "To curry favor with the men (by whom they were chosen and on whose smiles possibly they may think they may again rely) seems to be one of the principal objects of their attention." The commander in chief was indefatigable, yet improvement came but slowly. Bitterly General Greene wrote to Governor Cooke in October 1776 after the disastrous New York operations: "There has been, it must be confessed, some shameful conduct in this army this campaign, in a great measure owing to the bad conduct of the officers." But against such dispiriting testimony can be set the devotion of the men to those who were both brave and skilled—their devotion to Morgan, to Arnold, and to the great commander himself.

It was a merit of the systematic instruction conducted by General Steuben at Valley Forge in 1778 that the effectiveness of the Continental officers was enhanced simultaneously with the disciplining of the troops. What was achieved in the creation of an *esprit de corps* is vibrant in the "Creed Adopted by the Officers of the American Army" at Verplancks Point in 1782:

We believe that there is a Great First Cause by whose almighty will we are formed; and that our business here is to obey the orders of our superiors. We believe that every soldier who does his duty will be happy here, and that every such one who dies in battle, will be happy hereafter. We believe that George Washington is the only fit man in the world to head the American army. We believe that the evacuation of Ticonderoga was one of those strokes which stamp the man who dares to strike them, with everlasting fame. We believe that Baron Steuben has made us soldiers, and that he is capable of forming the whole world into a solid column and deploying it from the center. We believe in his Blue Book. We believe in General Knox and his artillery. And we believe in our bayonets. Amen.

This spirit was stuff too fine to let perish. As the prospect of peace became certain, nostalgia for keeping it in remembrance moved General Knox, in April 1783, to suggest the formation of the association which took the name of the Society of the Cincinnati. Its membership was composed exclusively of officers in army and navy whom the years of common service, hardship, and sacrifice had united. But it was a military order, its perpetuity was assured by the adoption of the hereditary principle, and very soon it was bruited about that the society held secret deliberations upon the state of the Union. Incredible as it may seem, the outcry against the order reached such a pitch in some states that the legislatures began to consider action. In Massachusetts committees of both Assembly and Senate made hostile reports; Connecticut refused to incorporate the local chapter; Rhode Island was reported to have enacted a law disfranchising the members, and a bill to this effect was presented in the North Carolina legislature. A committee of the Continental Congress made a report against granting rights of citizenship to anyone holding a hereditary title, a move that Washington thought was directed at the Cincinnati. Patriot John Adams, who had scolded his way through the war from comparative safety, joined with his cousin Samuel in denunciation. Jefferson drove his sharp pen in opposition, and even Dr. Franklin had derisive things to say. To this ardent fire, fuel was added by the agitation over the pensioning of the officers.

Even before the war was over, Washington had bestirred himself for the compensation of his officers. He had urged half pay for life, distinguishing officers from men, because the latter had received large bounties from the states, donations of lands and arrearages of clothing and pay. Congress had passed a resolution to this effect, but as the war drew to a close, civilian opposition grew clamorous. Proposals for some manner of commutation were debated in Congress, and in 1783 the so-called Commutation Act was passed, providing that in lieu of half pay for life the officers should receive five years' full pay in money, or securities at six per cent per annum, as Congress should find more convenient. Public reaction was painful. It was most bitter in New England, where the papers screamed that an impoverished country would have to be taxed to build up and maintain an aristocracy. A general convention of towns was held at Middletown, Connecticut, where resolutions of protest were passed. A similar plan was attempted but failed in Massachusetts. The storm soon spent itself, but old animosities had been revived. No wonder that in 1784 the Continental Congress voted to disband the army.

Fear of a standing army and suspicion of an officer class in combination had a profound effect upon the terms of the Constitution. It is significant that the Federal power is conceived in terms of defense, that the core of our military might was to be a militia, the sword of the several sovereign states, which the Union could wield only in emergencies. Washington himself believed in the citizen-soldier principle. At the conclusion of the war he had written his *Sentiments on a Peace Establishment* in which he had expounded a plan for a small army of regulars completely in Continental control to be used for garrison duty, and had elaborated his design of a "well-regulated militia" involving consistent and carefully supervised training of the citizen. After the establishment of the Federal Government both parts of this plan were submitted to Congress. That dealing with the standing army was made law in 1790, but a Federal militia act was not passed until 1792. The proposed Federal supervision of training which would have implied a corps of officers not subject to state control was rejected. In consequence our first militia law was a toothless affair which ignored both the Revolutionary experience and the lesson that should have been learned from the inefficiencies of the tiny new United States army. In 1790 the western Indians had given General Harmar a drubbing and had repeated on the luckless General St. Clair. The latter returned to the East amid jeers of the populace in the towns through which he rode. It was after these events that the militia bill was passed. The East disapproved of the Indian War. Anthony Wayne's subsequent brilliant execution of what Washington planned and desired, by creating a winning force out of raw recruits, came two years too late to affect our national military policy. In any event, elation over Wayne's success was canceled by reaction over the use of soldiers to suppress the Whisky Rebellion.

It is difficult at this day to realize how profoundly the national measures for defense were affected by the political predominance of the states as sovereigns and by popular attachment to the militia idea. The Federal Government was driven to the device of the expansible Regular Army, partly because the states retained the prerogative of releasing militia for service (Massachusetts and Connecticut both refused to supply militia in 1812) and partly because of resistance to any Federal peacetime supervision of militia training. As a result the Regular Army became a sort of accordion extended and collapsed by Congress as successive emergencies occurred. It was expanded in 1798 during the French war scare and two years later was reduced in spite of the still threatening aspect of international affairs. The old fears of standing armies had revived.

In Congress, Randolph of Roanoke, making his maiden speech on the bill to reduce the military establishment, ridiculed the regulars as ragamuffins and a body of loungers. Two nights later, at a theater, some marine officers took it upon themselves to make provocative remarks to the congressman, who promptly addressed a protest to President Adams claiming that the independence of the legislature had been attacked. In a special message the letter was laid before Congress, which referred the matter to committee. Its report characterized Randolph's action as a deviation from the ordinary forms of decorum, and Congress passed the proffered resolution that there had been no sufficient cause of complaint. The episode supplied the anti-Federalist papers opportunity for a scathing attack upon commissioned officers and gave to the Army its most bitter-spoken enemy in public life.

The Burr conspiracy and the suspicions that army officers were involved in it did nothing to enhance the prestige of the regulars. The highhanded conduct of General Wilkinson at

New Orleans, when, panicked into clearing his shady coattails, he resorted to arbitrary arrests and to defiance of the courts, received a thorough airing at the trial of Burr. No matter how ill-disposed the citizen might be toward the defendant, it was disquieting to read the bitter words of counsel: "We have been subjected to a military persecution unparalleled in this country; given to the custody of the satellites of military despotism and guarded by the rigid form of military law."

The debates in Congress on defense in the years 1811 to 1815 are instructive reading. There were those, like Randolph, who declared that seven million free Americans had no idea of entrusting their defense to ten thousand mercenaries picked up in brothels and tippling houses. There were others, like Webster, who opposed conscription because of the corrupting effect of the regulars upon the clean-living civilians. In the face of congressional qualms, the regulars and the militia as well proceeded to cover themselves with shame in the second war with Britain. No other American war has produced a more disgraceful sextette of regular generals than the Revolutionary veterans Hull, Dearborn, Wilkinson, Hampton; the new warriors Smyth and Izard. Nor were they alone. The officers commissioned after 1808 were described by Winfield Scott as indifferent or positively bad; swaggerers, political dependents, or decayed gentlemen. Three generals emerged with laurels: Harrison, Jackson, and Scott. Two of these were citizen generals—a fact to be marked. The West was shortly to furnish presidents. Harrison's victory at the Thames and Jackson's at New Orleans had saved the West.

The few successful actions in the War of 1812 had demonstrated that citizen soldiers were good when properly trained. Nevertheless the Army was reduced upon the conclusion of peace; the lessons of the war were ignored, for no measures were enacted to repair the glaring defects of current militia laws. In 1817 General William Henry Harrison, chairman of a House Military Committee, who had had some lamentable adventures with militiamen, reported in favor of a scheme of military training. He declared that the defense of the country against foreign invasion, the defense of democracy against the few, symbolized by a standing army, lay in the militia, and to this end he suggested that military training be made a branch of education in every American school and that a few weeks' training each year be made compulsory. Harrison's declaration of principle echoed the sentiments of his countrymen. His practical plan did not, and it was shelved.

It would be tedious to detail the occasions upon which, with endless monotony, the refrain against a standing army was repeated. Despite the fact that the regulars scattered along our frontier were engaged in the useful task of breaking trails, building roads, making the backwoods safe for settlers, and exploring the further wilderness, there was no lessening of prejudice. There were unfortunately episodes which heightened it. The fact that volunteers won the Battle of Bad Axe against Black Hawk (1832), when the regulars took the wrong road, proved the soundness of the citizen-soldier principle. The sour remarks of Zachary Taylor about the craven behavior of the Missouri volunteers in the Seminole War (1835–42), enraged the legislature of that state into a resolution against the general and precipitated an inquiry into Taylor's use of bloodhounds to hunt down the Indians. The fact that the campaigns against the Seminoles had cost the nation some $30,000,000, which competent opinion thought could have been quartered if our military policy had been sounder, gave no one pause. Indeed, when Secretary of War Poinsett proposed a Federal training of militia, the usual cries against invasion of states' rights arose, the basso profundo of the "Godlike Daniel" shaking the rafters at the Richmond Whig Convention of 1840.

One might assume that, with most of our tiny army dispersed in isolated places, its presence would have been too unobtrusive for constant or unflattering appearances in public debate or in the public prints. One reason for this prominence was the strength and loquaciousness of the peace movement in the two decades before the Mexican War. Agitation by meetings and by a flow of tracts rose to a climax in the grand assault by orator Charles Sumner in a Fourth of July address in 1845. Adorned with a flashy rickrack of classical allusion, the grievances of colonial days were unearthed, the "farcical and humiliating exercises" at West Point declaimed, the pathetic garrisons at New London and Newport derided, and even the militia abused for "sucking the life blood" of the country. Copies of this speech were printed by the thousands, and lest the effect of such efforts be discounted, let us not forget what the peace movement of our own times achieved.

Damage of perhaps more hurtful political effect than the outcry of reformers resulted from the periodic use of troops in domestic disturbances. Jackson's orders for protection of revenue officers at Charleston by the military when the nullification row was seething (1832) did not soothe the South Carolinians; nor did the dispatch of General Scott to the Canadian border (1838), when the upstate New Yorkers were conniving in the Canadian Rebellion, gratify the fire-eaters in that state. Our history has been punctuated with a variety of episodes of this character where the ambit of anger has been greater or less, depending upon the occasion. There were few voices protesting at the use of troops against the Mormons in 1857, but three years earlier, when Federal soldiers, after a riot in Boston, escorted a fugitive slave to a revenue cutter for deportation, the repercussions were immense.

Although the Fabulous Forties still heard the well-worn clichés about standing armies, there had already been signs that the officer class was about to become the focus of democratic distaste. Taylor's censure by the Missouri legislature was an early harbinger of what was coming. In the years after 1815 a considerable group of men had made a career of soldiering, and the quota had been annually swelled by graduates of the military academy. It was, however, the Mexican War with its lusty crop of political generals and its volume of volunteer fighters that brought collision between professional standards of discipline and civilian nonchalance. Mutual recrimination was inevit-

able. The volunteer soldiers complained about the army marti-
nets, and an Englishman serving in this war has reported a favorite song, "Bucking and Gagging":

> "Sergeant, buck him, and gag him," our officers cry,
> For each trifling offence which they happen to spy;
> Till with bucking and gagging of Dick, Tom, and Bill,
> Faith, the Mexican ranks they have helped to fill.
> > Derry down, &c.

> The treatment they give us, as all of us know,
> Is bucking and gagging for whipping the foe;
> They buck us and gag us for malice or spite,
> But they're glad to release us when going to fight.
> > Derry down, &c.

Lieutenant George Gordon Meade, later to ride to glory
at Gettysburg, has left us a bill of particulars about the shortcomings of the volunteers and what he calls the "utter incapacity" of their officers. There were sneers about the bravery of
Brigadier General Franklin Pierce, commissioned out of a New
Hampshire law office, and a first-class scandal about the personal honesty of Major General Gideon Pillow, the former law
partner of President Polk. Neither the credit of the Army nor
that of the regular officers was improved by the desperate quarrels between Pillow and General Winfield Scott, which culminated in a court of inquiry at which Lawyer Pillow succeeded in
clearing himself.

Exultation over American victories carried General Taylor
into the presidency, and backbiting subsided, but not for long.
The election of 1852 was a contest between the volunteer "veteran" Franklin Pierce and Major General Winfield Scott of the
regulars. Jeers at the fact that Pierce's glory was only "two
somersaults and a faint" were met with attacks on Scott's vanity, his aristocracy, and his ill-treatment of the citizen soldiers.
The anti-Scott literature was much the more devastating, and
upon the public was impressed the picture of army men as a
set of arrogant coxcombs. It is regrettable that Scott's conduct

subsequent to his defeat did nothing to eradicate this impression. With Jefferson Davis, Pierce's Secretary of War, the old general became involved in a most acrid dispute over salary, allowances for travel, and his so-called prize money. Ill-tempered and denunciatory letters were fired on both sides and were finally delivered to the public in the form of a Senate Executive Document. Since Secretary Davis was himself a West Pointer, a reader could hardly be blamed for regarding this opus as a revelation of the military mind.

Whatever may have been the degree of disfavor that army men had acquired in the decade before the Civil War, this was as nothing when, upon secession, the parade of West Point graduates to the Confederate colors began. Popular feeling about this was intense. And although military writers like General Upton and General Cullum later demonstrated that only some 23 per cent joined the rebels, the Secretary of War himself admitted in his report of July 1, 1861, that "but for this startling defection the rebellion could never have assumed formidable proportions." Psychologically more significant was the fact that it was Beauregard, a West Pointer, who fired the first shot, and that for dreary years the northern public had to swallow bitter doses compounded by West Pointers Lee, Stonewall Jackson, Joseph Johnston, Stuart, Early, and others.

In the North as in the South, the standards of discipline and military usage by which the armies were perfected as fighting instruments were the contribution of the trained soldiers. Diluted though the forces were with hosts of volunteer officers, the substance of the regulars was never dissolved, and it was least affected in the heart of things—the command. In the North, so far as any vestiges of bias about the Regular Army survived, it polarized inevitably about the West Point men. The initial misfortunes of the Union armies shed no glamour upon the profession, and the perennial frictions developed between the volunteer officers and the regulars. This assumed significance in relation to the persons affected. Volunteer General James A. Garfield's experiences with regular General Wood prompted him to write his friend Rhodes (1862) that he suspected lead-

ing officers in the Regular Army of a virtual conspiracy in favor
of slavery:

> A command in the army is a sort of tyranny and in a narrow and
> ignoble mind engenders a despotic spirit which makes him sympathize
> with slavery and slaveholders. There is at the same time in the position
> of the soldier in the ranks that which makes him feel the abridgment of
> liberty and the power of tyranny.

Garfield wrote more about what he conceived to be the inefficiency and corruption of the West Pointers, and he expended
much energy in efforts to avoid serving under them. Later,
under the duress of association, Garfield altered his attitude
and, when he subsequently went to Congress, became the champion of the regulars.

Rutherford B. Hayes, who was fortunate in an acceptive
temperament and who fought his campaigns with a sort of
adolescent high spirits, was also not impressed by army men.
He was often bored and impatient with his superior, Colonel
Scammon, who liked to talk about West Point and genteel
people, but Hayes obviously did not share Garfield's suspicions.
Although his diary records instances of what he thought to be
unnecessary brutality and a want of consideration for the
citizen soldiers, he took men as they came. He possessed indeed
so much Christian forbearance that he refused to harbor resentment even at a humiliating and undeserved castigation by regular General Reno for permitting soldiers to use fence rails for
making fires.

Adversaries of a different stripe were Generals Benjamin F.
Butler and James A. Logan. Both were out of civil life, and
both had held responsible commands. Butler, whose war
against the ladies of New Orleans will insure him an enduring
name in the South, was not competent. His bungling in the
spring of 1864 had been criticized; his conduct at Fort Fisher
had been arraigned by Grant in a telegram to Lincoln, and he
had consequently been superseded. His antipathy to Regular
Army men stemmed from this humiliation. Logan, on the other
hand, possessed Grant's confidence, for he esteemed him to

have been one of the best division generals in the Army and "equal to a much higher command." General Sherman, however, had reservations about political generals. When McPherson, in command of the Army of the Tennessee, was killed in the Atlanta campaign, Logan had taken temporary command by virtue of seniority. Although Sherman recognized Logan's capacity, he considered him to be a politician "by nature and experience" and "it may be for this reason mistrusted by regular officers like Generals Schofield, Thomas and myself." In consequence the command was given to General O. O. Howard.

The chance of evening old scores was not long postponed. Before the Fortieth Congress in 1867 came a bill to reduce the military establishment designed to save the "rights, honor and dignity of every officer." Butler and Logan led the battle, which, as debate developed, took on the color of a savage attack upon the West Pointers. The bill was recommitted and offered again in the following session. Through careful generalship of Garfield and Blaine, it was passed after as "ugly a fight against the Army" as the former had ever witnessed.

In the post-Civil War years, the discharge of three major policing jobs kept active political sentiment against the Army. The first of these was the garrisoning of the South and the frequent use of troops to suppress the riots incident upon the execution of congressional reconstruction. The second job was that of Indian patrol in the West, an equally thankless task which, after the defeat of Custer, multiplied the censures of eastern humanitarians and brought ugly charges of brutality. The third job was occasional and, for the Army, pregnant with future hate—the use of regulars in labor troubles. The effective employment of Federal troops in the Pittsburgh railroad riots of 1877 was an example to which anti-labor newspapers constantly adverted in succeeding years of strikes, and which, repeated at Coeur d'Alene in 1892 and during the Pullman strike in 1894, arrayed against the Army a new element of opposition. For every homesteader who had mourned the death of Custer, there was a score of urban dwellers who cursed the military reluctantly patrolling the streets of Chicago.

Except for the opinion of organized labor, which continued to harbor the ancient prejudice against the Army as an instrument of tyranny, the grip of old fears relaxed its hold upon the public during the years before the Spanish War. Nor was it galvanized by the events of that conflict. On the contrary, there was amazement and criticism of the Army's shortcomings, and when the Dodge Commission (1899–1900) laid bare in eight volumes of evidence the truly monumental dimensions of the inefficiencies, it seemed that even the most anxious lover of liberty no longer need feel a compulsion to look under the bed. But at this very juncture, with the interjection of the issue of imperialism into the national arena, suspicions were revived. The question of what our future course in the Philippines should be and the irruption of a rebellion there together gave to the threat of a standing army a new and peculiar twist. The opponents of expansion warned of the dependency of empire upon military might. The hostilities in the Islands, like Washington's troubles with the Indians, were branded as an undeclared war which the President alone had promoted. The inference as to what might be in store for America if he was not checked was obvious. In March 1899, at Boston, Samuel Gompers spoke for labor. He declared that expansion meant a large standing army, "and standing armies are always used to exercise tyranny over people and are one of the prime causes of rupture in a country." The American Anti-Imperialist League was quick to enlist such sympathetic ears. George S. Boutwell warned "the laboring and producing classes" that they would have to furnish the men for the Army to set up an empire where underpaid and half-clad laborers of Asia would produce a never ending competition. It remained for Bryan, the Nebraska Habakkuk, beholding grievance and crying out against iniquity, to discover that in New York a fort was to be built and a large army to be used "to suppress by force that discontent that ought to be cured by legislation."

Although the political issue over imperialism was settled by the re-election of McKinley in 1900, the Army continued to draw unfavorable attention by rumors of brutality in the Philip-

pines and tales of torture with the now legendary "water cure."
There can be no doubt that there had been bad incidents, but
it is equally apparent from the testimony of William Howard
Taft, General Hughes, and General Otis before a Senate committee in 1902 that the American officers had attempted to
prevent such happenings, but since the insurgents constantly
resorted to acts of savagery, it was nearly impossible to keep
the men from isolated acts of revenge. It is significant of the
fugitive character of the postwar prejudice that both the War
Department's reorganization bill and a new militia law were
enacted in 1903, and only the faintest echoes of former odium
were heard in Congress. When it was discovered in 1905 that
army maneuvers could not be held because there were not
enough troops in the United States, the democratic drumbeats
were virtually stilled.

It became the mode in high places to speak of the Army in
the icy language of academic restraint. Scientific scrutiny reduced the werewolf of frontier days to a formula. "It is the
traditional policy of the United States that the military establishment in time of peace is to be a small regular army and that
the ultimate war force of the nation is to be a great army of
citizen soldiers." Thus wrote a Committee of General Staff
Officers in 1912, and in nearly identical words President Wilson addressed the Congress in 1914. Gone are the florid warnings about tyranny and the dangers to democracy that colored
even Jackson's references to standing armies. The policy remained, but it would be stated without rattling of chains and
phantom thumpings.

Yet, at the very moment old ghosts were thus laid, occurred
the popular discovery of "militarism." This was a word destined for a long sojourn in the dictionary of democracy. It was
more than a mere epithet. Catapulted into general use at a
moment when German soldiers were tramping through Bel-
gium, it evoked a rush of mental images—atrocities, ruthless-
ness, suppression of democracy, and bloodless efficiency. It
possessed, in consequence, a verbal fire-spread hitherto achiev-
able only by an oration. With startling rapidity and in pace with

the encroachment of war, the nation was divided on issues of military preparation. The forces of pacifism exploited the new word with telling effect. The inadequacies of the National Defense Act of 1916, by which the standing army was enlarged and provision made for the increase of the National Guard, were in a measure due to the power of the anti-militarists.

Conviction that one of our aims in the war against the Central Powers was the suppression of militarism was so strongly founded that it remained a factor of intense political importance. In combination with postwar isolationism it determined the immediate direction of foreign policy. It colored the discussion of the 1920 Defense Act. It gave to the peace movement of the twenties and thirties the practical appeal that the homilies of the pacifists a century earlier did not possess. It kept the WPA away from works of military merit and the CCC from instruction in the use of weapons. The goings on in Europe and Asia supplied us with constant and terrifying reminders of what the worship of Mars may signify.

The grip which dislike of militarism has had upon American imagination has been made firm by contemplation of the unhappy European scene, and in some quarters by a studied deprecation of American wars and the virtue of valor. The dislike itself has owed much to the emotions, opinions, and happenings here related. In a left-handed sort of way it was begotten by the military policy devised as the best insurance of democracy. The thing has a saga-like quality, for in an age of books and printing, education and propaganda, it has been nurtured by a word-of-mouth tradition among the people themselves. Our wars have been so spaced and have been so waged that every generation of citizens has experienced or has touched hands with those who suffered the collision of tyro and professional soldier. Out of the sum of individual adventures or the telling of them has been compounded the prejudice of common men. The historian must rummage in memoirs, in speeches, and in congressional investigations to find the ever-fresh spoor of prejudice. Among the people each war brings back the teller of tales with stories to match against his sire's that like old wounds still ache when the day of glory is past and forgotten.

As long as technical preparedness rests in the hands of experts, and as long as the citizen's military duty continues to be performed spasmodically and upon emergency, the civilian and the professional will have the problem of adjustment. The stronger and more perfect the organization of the standing army is, the more difficult this adjustment will be. Any organization excretes red tape and propagates rules and patterns of conduct just and comprehensible to its members, unjust and incomprehensible to the outsider suddenly inducted. On the other hand, the soldier who has slowly picked his way along the desolate road of peacetime promotion is understandably wounded when precipitously outranked by some lawyer or broker whose life has hitherto been his own to spend. The National Guardsman who has sacrificed his evenings in pursuit of an ideal is obsessed by the delusion that to the journeyman soldier he remains a mere apprentice. An old Guardsman (formerly a brigadier general in the National Army) testified to this before the Senate Military Committee in 1919:

SENATOR CHAMBERLAIN. Did you see any disposition among the Regular Army officers to discriminate against the Guard officers?
MR. SHERBURNE. Why yes; there is no question about that.
SENATOR CHAMBERLAIN. I would like you to enlarge on that. I have heard a good deal about it. If it existed, how did it manifest itself?
MR. SHERBURNE. Of course the original step in that was in passing the 119th Article of War, which subordinated all officers not of the regular service to all regulars holding temporary commissions in higher grades. In other words whenever I was with six or eight general officers I was always the last one to go in the door.

Part of a soldier's armor is his pride. Those who would smile at General Sherburne's disclosure should remember Washington's testy reaction to the British regulations about rank when he wrote his agent in 1758: "You are pleased to dub me with a title I have no pretentions to—that is ye Honble." Nearly all of our military history is crammed between these two bits of evidence. Still committed to the citizen soldier, we have learned, it would seem, but little about him.

In the face of this long and dolorous tale of prejudice stands the opinion which the voters have repeatedly registered at the polls. What has led to the nomination of generals, why have some been elected to the presidency and why have others failed? The careers of the several General-Presidents will furnish us details, and at their records we propose presently to look. In nearly every case the military career was the condition precedent to political availability. The one common denominator is the fact of being a general. What makes a general?

III

What Makes a General?

———◆◆———

WHAT MAKES A GENERAL? To this question Captain John Montresor, chief engineer of His Majesty's forces, was writing bitter answers into his journal during the winter of 1777–78 as he contemplated the incredible ineptitude of Sir William Howe. To this question Generals Horatio Gates and Thomas Conway were then conspiring to compel the Continental Congress to a new solution. On this question General Washington was pondering in that bleak suburb of Philadelphia as he weighed the capacities of Frederick von Steuben. Somewhere in the minds of each of these men was a portrait of qualities. Each of them was answering the question as if it read, What makes a *good* general? This has been the way of soldiers from the beginning of time. This is how Xenophon approached the matter, and "The Good General" is what Sir Archibald Wavell called his first lecture on *Generals and Generalship* in 1939.

It is a truism to speak of soldiers as the great romantics. If there were nothing else in their way of life to prove it, the quest for perfection in their answers to our question should be conclusive. Engaged in the cruelest and most destructive of human activities, they have persistently sought what virtues can be wrung from it. That is why their standards of soldiery are replete with moral tone; that is why their analyses of a general's qualities are traditionally in terms of an ideal.

Professional inquiry into the essence of generalship has been pursued, not merely for the purpose of illuminating military history, but for the practical end of instruction and of fixing a standard of selection for command. We shall see in a moment the obstacles which have beset the achievement of this last and most important purpose. But first we must consider how stand-ards of excellence have been established by soldiers themselves.

At a very early date it became customary to speak of the military "art" and the "art" of war. This manner of speech in-duced the belief that certain rules and certain standards under-lay the conduct of matters martial just as in the art of music there are rules of harmony. It was not difficult to evolve for-mulae for the deployment of a company or for "Plain Firings and Figures of Battail." The broader questions of strategy and the qualities essential to its direction were more baffling. In de-fault of any better means of analyzing the elusive quality of genius which sets the great leader apart from lesser men, some early European writers approached the matter as if it were a problem of ethics and emerged with a catalogue of virtues. In so doing they were profoundly influenced by the prevailing veneration of classical culture, for Greek and Roman learning occupied even the crevices of human thought, and the art of war was no exception. A distinguished military historian has described the renaissance of military art in the sixteenth cen-tury as "a long musical passage in pedal point on the deep bass note of classical tradition." This bass note was still loud in the succeeding century, and it can still be heard in the *Rêveries* of Marshal Saxe, written in 1732. Nor was it the ancients' mili-tary science alone that was respected, for the qualities of a general listed by that veteran of the Thirty Years' War, Field Marshal Montecuccoli, in his *Aphorisms,* has supporting refer-ences to the *Rhetoric* and *Politics* of Aristotle.

Although the wisdom of antiquity had a sort of Biblical hold upon military writers, men could not and did not shut their ears to the experiences of contemporary commanders. Montecuccoli himself had not disdained in another work upon the art of war to fortify his discussion of the general with allusions to things he knew. When he declares a general must first of all secure the attachment of his men, we realize he is talking of the mercenary troops he commanded. When he says a general must have luck, we remember he was writing while a prisoner of the Swedes. The general must be brave but not foolhardy, as Gustavus

Adolphus once was. He must hold councils of war as did the Duke of Saxony and Hatzfeld at Wittstock. He must be open-minded and constantly consider how to injure the enemy; and when his own wit fails, he may, like Wallenstein, consult astrologers—an expedient which has recently again come into favor in Central Europe.

There were other soldiers who wrote their formulae from experience. Lieutenant Colonel Richard Elton, a Roundhead officer who served under Fairfax, compiled his *Compleat Body of the Art Military,* an elaborate disquisition on tactics, in 1650. He included in it ideas derived as well from the English Civil War as from the operations of the Swedes and the Prince of Orange. Elton reflects the high disciplinary standard of Cromwell's New Model Army in his specification of the exact duties of every officer. The leveling spirit then abroad in England is, however, obvious from his comment that "a Commander should be qualified with much Knowledge, Courage and Faithfulness, the only accomplishments of a true soldier." On the Continent the aristocratic Saxe, for all his study of the Romans, opens what he calls his picture of a "General Commanding" with the blunt statement, "I have seen such men." Valor, intelligence, health are first in his recipe. Thirteen years later he gave the lie to the last when, too ill to move, he beat the detested "Butcher" Cumberland at Fontenoy.

Military writing in the eighteenth century had an international vogue. Montecuccoli's *Aphorisms,* like Saxe's *Rêveries* and later Frederick's *Instructions* to his generals were translated and in various editions were widely circulated just as today Von Clausewitz's *On War* has girdled the globe. In the American colonies Nicholas Boone of Boston published, as early as 1701, *Military Discipline—The Compleat Souldier or Expert Artilleryman,* compiled from Elton's work and others, and although most of the native prints were mere militiamen's manuals, the importation of foreign works was considerable. The titles in Washington's military library illustrate the eclectic nature of the study of warfare at the dawn of our Republic and how the thoughts of dead commanders might weigh with the living. Nathanael Greene studying Turenne, William Henry Harrison conning Saxe in the backwoods, and James Garfield feverishly translating Frederick in 1862—how long the arm of the past!

The early professional analyses of war and leadership, being bounded by personal experience and the contemporary manner of waging war, were in reality period portraits. In the era of self-instruction, Americans who studied such books, eager to acquire an understanding of tactics and strategy, tended to view them as patterns of principle. This is commented upon by Grant:

> Some of our generals failed because they worked out everything by rule. They knew what Frederick did at one place and Napoleon at another. They were always thinking about what Napoleon would do. Unfortunately for their plans the rebels would be thinking about something else.

Grant's criticisms were directed less to the study than to the misuse of history. He himself, as an intimate reveals, possessed a detailed and profound knowledge of military history. He differed from others in that he had assimilated the wisdom that was to be extracted from such study. The generals he criticized were doing on the field what they had done in West Point classrooms—executing by rote as they had once repeated lessons by rote. It would hardly have occurred to a field officer that there was wisdom to be derived from the writings of an army surgeon. Yet the young captains and lieutenants of the Mexican War would have done well to ponder the sage words of Robert Jackson, published the year before that war was begun: "Promptitude in the field is what may be called military knowledge. It cannot be learned from books but it may be matured and systematized by observation and reflection." Of all the men who followed Taylor and Scott and later bore the stars of high rank during the Rebellion, only Grant and Lee possessed this capacity in its quintessence.

Since the United States has pursued the policy of selecting general officers, an accumulation of knowledge regarding their expected qualifications might have been of decisive importance if the professional soldiers who possessed this knowledge made the decisions. But the authority to appoint rests ultimately in the President as commander in chief, subject to confirmation by the Senate. The Secretary of War has, of course, never been without a voice in the matter. The position of the professional soldiers has been purely advisory. In other words, their criteria have always been available, although they have not invariably been acted upon. The matter has always had its pathology, especially during a war, of which more later. At the moment let us consider the process of choice at its best.

It is told that Secretary Newton D. Baker, before the selection of General Pershing for the expeditionary army, studied the efficiency records of every higher officer—his varied experience, his intelligence, his character, his tact, his industry, his energy, his capacity to lead, his resolution under difficulties, his physical power and endurance. The items on this list compel attention, compiled as they were in a department which had dealt with soldiers for 128 years. They are still embodied in the contemporary army "Efficiency Report." Together they are the conditions of soldierly conduct to be fulfilled by one whose goal is generalship. In making the decision, Baker, like any other employer, had his own conception of what the job to be filled demanded.

General Palmer, who relates this story, himself a distinguished soldier and historian, at another place revealed the share of history in the final judgment. Testifying before a Senate committee in 1919, he said:

The military efficiency of an officer might be indicated by an equation: $E = AK$, in which E is his efficiency and K is his knowledge and A is a coefficient, an applicative coefficient determined by his character, his energy, and other practical factors.

Now if you take a soldier like Napoleon, K is very high, and A is also near its maximum value. In the case of a theoretical soldier like our General Halleck, of Civil War fame, K was probably as high as it was in the case of Napoleon, or nearly so, but this practical or applicative coefficient was very low, so therefore his efficiency as a whole was low. Take a man like Forrest, a man so illiterate that he could not write an order; yet one of the greatest cavalry soldiers the world ever produced. In that instance K was perhaps very small, but A was exceptionally large, and whatever he did know he could apply. In this case the product or total efficiency was very high.

Shorn of its equation, this statement is persuasive of the fact that study of command in old battles and campaigns is still supplying premises on which generalship is judged and capacity predicted. Military science, like the law, finds past example indispensable.

If in the past the selection of general officers had invariably depended upon a consistent search for the qualities expounded by soldier students of war, the fate of nations would have been very different from what it has been. Armies and wars, however, being instruments of national policy, the question, "What makes a general?" has always had a political answer. This has not always coincided with the professional answer. When this has happened, it has been mere chance, for the professional answer has been concerned with capacity, and the political answer with a host of other considerations.

The word political we use here in its most comprehensive sense. A political answer is one which is formulated with reference to factors like our Constitution, our military legislation, and finally what is called practical politics. It is addressed chiefly to the process of acquiring a commission and only incidentally to the qualities of the officer commissioned. Such answers will differ in every nation, and nothing illustrates the violence of difference more vividly than our own rejection of the English answer book. We rejected the basic theory of the Crown's prerogative to provide for defense; we rejected the uncontrolled royal prerogative to commission; we rejected the idea that a military commission was a piece of property to be purchased; we rejected the social commandment that only "gentlemen" could be officers.

Whatever the American conception of military duty and military preferment owed to England by way of democratic reaction, it owed more to practices connected with colonial militia, especially in the matter of commissioning, and to the experiences of the Revolution. It was out of the bedlam of the war for independence that our constitutional solution emerged.

In the first measures taken for defense by the Continental Congress the pattern of ensuing tribulation appears—state interest, sectional interest, patronage and self-seeking. The South and Virginia were attached by the appointment of Washington, Massachusetts placated by the choice of the adipose Artemas Ward, first major general. Charles Lee, an ardent self-seeker, was made second major general; the third was Schuyler of New York; the fourth, Putnam of Connecticut. All of the brigadiers except Gates hailed from New England. "Nothing," wrote John Adams, "has given me more Torment than the Scuffle we have had in appointing the General officers." There was torment and scuffle to come.

These first appointments were made in a manner resembling the diplomatic apportionment of command at a conference of military allies. That is more or less what the colonies were in 1775, and subsequent dealings in matters of defense never quite lost the odor of protocol. The Continental Army was created to establish a force of greater stability than a congeries of militia. But fear of a standing army and reaction against executive authority prevented Washington's dreams of a true national army from being realized. As we have noticed, the Continental Army was organized by state lines; that is to say, each state was responsible for recruiting, for the bounties of its quota, and for the appointment of officers below the rank of general. The prerogative of appointing general officers Congress retained, and it turned a deaf ear to Washington's intimations that such appointments should be dependent upon his recommendation. It was only in the two intervals when the commander in chief was voted brief "dictatorial" powers that he possessed a free hand. The rest of the time he had to struggle as well with Congress as with state committees.

Once the war was well under way, the principles of promotion up to the grade of colonel and the relation of any such scheme to the congressional selection of general officers became a serious problem. The officers were almost unanimously in favor of a rule of seniority, and in August 1776 Washington reluctantly admitted this was the most practical scheme. Congress, however, insisted upon and never surrendered its right to promote for "distinguished merit." This left the way open for state pressure both on promotions and on assignments, as when Schuyler was sacrificed in 1777 at the insistence of Massachusetts. When the foreign adventurers came upon the scene the army resentment of congressional prerogative reached its height.

Like a potato too hot to handle, the promotion problem was tossed back and forth between Washington and Congress. Finally, in 1781, the latter decided that promotions in the infantry were to be by state lines under the rank of brigadier. The country was divided into seven districts in which the senior colonels were to rise to brigadier rank. In the cavalry and artillery, promotions were to be by regiments to the rank of commanding officers. Brigadiers there were to be commissioned by seniority. All major generals were to be chosen according to seniority from the whole army.

The mechanics of how to get ahead in the Continental Army appear duller in brief outline than they do in the full record —in particular, in Washington's correspondence. The hue and cry after commissions was hot. Squabbles about rank and precedence were incessant—hardly a court-martial could be held without such strife. Lavishness had gone to such lengths that even wagon masters were commissioned, with the result that "absurd fancies of gentility" made them too good for their jobs. Experience with the practical workings of congressional and state policies is reflected in Washington's *Sentiments on a Peace Establishment,* written in 1783. For his proposed Continental Army he rejected the principle of seniority and suggested selection by a board of officers, the Congress to make appointments.

If knowledge of events as much as political expediency decided the substance of what the sovereign states were surrendering to the Union in the new Constitution, it is not idle to suppose that the career of the Revolutionary commander influenced the decision to make the President commander in chief of the Army and Navy. True, a paper of Hamilton's in the *Federalist* justified the provision by reference to existing state constitutions. But his words, "the direction of war implies the direction of the common strength," were scarcely inspired by the ineffectual performance of Governor Jefferson when the British came raiding through Virginia tidewater.

More germane to our present question was the constitutional provision giving the President power to nominate officers of the United States, subject to senatorial confirmation. Appointment of inferior officers Congress might vest in the President alone or in heads of departments. At the time of the Convention, this appointing power was not formulated with reference to army appointments, nor was this matter raised. Nevertheless, since the purpose of the article on the executive was to center in an individual the executive powers theretofore wielded by the Congress, the implications of the clause must have been understood. In any event, it approximated Washington's conception of a proper executive control of appointment of army personnel envisaged in his memorandum four years before.

No less significant than the appointive power was the Constitution's grant to Congress of authority to raise and support armies, with the proviso of a two-year appropriation limit, which fear of a standing army made inevitable. This provision, as time was to prove, was to give Congress something to say in answer to "What makes a general?" If, as it almost decided in 1828, the office of major general was to be abolished, there would be no such general to make.

Apart from what was embedded in the Constitution by way of reaction to Revolutionary muddling, two further legacies were derived from the conduct of army affairs during the Revolution. The most important was the tradition of a state voice in the organization of defense. The perpetuation of this was to some extent assured by the militia provision in the Constitution. The second legacy was the principle of promotion by seniority. If the Army was to furnish from its ranking colonels

the candidates for the making of a general, it was certain they
would be properly aged.

It would be tedious to relate the details of successive statutes
regarding the organization of officer personnel and promotion
in the Army. The latter was entirely in the hands of the executive until 1812, when Congress affirmed the established rule
—promotions to the rank of captain were made regimentally,
to the rank of colonel by line of service. The army regulations
established the principle of seniority. General officers alone
were selected. Not until 1890 were examinations to determine
fitness introduced—and then only for officers below the rank
of major; the next rungs depended upon seniority. The sanctity
of the latter principle still is rooted in the modern promotion
list.

Thus, in brief, were fixed the prerequisites of availability
for translation to the estate of a general officer. The chances
of promotion were small in the ordinary years of peace, for
until after the Civil War no system of retirement for wounds
or disability was contrived. Officers continued in service until
death. The results of this illogical arrangement were painfully
apparent when the war with Mexico broke out. There was no
regiment that could take the field with its full quota of field
officers, owing to illness or disability; one colonel, indeed, had
reached the ripe age of eighty-two.

If Constitution, statutes, and executive orders give to our
question, What makes a general?, a political answer of the
most respectable complexion, our curious military policy has
furnished a more raffish one. The periodic inflation of our fighting force when danger loomed and the necessity of recourse
to militia or enlistment of volunteers invariably entailed legislation authorizing the commissioning of more generals. Since
the Constitution treated the states as copartners in matters
of defense, and since we began our national existence with a
strong tradition of state responsibility, the emergency quest
for leadership was not hampered by academic considerations
of professional competence.

The War of 1812 was the first important occasion for the

exercise of political genius in the selection of generals. The affair began with taking some Revolutionary officers out of moth balls, among others the unhappy Hull, Dearborn, and Winchester. On paper the appointments were defensible, but none of these men had seen fighting for thirty years. Their several performances against the British were nothing to increase confidence in the value of military experience. There was at the time no such office as general in chief of the Army. War planning as well as army organization was completely in the hands of the President and the Secretary of War. Since the directions issued by the Secretary to the commanders in the field were of the sketchiest sort, it was of extreme importance that each commander be chosen with perspicacity. Yet it was not wisdom that governed, but chance or expediency. Two men whose careers concern us, Jackson and Harrison, are exhibits.

What made Jackson a general? He was a citizen of Tennessee, where command of the militia was an elective office. The field officers of each of the three districts elected the brigadier for the district, and all the field officers and the three brigadiers elected the major general. By 1797 Jackson had risen to a colonelcy in the militia and had been beaten in an election for major general. His successful rival died in 1801, and at the ensuing election Jackson finally won the coveted post when his friend Governor Roane cast a deciding vote. In 1812, therefore, Jackson was an important military figure in the state. He had been a judge of the Superior Court, and he was politically eminent.

Shortly before the outbreak of war, Congress authorized the enlistment of 50,000 volunteers. General Jackson forthwith issued a call to arms: "Are we the titled slaves of George the Third? The military conscripts of Napoleon? Or the frozen peasants of the Russian Czar?" A week after war had broken out, on June 25, 1812, he offered President Madison 2,500 volunteers. He had already tendered his own services. The Administration was apparently not interested. General Jackson had been suspected of befriending Burr. He had made a speech deriding Jefferson at Richmond while Burr's trial was

going on. He had written a nasty letter (1807) to the late
Secretary of War, now General Dearborn, in which he had
said, "You stand convicted of the most notorious and criminal
acts of dishonor, dishonesty, want of candour and justice."
Small wonder that his patriotic overture was rejected.

In October 1812 a request for 1,500 volunteers to defend
New Orleans was received by the governor of Tennessee. They
were intended as reinforcements for the sleazy General Wilkinson. Nothing was said about Jackson or how the troops were
to be commanded. Governor Blount, however, had received
from Washington seventy blank commissions ready-signed. He
took what is described as "legal advice" and filled in the name
of Andrew Jackson, who thus became major general, United
States Volunteers.

Jackson got his men as far as Natchez when he received a
letter from Wilkinson ordering him to halt, as the latter had
no commands with regard to the expedition. After an uneasy
wait of weeks, an order of the Secretary of War dismissing
his corps from service arrived. To get the men home, Jackson
pledged his personal credit.

Back in Tennessee, Jackson spent the summer of 1813 chafing for further orders. It was his good fortune that a rising
of the Creek Indians precipitated an expedition which the state
of Tennessee organized and dispatched under his direction
while the War Department, aware of the danger, was dithering
over a plan. In this campaign Jackson acquitted himself with
distinction. Before the fighting was over, Major General Pinckney, in whose district it was happening, recommended promotion. Secretary Armstrong in May 1814 offered a brigadier generalship with a brevet major generalship. But within a few
days occurred the resignation of Major General William
Henry Harrison, and the vacancy was tendered Jackson. Thus
he became major general of the regulars, in command of the
Seventh Military District.

The elevation of Harrison, in whose room Jackson was
appointed, had followed a different pattern. As we shall later
see, Harrison had served in the Regular Army from 1791 to

1798. He next held various public offices and was governor of Indiana Territory when he fought the action at Tippecanoe. When the Army was increased in the spring of 1812, Harrison's name was not included in the list of brigadiers. There had been criticism of his conduct, and the Administration was opposed to his plans for vanquishing the Indians. Harrison mobilized his friends. Governor Scott of Kentucky and Henry Clay took up the cudgels for him, but without success. Meantime the siege of Detroit precipitated a crisis which led the Kentucky leaders to commission their friend Harrison major general in the Kentucky militia, disregarding the state law that limited militia commissions to Kentucky citizens. Armed with this rank, Harrison proceeded to supply himself with an army by claiming command of the Kentucky militia, then under the control of Brigadier General Winchester (U.S.A.). Strangely enough, the latter yielded, and Harrison was about to lead his troops to relieve Detroit when orders arrived from the Secretary of War giving command to Winchester. At the same time came news that Clay's importunities had been successful—a brigadier's commission in the United States Volunteers had been secured. Harrison was in acute distress. Acceptance meant he was junior to Winchester; balancing the relative glory of militia major general versus a brigadier general in the volunteers was difficult. Fortunately the President relieved the anguish of decision, for in September 1812 he placed Harrison in full command of the northwestern army.

Although Harrison's winter campaign in the wilds eventuated in little, the maneuvers of Clay and other friends in Washington accomplished much. Congress having authorized the commissioning of more major generals, Harrison's name was submitted for one of the posts, and on March 1, 1813, the Senate approved. If Jackson's adventures exemplify the power of the states in matters of defense, Harrison's exemplify the power of a Washington lobby.

The War of 1812 demonstrated beyond all doubts that the political answer to the question, What makes a general?, however chastely it lay revealed in the statute book, had acquired some ravishing footnotes. Some of the men who helped to write these footnotes were well aware of the darker aspects of preferment during the Revolution; and it is not to their credit that they tolerated revival. It was mere luck that the political art practiced in the case of Harrison and Jackson had a favorable outcome. Chance had been spiteful in other cases, but it is success which men remember. No wonder the Regular Army itself did not disdain the extrastatutory magic, and that a cynical congressman could quote as a proverb in 1821 : "A tour of duty in Washington is worth two in the field."

When the Mexican War came upon us, Senator Thomas Hart Benton says that the Administration had decided it was to be a small war. There is no doubt that Polk and his advisers were determined it should be the Administration's own war and that the Whigs were to squeeze no glory from it. After the declaration of war, President Polk consulted Winfield Scott, the general in chief, and offered him the command. He records that he did not consider Scott in all respects suited to such an important command, but he thought his position entitled him to it. Polk's dilemma arose from the fact that Scott was a Whig and that he was the most eminent American soldier. Scott remembered the unpreparedness of the War of 1812. These mistakes he set about to forestall. Unfortunately he preferred letter writing to conferences. He accordingly addressed a long communication to Secretary of War Marcy detailing the measures he was taking to organize the Army and justifying his continued presence in Washington. He then proceeded to destroy his argument by naïvely adding that he did not wish to expose himself to "a fire upon my rear from Washington and the fire in front from the Mexicans." His suggestion that he stay in Washington was accepted. There followed the victories of General Zachary Taylor and his espousal by the Whigs. This precipitated the decision that Old Zach be halted in his tracks and that a new expedition be launched at Vera Cruz. At this moment Polk was toying with a project to make a lieutenant general of Senator Benton (briefly an 1812 lieutenant colonel who had seen no fighting) in order to give him the necessary seniority for supreme command. As this involved legislation, and as something immediate had to be done to off- set Taylor, Polk felt compelled again to turn to Scott. The proposition which was made was simple. If the President could be sure Scott had proper "confidence" in the Administration and was willing to "co-operate," Polk would let bygones be by- gones. The implications of "co-operation" were fully under- stood by the general in chief. Polk records that Scott "was so grateful & so much affected that he almost shed tears. He then said he would take with him any of the Volunteer Generals whom I might indicate." He received a list of men, deserving Democrats, only one of whom had had recent military expe- rience.

The full measure of Polk's perfidy is revealed in later diary entries. The manipulations to secure a lieutenant general's status for Benton, to give him rank superior to Scott, continued for weeks until it became manifest Congress would not con- sent. Benton was then commissioned a major general, but when he discovered he could not thus achieve supreme command he resigned. Frantically General Pillow, the President's intimate, wrote from Vera Cruz imploring the appointment which Ben- ton had declined. It was essential, he wrote, that the Demo- crats have a major general. The party "might well expect in that officer to build up in the army a power to counteract that of the *Privates* which is exclusively Whig." Pillow was re- warded. But in spite of Polk's precautions the barn door had not been locked betimes. Taylor, the general who had come up the hard and statutory way, was to win the immediate political fruits of victory.

If achievement of rank in the militia had involved familiarity with more than the manual of arms and had been a real train- ing ground of officers, Polk's frivolity in treating the choice of general officers on the same basis as the selection of a post- master would be less incredible. But the training of militia had drifted from bad to worse, and in many states where office was elective, talents no different from those needed to be an assessor or a supervisor were essential. The perversion of principles of equality in naming incompetent commanders to lead incompetent volunteers would be ludicrous except that the stakes were so desperate. Considering the fact that in 1846 there were available some five hundred graduates of West Point who had resigned from the Army, the political answer of Polk was shameful.

In 1861 the situation which confronted the Union as southern states seceded one by one was appalling because of the creeping paralysis which immobilized Washington. In the words of the Joint Committee on the Conduct of the War: "There was treason in the Executive Mansion, treason in the Cabinet, treason in the Senate and House of Representatives, treason in the Army and Navy, treason in every department, bureau, and office connected with the Government." Among the states there was a great divergency of interest and enthusiasm with respect to impending conflict, but in the face of the feeble condition of the Federal Government vigorous state administrations like Wisconsin, New York, Massachusetts, and New Jersey took the initiative in preparing for war and in recruiting troops. This situation revivified and strengthened the tradition that in national defense the sovereign states were peers of the Federal Government. The speed and vigor of state action contributed incontestably to the salvation of the Union. For purposes of military efficiency it had, however, its eventual irksome features. General Upton, who perceived how the thread of tradition ran back to the Revolution and who knew at first hand the Civil War problems, later remarked: "With certain State Governors during the late War of the Rebellion, the combined recommendations of division corps and army commanders were powerless to influence the advancement of officers of known skill and ability."

There is no episode more revealing of the early power of the states than that which led to the apotheosis of McClellan. Little Mac had attended West Point and had resigned from the Army, a captain. He was president of a railroad when Governor Dennison of Ohio made him major general in the militia. When Lincoln delegated to Ohioan Salmon P. Chase, Secretary of the Treasury, the organization of the new army, opportunity could be heard knocking. Chase had three army officers helping him, but he was strong-minded. He told Captain Franklin "he would rather have no regiments raised in Ohio than that they should not be known as Ohio regiments." This mind was receptive to Governor Dennison's telegram: "Can McClellan get a commission for three years at once, so as to make sure of his holding the chief command here? Ohio must lead throughout the war." Chase replied two days later, "We have today had McClellan appointed a Major General in the Regular Army."

Clothed in his new rank, McClellan led into West Virginia the expedition initiated and planned by Ohio. The Confederate forces were defeated and dispersed, and the Union was given a sip of victory. On the heels of this success came the disaster at Bull Run. In no time at all McClellan was put in command of the Department of the Potomac.

Ulysses S. Grant was also a West Pointer and had resigned, a captain. In 1861 he was clerking in his father's leather store at Galena, Illinois. A chance meeting with Governor Yates landed him in the office of the state adjutant general helping with the mustering of volunteers. There Grant renewed acquaintance with Brigadier General Pope, who was "well acquainted with most of the prominent men in the State. I was a carpetbagger and knew but few of them." Pope advised Grant to write to the adjutant general in Washington. This he did, but no reply was ever received. In the same month Grant traveled to Cincinnati to request a position on McClellan's staff, but after two days' wait he gave up in disgust. Fortunately the 21st Illinois, mustered in by him at Mattoon, refused to go into service with the colonel of their own choice. Governor Yates then appointed Grant. The regiment moved into Missouri. While on duty there, the new colonel read a newspaper account that the President had requested the Illinois delegation in Congress to recommend some citizens of the state for the position of brigadier. Grant's name headed the list. "I was very much surprised because . . . my acquaintance with the Congressmen was very limited and I did not know anything I had done to inspire confidence." In due course the appointment was made and confirmed. After Fort Donelson came the commission as major general in the volunteers.

The difference in the quality of McClellan's and Grant's status as major general was due to the strange plan of retaining and expanding the Regular Army and building alongside the volunteer army. The latter, of course, was the resting place of most of the so-called "political generals," and thither drifted many of the West Pointers who had previously resigned. The latter were certain of some sort of rank, usually on the staff of a politically appointed colonel. Once landed, training and skill had a better prospect of advancement in the morass of volunteer ineptitude than did equal qualification in the regulars, where slow promotion still ruled. There were a few—and Sheridan was one of them—who were lucky enough to be transferred from the regulars to the volunteers. The spawning of political generals was unavoidable because of the peculiar military system. In the promotions which occurred as the war continued, Lincoln, who has been criticized for his nominations, of necessity had to fish his brigadiers from the teeming pool of political colonels created by the state governors in 1861. It was the mercy of Providence that the ultimate political answer in that war was the man of whom Governor Yates boasted: "God gave him to the country and I signed his first commission."

The Rebellion gave us the last of our General-Presidents. The laurels of the Spanish-American War were worn by the Navy, for the actions fought by the Army were inconsequential and even the sheen of these achievements was dimmed by the furor over maladministration. It was miraculous, under the circumstances, that once more the political formula worked its magic. Congress had authorized the recruiting of special bodies of troops from the nation at large, and one of these was the First Volunteer Cavalry, immortal as the Rough Riders. Leonard Wood, a medical officer, became colonel; Theodore Roosevelt was lieutenant colonel. Colonel Wood rose to the rank of major general, and in 1910 he became chief of staff. Colonel Roosevelt became President.

For the sake of the record and not because we need the data for historical calculations, a final word must be said about what our own century has contributed to the political answer. There has been, in the first place, the creation (1903) of the general staff and the chief of staff, two agencies, one planning, the other executive, which in combination with schools of postgraduate study have produced scientific soldiers basically different from those who glittered on the staff of "Old Fuss and Feathers." In the second place the resort to conscription in 1917 and the almost successful eradication of the state identity of Guard units then drafted into Federal service emphasized the national character of the war enterprise and reduced the states to nearly silent partners. There were reverberations against this in 1919 at the hearings on the National Defense Act that produced change of plan. But it is to be noticed that in the statute as finally passed a reservoir of effective officer personnel was assured by the continuance of the officer reserve corps and by setting up criteria for commissions in the Guard. A long step had been taken to make the military and the political answers to our question coincide. The door to fame, wide open in the nineteenth century, seemed closed. But not quite. Federal legislation could fix standards, but it could not overturn the powers of the several states over their militia. In the crisis of 1941, as in 1917, the President was empowered to commission emergency officers. It was an emergency officer become a brigadier who achieved the limited distinction of the vice-presidency in 1924. Let us say, then, the door is open a crack; America may still be the land of opportunity.

Our military policy and the fortunes of war have, between them, tossed a long array of soldiers upon the treacherous sands of public prominence. There has been hardly an election in the United States at which, either in preconvention months or in the campaign, strains of a *marche militaire* could not be heard, faintly or with vigor, in response to the dictates of popular taste. Party leaders have never been deaf to such music, but they have always remained cognizant of the existence of native prejudice and have had to take as a premise popular trepidation over soldiers, dictatorship, and what is called the military mind. It is something as palpable as a religious, a regional, or class prejudice and equally to be reckoned with. The distracting element has been the antic quality of the military prejudice, the remarkable capacity of the nightmare to transform itself into a happy dream. There have been occasions when the transcendence of public enthusiasm has been so plain—the adulation of Zachary Taylor, the acclaim for Ulysses S. Grant—that prejudice had hardly to be reckoned with. There have been other occasions, like the nomination of Winfield Scott in 1852 and George McClellan in 1864, when miscalculation has been fatal to party triumph. There are few episodes in our politics more diverting than the Whigs' theft of the Democrats' corner on the War of 1812, when by reviving with proper trappings the battles of Tippecanoe and the Thames, they swept General Harrison into office. There is no more sardonic spectacle than the Democrats' post-mortem exploitation of Andrew Jackson's fame, first for Lewis Cass, and then the "Young Hickory" promotion of Franklin Pierce. "Like a horde of hungry ticks you have stuck to the tail of the Hermitage lion to the end of his life, and you are still sticking to it, and drawing a loathsome sustenance from it after he is dead," jeered Abraham Lincoln. But his own party used a similar artifice in 1888 for the election of Benjamin Harrison, grandson of the hero of Tippecanoe.

The military theme in our politics has not been woven into the most uplifting of music. Much of it has been composed for the bedazzlement of the emotional voter; little of it has been written for the dour fellow who can read a score. When he hears the band playing in the distance, if he has preconceptions about the civil capacities of military leaders, he may well ask, "What manner of generals have become presidents? Were they competent? Did their military careers fit or unfit them?" The answers are various. There is no glib reply for any single General-President. Let us look at the record.

IV

General Washington

———————◆——————

THERE IS SOMETHING about the red earth of Virginia which
has inspired in her sons a singular devotion to that land. It was
in this loyalty that Washington was born, and yet as a man he
was one of the first few who perceived and felt that being an
American was a greater pride. While some of his distinguished
contemporaries whose talents had been better spent were
wrapped in the parochial concerns of colony and state, this Virginian, with a handful of like-minded zealots assembled from
the ends of the revolting provinces, was engaged in the libera-
tion of a nation. What set the flame in him can only be conjec-
tured. But he was a hater of faction, a lover of glory, and what
he set his hand to was grandly conceived, as if the spaciousness
of the conception was a spur to accomplishment.

The circumstances of Washington's election as commander
in chief in June 1775 have been remarked upon. Undoubtedly
the delegates in Philadelphia knew something about his military experience. But the problem of a leader was obviously not
treated as a matter of finding the best provincial soldier. On the
record as it then stood, Washington's capacities were fortunately as good or better than those of any other patriot. At
the age of sixteen and for two years thereafter he had been
employed surveying lands in western Virginia and had thus
acquired knowledge of terrain. In 1752 he was appointed major in the militia, and the following year was sent to investigate
the encroachments of the French in the Ohio Valley. Promoted
to lieutenant colonel, he was again sent to the Ohio, where he
was worsted by the French. He next served as an aide to the
heedless Braddock, and after the disastrous defeat on the Mo-

nongahela devoted three years to almost fruitless efforts at organizing the defense of the border. He had accompanied Forbes on the expedition which finally ousted the French from the Ohio. During all these years Washington was a book student of the military art.

These experiences were to be fruitful. In the first place, Washington acquired an exact knowledge of the limitation of militia training and of how the independent American soldier could best fight. He had gained an intimate acquaintance with the inflexible British military mind. His efforts to fortify the frontier had taught him the pains of dealing with politicians upon whom the supply of men and arms depended. No contemporary European military pundit would have admitted that any of this qualified Washington to be a general, for his experiences did not fit the orthodox pattern of the profession as it was then understood.

The commission which Washington accepted in 1775 furnishes the premises by which his career is to be judged. He is named "General and Commander in Chief of the Army of the United Colonies." The Congress probably intended to grant thereby little more than superiority over all other commanders; the reservation of Congress' own ultimate control is apparent in the instructions that accompanied the commission. As events unfolded, however, as the conflict assumed greater magnitude, as various theaters of war developed, it was inevitable that Washington had to act in two capacities. As general he commanded his own army in the field; as commander in chief he had responsibility for problems of organization, logistics, and over-all strategy. We propose therefore to assess him first as commander in chief and second as a general in the field.

The evolution of the commander-in-chief role is forecast in the instructions which, in the sixth paragraph, permitted the exercise of discretion. At the moment this did not imply very much. Congress had not yet learned of Bunker Hill. The avowed purpose of military action was the defense of American liberties and the repulsion of invasion. A reconciliation with Britain was still anticipated and planned. Washington shared this hope, and in New York he publicly expressed it (June 24, 1775). A little over six months later he wrote Joseph Reed that after he learned of the measures adopted in consequence of Bunker Hill, "I have never entertained any idea of an accommodation." Such political prescience is remarkable, for it predetermined the things done to transform into an army the motley crew besieging Boston. Again and again there are manifestations of his peculiar sagacity. "To direct a whole war or its greatest enterprises (which we call campaigns) to a brilliant goal, requires great insight into higher political relations. The conduct of war and politics merges here, and out of the leader in the field emerges the statesman." So spoke Clausewitz; Washington could have been his example.

The military advantages which might have been gained by a full exploitation of this capacity of prophetic insight were rarely realized, because of a second characteristic which we may call Washington's constitutionalism. This may seem an odd word to use about a leader of a rebel army, yet no other quite expresses Washington's attitude. It possessed the elements of religious conformity. His commission stated that he was to observe orders and directions from Congress or its committees. To this he was obedient. In one of his first official acts —his orders to Schuyler—he makes this clear. Schuyler is to keep an eye on royal governor Tryon of New York—"if forcible measures are judged necessary I should have no difficulty in ordering of them if the Continental Congress was not sitting." And so he refers Schuyler to that body. He defers to provincial congresses, as his correspondence with the New York body illustrates. He requests of Congress (1777) a ruling on whether the instructions to advise with his Council of War mean he is to be bound by the majority. If there is something in the constitutional setup which irks him like the matter of promotion, he tries to have it corrected, he does not transgress.

Washington's quality of law abidance hampered his work as commander in chief because the American reaction against executivism compelled him to deal with a basically ineffective political setup. His military policy demanded first a cohesive army enlisted for the war and subject to centralized authority. This we have seen he did not get. Secondly, the army had to be well trained, well supplied, and well paid. Only the training objective was approximated, and this due to his own and his officers' efforts. Thirdly, the planning of campaigns was a soldier's job and not one for a civilian legislature or a committee. Here the pendulum swung back and forth, for sometimes Washington exercised this function and sometimes he did not. This phase of his policy was also profoundly affected by Congress' insistence upon appointment of general officers and its interferences in assignments. On the most important strategical questions, when and how battle was to be joined, Congress was anything but silent, yet the decisions were usually Washington's. This was chiefly because such decisions depended upon what the British did, and because he had to make the best of what at the moment he possessed in the way of an army.

The first task of the commander in chief when he reached Cambridge in 1775 was to fashion an army out of the militia levies. The manual of arms and the articles of war were administered as the recognized nostrum for undiscipline. The medicine was not utterly effective, partly because of the here-today-gone-tomorrow character of the army, and partly because of the deep-rooted independency of the private soldiers. They were disposed to do things on their own initiative, and they were quick to argue. Steuben wrote his friend De Gaudy in 1787:

> The genius of this nation is not in the least to be compared to the Prussians, the Austrians or the French. You say to your soldier "Do this" and he doeth it, but I am obliged to say "This is the reason why you ought to do that" and then he does it.

This individualism made good soldiers in certain types of combat, but it was their undoing in other situations, as the battle at Germantown demonstrated. Washington's efforts to create a stable and efficient corps of officers were intended to meet both difficulties, the shifting personnel and the insubordination. He was not entirely successful, for he never had appointments and promotions sufficiently under his own control. It was the drilling at Valley Forge both of men and officers that finally turned the trick.

Making an army in 1775 presented another problem which was to harass Washington to the end of the war. This was the canker of localism which corrupted union and was manifested in the form of intertown rivalry, interstate rivalry, and even interregional rivalry. The new bonds of common defense and the achievement of liberty were not proof against an old history of quarrels about boundaries, extraditions, religious antipathies—indeed, the whole grab bag of colonial contentions. Washington discovered at once that you could not put a Connecticut officer over Massachusetts men, and that in some quarters a Britisher was preferred to a Virginian. Out of his dilemma sprang his strong feeling of nationalism and the impassioned efforts to make at least of his army something truly American. This spirit animates all of his correspondence with Congress on the state of the Army. But the fear of a standing army, the defensive-alliance quality of our first political association were too strong. As we have seen, the Continental Army was organized on state lines. Only among his officers, and here chiefly by force of his own personality, did Washington approximate his objective.

The rivalries and prejudices which frustrated the creation of a national army resulted likewise in limitations upon the office of commander in chief. Washington's conception of his constitutional obligations played into the hands of those intent upon making him the utter servant of the Continental Congress, and lack of sympathy with his strategical conceptions put upon him the alternative burden of cajoling, or repairing damage already done. Decision was wanted of him only by way of agreement.

From the beginning, Washington, aware of the state of preparedness, pursued the strategy of defense. His letters show a clear grasp of the military principle that interior lines are superior to exterior lines of operation. His experience at the siege of Boston convinced him that if the British could be penned in at a port of landing they would have to live off their ships and not off the land. This was the basis of the New York campaign of 1776 and of the later raids on Trenton and Princeton that forced the British out of New Jersey. It was the policy pursued after Brandywine and Germantown. It was what he expected would be done when Charleston was invaded in 1780. Washington gave battle only when considerations of morale and political effect made it imperative. As long as he could hold an army in the field, however small, America was not yet subdued. He understood completely and practiced the war of nerves, although he would not have called it that.

The Fabian strategy was not appreciated by many state delegates in Congress who believed in what has been called the "power of untutored impetuosity." Some gauge of the military genius of this group can be found in the opinions of John Adams, who was one of them. Adams had started reading military books in 1775 and was consequently schooled in the rudiments of how warfare was conducted. His military prescriptions, however, were of his own compounding, and they were truly remarkable. He thought that shooting a general after a retreat would give an impulse to victory; he wanted a short and bloody war; he advocated annual election of generals. If the activities of the opposition had been confined to speeches, such notions would have caused little trouble. Unfortunately, machinations were directed toward getting rid of Washington, a project which collapsed with the unmasking of the Conway Cabal, but did not entirely subside. The effect of such politics upon Washington personally was to confirm him in a lifelong dislike of what he called faction. But in spite of his private resentment he was careful to give no sign of taking personal offense, for he possessed a patient detachment, the capacity to submerge his own feelings, and to make his decision entirely upon the basis of the good of the cause. He continued to deal with Gates, Reed, Mifflin, and others, outwardly as unperturbed as if they were his friends.

But if Washington could ignore personal affront, it was less easy to cope with resolutions that carved away large portions of his authority as commander in chief. This was a situation that developed out of the war-planning powers which the Continental Congress had clearly reserved in 1775. At that time no one could have foreseen that intrigue would pervert this prerogative into encroachment upon the functions of the chief command. The creation of a separate Northern Department to meet the menace of invasion from Canada did just this. Washington's friends in Congress secured a resolution authorizing him to select the commander. This he refused to do in the interest of unity. There was, in any event, no need for him to act. The strategy of the campaign had already been laid out in his letters to Schuyler, and his detail of Arnold, whose military qualities were great, was an insurance that the plan would be executed. It was characteristic of his modesty that Washington let others have the credit.

The second Canadian expedition projected in the winter of 1777–78 was another congressional plan which Washington did not touch, for it was fomented without consulting him. He did not approve of it, but knowing that it depended upon the ability of Gates and Conway to raise men and supplies, he permitted these geniuses to dig the grave of the project with the shovel of their own incapacities. However, in the following year when Lafayette, fired with dreams of restoring the French Empire, resurrected the scheme, Washington made haste to scotch it. He had no desire for a French Canada to the north and a Spanish New Orleans to the south, with Indians friendly to the French at our backs. For thus, wrote he, would France "have it in her power to give law to these States." It was not for the integrity of his command but for the integrity of the nation, present and future, that he was fighting.

Congress' second drastic intrusion upon the supreme command was in the Southern Department. This had been established in 1776 but did not become a major theater of war until later. When British designs on Georgia and South Carolina became apparent, Congress, without consultation, put General Lincoln in charge. After Lincoln's surrender at Charleston, Gates was chosen to lead the defense—again without Washington's advice. The defeat at Camden and Gates's two-hundred-mile gallop to the rear led the Solons of Philadelphia finally to appeal to the commander in chief, who dispatched the competent Greene to the scene. The scrupulousness with which Washington thereafter maintained the role of a mere adviser can be read in his communications to his comrade in arms. After the Yorktown operation had been planned, Greene suggested a joint expedition against Charleston. Washington sent Colonel Morris with a message:

Col. Morris will inform General Greene in the sincerest manner that there are but two motives which can possibly induce Gen'l. W——— to take the command to the southward; one the order of C——— [Congress] to repair thither; the other the French army going there. In the last case Count R——— [Rochambeau] would command if Gen'l W——— did not go in person.

The Yorktown affair exhibits at once the genius of Washington in seeing the war as a whole and his capacity to make bold plans. In the summer of 1781 the chance for the long-hoped-for assault on New York seemed at hand with the presence of French troops and an available French fleet, and plans had actually been laid. When the news arrived that Cornwallis had walked out onto a limb barer than Boston, New York, or Philadelphia, the priceless opportunity of a coup brought quick decision. The New York campaign was shelved and measures taken to beguile Sir Henry Clinton with a *petite guerre*. With astonishing swiftness and secrecy, the Continentals and French were marched and transported to Virginia, where Lafayette had been holding Cornwallis' attention. The risk was great, for the operation depended upon a French blockade of the Chesapeake, and no one could be sure that the fleet had arrived. When this proved to be the case, the commander in chief once more displayed his consummate political gifts in persuading Admiral De Grasse, anxious for a West India rendezvous, to stand by. De Grasse, in signifying agreement, assumed paternity for the plans which were, in fact, perfected by Washington. But the latter, aware of the Gallic hunger for renown, applauded De Grasse's "personal sacrifices" and added, "I flatter myself that the result of the operations conducted under your auspices will compensate them by its utility to the common cause." The issue was the common cause; the credit could go where it would.

Washington's work as commander in chief was considerably affected by his own experiences as a general in the field. He had discovered in the course of the New York campaign of 1776 that, bad as the militia was, the presence of a core of veterans had a steadying effect, and that green troops did better when the danger was immediate to their own neighborhood. The forces to oppose Burgoyne were planned in this way, and he refused to let southern troops be detached for these operations because he thought the New Englanders would fight better. The same ideas were applied in the southern campaign of 1780. Similarly, the intelligence service which Washington developed in connection with the operations under his immediate direction was expanded for broader uses. A striking use of this, exemplifying his prudence, was the elaborate investigations made through persons on the western frontier before Sullivan's expedition was dispatched in 1779 to extirpate the Indian menace.

As to Washington's generalship and handling of the troops at his own immediate disposal, the greatest controversy existed at the time of the Revolution. No one ever denied his mastery of the art of retreat; it was his command in action that evoked criticism. There is no doubt that he made mistakes, but many of the errors attributed to him were due to the incompetent execution of assignments by some of the general officers with whom Congress had saddled him. The outflanking of Sullivan on Long Island and again at Brandywine in 1777 with loss of both battles are typical instances of this. On two occasions Washington's generalship suffered because he succumbed to local political pressure. He could have inflicted serious harm on Howe's army if he had bombarded Boston in the spring of 1776. He could have made New York an empty conquest in August of that year if he had burned the town upon his retreat. In the face of misadventures with the capacities of his generals, it may seem remarkable that Washington so consistently consulted them. It has been said by General Cullum that whenever Washington acted upon his own judgment and did not yield his conviction to his subordinates' he outgeneraled his opponents. His instructions from Congress, however, had explicitly directed consultation, and the commander in chief was incapable of disobedience. The practice persisted with him even in the face of his experience before Monmouth (1778), where poor advice before the fight lost him a chance to repeat Frederick's success at Rossbach with one of the great Prussian's captains at his side. He was not to know until it was almost too late that in Charles Lee he harbored a rogue. His retrieval of almost disastrous defeat was one of the grand moments in his military career. Wrote Hamilton a few days later:

> I never saw the General to so much advantage. His coolness and firmness were admirable. He instantly took measures for checking the enemy's advance and giving time to the army, which was very near, to form and make a proper disposition. . . . America owes a great deal to General Washington for this day's work. A general rout, dismay, and disgrace would have attended the whole army in any other hands but his. By his good sense and fortitude he turned the fate of the day.

"Good sense and fortitude," these are the virtues which consistently characterize the generalship of Washington, which underlie the devotion of his men, and which kept the Army from dissolution. It is difficult to fathom how this general, so severe, so upright, and so detached, created that mystical bond of allegiance with the common soldier. Of its existence there can be no doubt. "See the poor Soldier," wrote Surgeon Waldo on December 14, 1777, at Valley Forge. "When in health with what chearfulness he meets his foes and encounters every hardship—if barefoot he labours thro the Mud & Cold with a song in his mouth extolling War and Washington." Deeper than the mere sharing of adversity or the glory of an occasional victory shared, the spell exercised by this tall, composed Virginian lies in the very impenetrability of his personality.

. . . where there is no royal magic in the person of the commander, heroism and unshaken courage in dangers and difficulties, a reserved wisdom which does not expose purposes that ought not to be known, and a firmness of character which does not yield to importunities, of whatever kind they may be, are the points which strike the soldier's mind, and assure his attachment beyond all other causes which act on man. If the general expose his designs prior to forming his order of battle, or, if he change purposes from wavering within himself, the soldier (and soldiers are ordinarily acute to perceive manifestations of weakness) loses confidence, and, whatever may be the eminence of the commander's rank, commits himself to his guidance with reluctance. The military chief, in order to assure the success of his enterprizes, must be supposed to command the confidence of his followers; and he cannot be expected to command it without the possession of a genius which cannot be penetrated or measured by common capacities.

Here, in the words of Robert Jackson, a surgeon serving with British forces, and written long after the war was done, is captured the essence of Washington's power. As military genius went, it had not the great and original quality of a Frederick or a Wellington, but it was a genius that fitted the circumstances of the war he was fighting, and its strength was such that its effects were communicated beyond the soldiery to the people themselves. His destiny as a leader in peace was thereby made inevitable.

II

When Washington stopped in New York City on his way to Cambridge in June 1775, the New York Provincial Congress took occasion to express to him its confidence that when the war was done he would resign "the important deposite committed into your hands and reassume the character of our worthiest citizen." General Washington replied with the unforgettable words, "When we assumed the soldier, we did not lay aside the citizen." How steadfastly he adhered to this precept has been related. But eight years of command inevitably left their mark. The soldier returned to private life, yet the convictions of the commander lived on in the Virginia planter. When the new Constitution went into effect, Washington was unanimously elected first President of the United States. In the minds of his countrymen his record as commander in chief had qualified him beyond all of his compatriots. He was to bring to his new office a mind and spirit tempered by the years of leadership in war.

Historians have represented the span of Washington's presidencies as a stage set for the duel between the able Hamilton and the multicolored Jefferson; Washington's figure has been relegated to the shadows of the wings. Yet it was Washington who played the decisive, if less dramatic, role, holding the balance firmly between the extremes and achieving a truly American policy.

The years 1783–89 have been termed the "Critical Period." But in many respects the years that followed were far more critical. Six years of peace had revealed clearly the basic weaknesses of the central government under the Articles of Confederation. No power to levy taxes (and as a result no means by which to pay the Continental debt) no control over commerce, no common currency, no control over state legislation contravening treaty provisions and inimical to the common interest, no separate executive, no authoritative judiciary! The indictment had been framed by Madison, Hamilton, Washington, Jay, and lesser hands; and the verdict given by the ratification of the Constitution. But the Constitution was only a blueprint, a working plan of government. Success or failure awaited the new experiment—but the event was not predetermined. Could the men assembled in New York to inaugurate the new government clothe the bare bones with flesh and blood and transform the skeleton into a living organism? When Washington took the oath of office on the balcony of Federal Hall on April 30, 1789, the answer was still uncertain.

Washington's administrations were the hazardous years of experimentation and of innovation now hallowed as precedent. Of this the President himself was keenly conscious. "In our progress towards political happiness my station is new;" he wrote in January 1790, "and, if I may use the expression, I walk on untrodden ground. There is scarcely any part of my conduct wch. may not hereafter be drawn into precedent."

In general, his was the nationalist voice. Schooled by the vicissitudes of the Revolution, his years of devotion to "the common cause," he had learned to take an overview of the whole, to value the ultimate and to subordinate the local and immediate. And the man who had borne the outrageous slings of fortune in 1777 could in his presidential years face faction and friction with outward composure. The record bears this out. In the conflicts first over the development of our governmental structure, and secondly over the evolution of our policies, domestic and foreign, Washington clung tenaciously to his purpose, creating the paradigm of the executive in the minds of the people.

During the Revolution Washington had repeatedly revealed his belief in the necessity of a responsible and stable executive authority. Upon his accession to the presidency, there was little in the Constitution itself to guide him. Specific presidential powers were granted, but little was said of the relation of the executive to the other branches of government. The practices developed under Washington, either by rejection or by acceptance of his ideas, have been determinative of the mold of our government.

Washington's main concept was that of a government linked by consultation. Here his experience in the war years shaped his thinking. Throughout that period he had been in constant touch with the Continental Congress by letter, by conference with committees, or in person. During his first administration he attempted to knit together executive and legislative, but with little success. His annual messages to Congress were delivered in person and were ridiculed as "the speech from the throne." The procedure aroused such a storm of criticism that with the exception of his immediate successor, John Adams, later presidents abandoned the practice for more than a century. His attempt in August 1789 to obtain the Senate's advice on a pending treaty met with sharp rebuff. "The President wishes to tread on the necks of the Senate," snarled Senator

Maclay of Pennsylvania, and his colleagues concurred. From that day to this the Senate has exercised but a truncated share of the treaty-making powers granted it in the Constitution; the "advice" which that instrument stipulates has been excised, and for it has been substituted the take-it-or-leave-it amendment of custom. In 1792 a bill was introduced to permit heads of departments to appear in the House of Representatives and explain their policies. Characterized by Jefferson as "an attempt . . . to give further extent to the influence of the Executive over the legislature," the bill failed by a vote of 35 to 11. The net result of Washington's efforts to integrate the executive and legislative branches was the sharpened separation of powers that is a marked feature of our unwritten constitution.

Washington was equally unsuccessful in his attempt to inter-relate executive and judiciary. Troubled over legal problems which had arisen in connection with the European war, he asked the opinion of the Supreme Court justices on the propriety of securing their advice on questions of law, and submitted a memorandum of problems for answer in case the justices agreed to give advisory opinions. Stiffly the Court declined. The justices were "against the propriety of our extra-judicially deciding the questions alluded to"—in other words, no opinions except in cases duly litigated.

In his relations with the members of the executive branch, however, Washington realized his consultative ideal and thus developed the Cabinet, that original feature of our unwritten constitution. On executive officers other than the President, the Constitution is brief. The President "may require the Opinion, in writing, of the principal Officer in each of the executive Departments, upon any subject relating to the duties of their respective Offices." On this slender foundation Washington built the Cabinet. Just as he had conferred with his generals on important occasions and called for their opinions on a projected course of action, so he followed the same practice in his relations with the men serving with him—Jefferson, the Secretary of State; Hamilton, his former aide-de-camp, Secretary of the Treasury; Knox, his trusted companion in arms, Secretary of War; and Edmund Randolph, his protégé, Attorney General. First by calling for written opinions, later by summoning meetings for joint consideration of particular questions, he developed the basic structure of the Cabinet. No exact counterpart can be found in our political antecedents; neither colonial council nor state senate furnishes a precise analogue. Washington's cabinet was patterned on the relations of the commander in chief and the staff of the Continental Army—consultation, then unity of action in a common cause.

"The mind is so formed in different persons as to contemplate the same object in different points of view," wrote Washington in 1789, before he assumed office. Here spoke the general, accustomed to the sharply divergent views of a Steuben and a Wayne. Here, too, was presaged the President who would value and make use of the talents of such opposing figures as Hamilton and Jefferson. Divergence of opinion Washington understood; faction and party he was always to deplore, from his entrance into the presidency until his Farewell Address. Although parties developed during his administrations, it is questionable whether Washington could ever be termed a party man. As he wrote Jefferson in July 1796, ". . . I was no party man myself and the first wish of my heart was, if parties did exist, to reconcile them." Rather, he stood out as an American, favoring the strength of the Union through the exercise of national powers. He coincided in view with the policies of the Federalist party, but in party politics he played little part.

Both in domestic and foreign matters Washington's weight was felt. Outstanding in importance among domestic issues was the troubled question of the debts incurred by the defunct Continental Congress and left as an unpleasant legacy to the new government. Out of the muddled years of the 1780s the urgency of one national policy had emerged. Officers of the Continental Army who had accepted "commutation" certificates in lieu of pensions, citizens who had staked their fortunes to win the Revolution, and foreign governments which (for diverse reasons) had supported the Revolutionary cause must be reimbursed. The future credit of the Government was at stake. The Constitution solemnly affirmed this obligation; Madison and Hamilton had defended the policy. Now the day of reckoning was at hand. The past debt must be funded and paid off as the new government gathered financial strength. To Washington, the problem must have appeared simple—a just man meets his obligations.

The Hamiltonian program was initiated in January 1790. Full payment of all outstanding debts, domestic and foreign, principal and interest, at face value to citizen and foreigner alike —this was the kernel of Hamilton's proposal. And the assumption of the state Revolutionary debts was added. All had been incurred in a common cause; all should share the burden.

On the rock of Hamiltonian financing, the unity of the Federalists of 1787 (the defenders of the Constitution) was shattered, and the first parties—or at least factions—arose. Cries were raised against Hamilton's proposals. The speculator and the capitalist would be enriched. This was a program designed to favor the rich and the seaboard at the expense of the poor and of the men of the back country. The Continental certificates were depreciated and should be paid at market value only. The arrears of interest should be canceled. Madison, the "Father of the Constitution," proposed that the original owners should receive the difference between the market and par value and thus reduce the speculator-buyer's profit. Some states had shouldered a large part of their Revolutionary debt and regarded assumption as unjust. The storm of discussion raged through the spring of 1790. Convinced at that date that defeat of the funding bill "would be tantamount to a dissolution of the government," Jefferson (to his later regret) was won to the assumption of state debts by a "compromise" locating the future capital on the Potomac. "The President of the United States has (in my opinion) had a great influence in this business," wrote Senator Maclay darkly in the conviction that "the President has become, in the hands of Hamilton, the dishclout of every dirty speculation, as his name goes to wipe away blame and silence all murmuring." The

Hamiltonian program was enacted and the Federal credit made secure. But public outcry against "Miss Assumption" was bitter. Jefferson and Madison, perceptive of the rising tide of agrarian protest, would soon emerge in the silhouette of opposition leadership.

A widening of the rift was precipitated in 1791 by Hamilton's project of a National Bank to facilitate the Government's financial operations. Here, as in the past, Washington consulted members of his Cabinet—Hamilton, Jefferson, and Randolph. The opinion of the Attorney General was negligible. But Hamilton and Jefferson produced two of the most important papers in our history—their reports on the constitutionality of the Bank. Hamilton's opinion was prophetic of the future, a justification of a broad interpretation of Federal powers. John Marshall and his successors in the Supreme Court from that day to the present were to utilize the Hamiltonian analysis of the "general welfare clause" and the doctrine of "implied powers." Jefferson's opinion (in essence, a swaddling cloth of strict construction to bind the infant government) was to exercise a potent influence until the Civil War put a sanguinary period to the issue of states' rights.

It was characteristic of Washington's constitutionalism that his decision was in favor of Hamilton's project. Financial problems lay in the Secretary of the Treasury's bailiwick. In the face of a division of opinion, he would follow the advice of the head of the department concerned. We can nevertheless be certain that in coming to this decision the President was not unforgetful of the commander in chief's painful experiences with the financial bedlam during the Revolutionary years in which state bickering played so great a part. He was consequently favorably disposed toward devices which would overcome local ambitions and local jealousies. With his approval, the Bank bill went to Congress and was passed. Posterity must echo Jefferson's later grudging characterization of the President as a man "who errs as other men do, but errs with integrity."

Another issue in our early history that aroused intense feeling was the "Whisky Rebellion"—that outburst of local antagonism to the Federal Government aroused by the excise tax. Hamilton had proposed, and in March 1791 Congress had enacted, a law placing a tax on every still that converted grain into whisky. The frontier farmer, lacking the facilities to ship his weighty bushels of grain to the East, bitterly resented the tax that fell on the manufacture of his more transportable and potable product. The frontier grumbled in 1792 and 1793. Democratic societies recently formed in the defense of the Rights of Man took up the cry; meetings were held; tax collectors were threatened or driven out. In July 1794 a mob burned the house of General Neville, the collector of western Pennsylvania. In short, the frontier, and back Pennsylvania in particular, defied the Federal law.

Washington stepped in. Under an Act of May 2, 1792, he was empowered "whenever the laws of the United States shall be opposed or the execution thereof be obstructed . . . to call forth the militia of such State to suppress such combinations, and to cause the laws to be duly executed," and furthermore, he was authorized to call out the militia of neighboring states if need be. Informed of the rioting at Pittsburgh, he issued two proclamations warning the malcontents to desist, and calling out the militia of Pennsylvania, Maryland, New Jersey, and Virginia. In person he accompanied the troops as far as Bedford, and issued orders for the organization of the undisciplined force. The affair soon took on the aspect of a pitiful *opéra bouffe*. The rebellion was dissipated, the army marched home, and the tax was collected. Washington by firm and timely action had vindicated without bloodshed the Federal powers.

It is, however, in his grasp of the problems of our foreign relations and his leadership in shaping these policies that Washington played his most significant role. In domestic issues he may have leaned on Hamilton for advice, but foreign policy was his own. Jefferson, that man of "sublimated and paradoxial imagination," was to turn against his policy and resign from office. Washington, as in the days of the Revolution, was to adhere inflexibly to his single purpose—the preservation of our independence.

The outbreak of the French Revolution kindled general approval and sympathy in the United States. The torch of republicanism was being passed to the Old World, and the evolution of the new order in France was watched with interest.

Washington wrote to Hector St. John de Crèvecoeur in April 1789:

I am very happy to find, by the translations which you were so polite as to send me, that there is so essential a change in the political opinions of the French Nation; indeed the American Revolution, or the peculiar spirit of the age seems to have opened the eyes of almost every nation in Europe, and a spirit of equal liberty appears fast to be gaining ground everywhere, which must afford satisfaction to every friend of mankind.

But as the tempo of the French drama quickened, the first enthusiasm was checked. The events of 1792 and the opening months of 1793 split the country apart. In general, the alignment of pro-French and anti-French corresponded with the demarcation already effected by domestic issues. Frontiersman and pamphleteer, hot against the funding of the debt, the bank, and the excise, were loud in the defense of the Rights of Man, eagerly forming "Democratic Societies" and erecting new-style liberty poles. Men of substance, the clergy and the conservative-minded, shocked by the execution of the amiable, if inept, Louis XVI and by the rising violence of the Terror, reacted sharply against the French Republic.

The outbreak of war between England and France in the spring of 1793 heightened the tension. What course should the United States pursue? On the one hand were our obligations to France. These were both moral and legal. French aid given against Great Britain lived in men's memories. The Treaties of 1778, although concluded with a king recently decapitated on the guillotine, hung over our heads. Should the new republic be accorded recognition? Was the treaty of alliance still binding? Must we be dragged into the European conflict as an ally of the French?

In dealing with these problems, Washington displayed the political acumen which is true statesmanship. Recognition was accorded the new government, despite Hamilton's stiff-necked reservations. A neutrality proclamation (of which Jefferson disapproved) was issued. The obligations of a neutral were steadily enforced in the face of Agent Genêt's willful actions and the violent outbursts of American "democrats," and in despite of the popular outcries evoked by the highhanded British treatment of our ships and our citizens. It was Washington who conceived this policy and Washington who insisted upon its maintenance. "If we preserve even a sneaking neutrality, we shall be indebted for it to the President & not to his counsellors," wrote Jefferson bitterly in May 1793. Public passions might rise, the adherents of Hamilton and Jefferson be inflamed by party animosities and predilection for monarch or Jacobin. Washington was firm in his determination to maintain our peace, our independence, and our frontiers.

For our frontiers were in fact imperiled. Alignment with France against the British-Spanish alliance would have affected us not solely in terms of a maritime war. No ocean separated us from the Allies. The danger was immediate and close at hand. In 1793 the United States was encircled by potential enemies. Our northern border from the St. Croix River to the Great Lakes faced British power. Indeed, in defiance of the Treaty of 1783, British troops still held the northern posts on American soil from Niagara to Green Bay, hotbeds of intrigue among their old allies, the Northwest Indians. In the Ohio country a deadly intermittent Indian war against the American settlers had broken out in 1790. Harmar's defeat was followed by St. Clair's failure in 1791. British prestige in the Indian councils rose, and British influence was bitterly anti-American. In the spring of 1793, when peace with England hung by a thread, Washington, following his in-times-of-peace-prepare-for-war policy, was struggling to secure by peaceful means a settlement of the Indian troubles while, on the other hand, the Army was being expanded in case of need. With a renewal of Indian war imminent, open conflict with Great Britain must at all costs be averted.

But the British were not the only peril to our frontiers. The situation on the southern border from Georgia to the Mississippi was a constant source of anxiety. The Spanish power stretched from Florida to Louisiana and from the Mississippi west to the Pacific. At odds with the United States over the southern boundary since 1783 and distrustful of republican ideals, Spain pursued a devious and unfriendly policy toward the United States. Uprisings of the Indians were encouraged, and the Spanish border lands were a refuge for Creek warriors. Agents and spies were employed in the United States; even a general in the United States Army, James Wilkinson, secretly drew a pension from Spain. With a throttle hold on New Orleans, Spain closed the Mississippi to American trade; for the men west of the Appalachians, the river was the only road to the sea and markets. Small wonder that Citizen Genêt found sympathy in Kentucky and Tennessee, or that discontent fermented against the eastern seaboard. The ties that bound the Southwest to the Federal Government were stretched thin. War must be averted lest the bonds snap.

Washington had written sagely in 1784:

> How entirely unconnected with them shall we be, and what troubles may we not apprehend, if the Spaniards on their right, and Great Britain on their left, instead of throwing stumbling blocks in their way, as they do now, should hold out lures for their trade and alliance. . . . The western settlers (I speak now from my own observation) stand as it were upon a pivot. The touch of a feather would turn them any way.

Thus, in Washington's view, frontier and foreign policy had long been fused. Never unmindful of our *rights* as neutrals, he sought to secure rectification of British and Spanish depredations on our commerce. Never forgetful of the dangers to our borders, he insisted upon the observation of our *duties* as neutrals. For this reason he put forth the Neutrality Proclamation of April 1793; for this cause he secured implementation of the neutrality policy by issuing executive orders to the collectors of customs in May and August 1793 and by wringing from Congress the Neutrality Act of 1794. All were designed to prevent unneutral acts on our soil, to preserve our peace, and to protect our borders.

It is in this light that one must read Washington's acceptance of the Jay Treaty concluded with England in 1794. Resentment against Great Britain had risen to fever he..t since the spring of 1793. British infractions of the Treaty of 1783, British refusal to open her colonies to our trade, British impressment of our seamen, seizures of ships and cargoes, had brought us to the verge of war. In 1794 John Jay had been charged with the duty of securing satisfaction for all these complaints. The treaty which goes by his name was the imperfect answer. Much was gained, but the West Indies trade was not made free, and impressment was not mentioned. Cognizant of the sins of omission of that document, its failure to secure our rights as a neutral, Washington finally bent his energies toward forcing its acceptance. Peace was essential and peace was secured.

"His Majesty will withdraw all his troops and garrisons from all posts and places within the boundary lines assigned by the treaty of peace to the United States," read Article II of the Jay Treaty. Here lay the triumph for the frontier; here la, the vindication of Washington's unpopular policy. He had warned Jay in 1794:

I will undertake without the gift of prophecy to predict that it will be impossible to keep this country in a state of amity with Great Britain long, if the [western] posts are not surrendered. . . . If they want to be in Peace with this Country and to enjoy the benefits of trade, to give up the posts is the only road to it. Withholding them, and consequences we feel at present, continuing, war will be inevitable.

The Jay Treaty removed this burr of irritation. The Northwest was saved for the United States.

Following the Jay Treaty came the Pinckney Treaty with Spain. The Jay Treaty proved to be a fulcrum in our negotiations with the latter power, for the attitude of reserve, if not contempt, which had characterized the Spanish attitude toward our diplomatic advances since Jay's mission during the Revolution was shattered by the conclusion of the Jay Treaty with England. In 1795 the Spanish proved conciliatory—nay docile. The Pinckney Treaty rescued the Southwest. Agreement was reached on all the critical issues that had been agitating the frontier. The boundary line was fixed in our favor at the thirty-first parallel. The navigation of the Mississippi "from its source to the ocean" was declared to be free to the subjects of both powers. Both parties (and this was a diplomatic flourish) bound themselves to restrain by force all hostilities on the part of the Indians living within their boundaries. New Orleans was opened as a place of deposit, and warehousing rights for the merchandise of American traders were secured for three years at least. The American concepts of neutral rights (particularly "free ships shall also give freedom to goods") were upheld. Obscured by the clamor against the Jay Treaty, the solid victory of the Spanish treaty has too often been overlooked. Yet, to be fairly judged, the conclusion of the Jay Treaty must be viewed as only a part of Washington's diplomacy—the pattern appears more clearly when the Pinckney Treaty is conjoined. War was averted, the Indian menace allayed, and the frontiers safeguarded—a consolation to Washington in the spiteful days of 1796, when he was enduring the vitriolic attacks of the democratic press.

The critical years were past. Long weary of public life, Washington could retire and obtain release from the burdens of the presidency. Much had been accomplished, much endured. His fortitude had been taxed by the defection of former friends —Jefferson, Randolph, Monroe. He had smarted under the offensive sneers of Callendar, Bache, and the hirelings of faction. He had known anger and resentment. But he had never swerved from his single purpose of service to his country. The words of the commander in chief of 1776 echo in the expressions of the President in his last years in office:

My ardent desire is, and my aim has been (as far as depended upon the Executive Department) to comply strictly with *all* our engagements, foreign and domestic; but to keep the U. States free from *political* connexions with *every* other Country. To see them independent of *all* and under the influence of *none*. In a word, I want an *American* character . . .

V

General Jackson

———————•◆•———————

ANDREW JACKSON became acquainted firsthand with war in 1780, when the British dragoons swarmed over South Carolina after the surrender of Charleston. At the tender age of thirteen he served as an orderly with Davies' partisan band and witnessed the fight at Hanging Rock. Thereafter he took a hand in the guerrilla warfare in the Waxhaw region, and following an unsuccessful attack was captured. The British officer who accomplished this coup ordered his young prisoner to shine his boots. In true guardhouse-lawyer style Jackson refused on the ground that he was a prisoner of war. The officer demurred to this plea with a saber cut and sent Jackson off to Camden jail. These souvenirs of the war were never forgotten. At New Orleans on January 8, 1815, the account was squared.

If the conditions of the time had been favorable, this early baptism of fire might at once have drawn Jackson into a military career. The critical years of his youth, however, were a period of demobilization when no man could anticipate more than the casual discharge of militia duty. Jackson turned to the law, a not unsuitable profession for a belligerent Celtic temperament, and as a lawyer he arrived in Tennessee, the base of his future operations in our history.

Jackson's elevation to the rank of major general of the Tennessee militia in 1802 has already been described. It was the result of a political process, usual in the States, and had nothing to do with military accomplishment. Indeed, as the militia was then constituted, some men without arms, the muster days convivial occasions with a minimum of drill, it is difficult to discover how any training was received by anyone. There is

no doubt Jackson sought to remedy matters. In one of his early
general orders (1803) he lectured the militia on the value of
discipline. He complained to Jefferson in 1808 about the lack
of arms, and two years later he wrote Governor Blount that
"under the laws of our State the militia will never be disciplined." Outlining a plan which bears some resemblance to
Washington's then unpublished project (1783) for a well-regulated militia, Jackson advocated congressional action, and as a
first step at home a change in the method of choosing officers.
Needless to say, Blount did nothing. It was going to take a war
for the Tennesseans to be made into soldiers.

The office of major general of the militia presenting so little
opportunity for self-perfection in the military art, some other
explanation must be sought for the proficiency with which
Jackson acted when he finally went to war. The aggressive
leadership, the daring and the coolness of his conduct, were
obviously not the sudden flowering of latent qualities; they
were the product of his previous career. It is not insignificant
that upon his first arrival in Tennessee Jackson had acted as
public prosecutor, and in 1791 had been appointed United
States attorney for the Mero district. In these two capacities
he campaigned against the bad men of western Tennessee. This
was a task which suited his natural pugnacity. And it was this
characteristic, rather than judicial detachment, which qualified
him when he was appointed judge of the Superior Court in
1798. In a turbulent frontier society it was coolness of courage
and not of intellect that the courtholder needed.

Although the years of Jackson's early manhood were occupied with the law, its enforcement, and its making (for he sat
briefly in Congress both as representative and senator), his
was a life lived dangerously. Much has been made of his
mother's last advice—never sue for assault or slander, "settle
them cases yourself"—an admonition which kept suits off the
dockets and made of the duel due process of law. This does not
account, however, for the extraordinary number of Jackson's
fights. He had a genius for controversy. And since, as a canny
priest once noticed, he possessed an innate piety, a strong

undertone of moral conviction colored his disputations. A correspondence with him was nothing for the timid to engage upon, for he penned his letters with the vigor and violence of a seventeenth-century Covenanter. A request for troops will read as if Gideon were pleading with the Lord; a letter to a superior, like Moses chiding the children of Israel. A subtle invitation to retort is usually implicit in his argumentative prose. But it was dangerous to accept, for it was unpredictable when warmth would burst into flame. Equally, a conversation had to be conducted with circumspection, for the Covenanter had a code of honor as delicate as that of the most captious Cavalier, and when he swore his favorite oath, "by the Eternal," the edge of patience had been reached. Hot in resenting affront, Jackson with a coldness no less ferocious would face the pistol of his adversary and with the least regret fire a dispatching bullet. This combination of rashness and imperturbability, the indifference with which he put his own life at stake, he expected in others. Here lies the key to the conduct of his military enterprises.

Covenanter and Cavalier—such was Jackson, an important figure in politics and in the militia, when the War of 1812 overtook him. We have seen the manner in which he secured his commission and his initial effort in the war. The expedition sent in 1812 to reinforce New Orleans and commanded by him in his capacity as major general of United States Volunteers had come to nothing at Natchez; but the return journey had earned him the asset of a soldier's nickname—Old Hickory. The journal of the trip downriver records the efforts to drill and discipline the troops, and the quick march back the Natchez "trace" establishes the effectiveness of the general's measures. He did not walk off his wrath at Secretary Armstrong and General Wilkinson, and it is unlikely he would have seen further service had not the massacre at Fort Mims by the Creeks spurred Tennessee into action in the fall of 1813.

Generalship in an Indian war was scarcely comparable to that required in operations against a European army. In either type of warfare, however, an American commander had certain

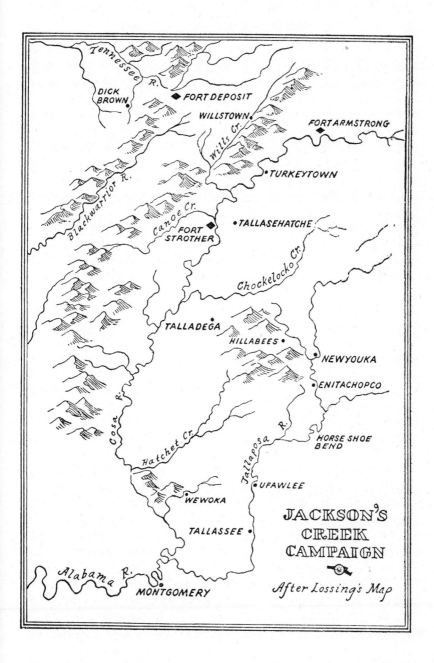

JACKSON'S CREEK CAMPAIGN

After Lossing's Map

basic problems, the organization and discipline of the army and the matter of supply. As to the former, Jackson had made a start with those volunteers who had followed him to Natchez. What hampered his direction of the new campaign was the old story of expired enlistments and the inflow of completely un-disciplined militiamen. These troubles, inherent in the military system of the time, were aggravated by the equally old story of a failure of supplies. At the very inception of his campaign Jackson was deviled by what he called "that meagre-monster 'Famine.'" The first set of contractors having failed him, the general promptly removed them and employed others. These proved to be little better and were the cause of nearly wrecking the whole enterprise. Historians have deprecated Jackson's lack of caution in embarking upon a winter campaign. What they have little appreciated is the astounding fortitude with which he literally stuck by his guns—such as he had.

The spirit which animated Jackson finds incidental expression in the stirring proclamation to his troops of October 24, 1813: "Your general laments, that he has been compelled even inci-dentally to use the word retreat. Never while he commands you shall you have any practical understanding of that word." He will make this promise again; in his letters, and no doubt in his mind, any movements not in advance are "retrograde." Retreat was banished from his vocabulary.

Early in November 1813 two successful actions were fought against the Creeks, but recall of troops and failure of supplies which the general derisively attributed to "some enchantment wrought by the Indian prophets on our contractors" compelled a "retrograde" to Fort Strother. Here occurred the troubles with his troops that, more than his Indian battles, showed the man's metal. On December 9 the volunteers demanded per-mission to go home, claiming their enlistment was up. Jackson paraded his militia and warned the volunteers he would open fire. The men submitted, but the spirit of mutiny was too strong, and he finally permitted them to leave. On January 4, 1814, the militia, except for one small company, departed.

Before this final defection a letter arrived from Governor

Blount advising evacuation of Fort Strother. To these "damd milk and water observations" Jackson replied in two letters. One, described by Jackson as a *gulger,* was an extremely robust lecture to Blount on his responsibilities. The other, "a good natured tickler," was more restrained:

> As the executive of the state it is your duty to see that the full quota of troops be kept in the field. . . . You are responsible to the government; your officers to you. . . . Believe me my valued friend there are times when it is highly criminal to shrink from responsibility or scruple about the exercise of our power.

Thanks to Jackson's indefatigability and the ardor of his officers who went home recruiting, a new army assembled, and in March 1814 the Creeks were crushed at Horseshoe Bend on the Tallapoosa River. In the following May Jackson was commissioned major general in the regulars commanding the Seventh Military District; in this capacity, on August 9, 1814, he made the treaty with the Creeks. The negotiations were conducted on the basis of an ultimatum which demanded from the Creeks a huge L-shaped tract so laid out as to protect the white settlements and insulate the Indians from contact with the Spaniards in Florida. Lands of Jackson's recent Indian allies were included. To the "noble red man" school of thinkers the demands have seemed brutal. The general, however, was moved by considerations that do credit to his political sagacity. He had experienced the damage done by British and Spanish incitation of the Indians. He was proposing a treaty that would minimize future trouble. His terms were accepted.

The reasons of defense on which Jackson grounded the treaty in his dispatch to Secretary Armstrong were sound. He had already received reliable intelligence of British designs for an attack on the Gulf coast, and the connivance of the Spanish at Pensacola was not to be doubted. His instructions from the War Department were of the sketchiest variety. With characteristic decision, he moved down to Mobile a few days after the Creek treaty was signed.

British troops had by this time landed at Pensacola, and

Colonel Edward Nicholls, "warm in the cause of the African race and the depressed and distressed Indians," was promoting the cause of racial equality by issuing British red coats and muskets to them. Jackson at once set about putting Fort Bowyer (guarding Mobile) in a state of defense, and owing to his energy an attack by sea was repulsed. The British advance squadron thereafter remained quietly at Pensacola awaiting the main forces, giving Jackson opportunity to assemble a larger army. On November 7, 1814, he made his celebrated attack upon Spanish Pensacola, after one of his aides bearing a flag of truce had been fired upon. He stormed the town but failed in his objective of catching the British. Their squadron moved out to sea.

The Pensacola affair is interesting on the political side of Jackson's generalship. As appears in his report to Monroe, his strategy was still concentrated upon removing the Indian menace. The old fear of the Indians, supported by foreign allies, still dominated his mind; Indians, being at hand, were more to be feared than foreign foes. Determined upon his own conception of immediate danger and his own plans for eliminating it, the harm the nation as a whole might have taken from an attack on neutral Spain was not weighed. Indeed, Jackson exults that he had "convinced the Spaniards that we will permit no equivocation in a nation professing neuterality, whilst we most scrupulously respect national, neuteral and individual rights." The Covenanter was certain of his own rectitude both in judgment and action.

The uncavalier behavior of the British in refusing Jackson's challenge to join battle at Pensacola lost them face with the Indians, and the American troops were buoyed by their success. Jackson's policy therefore brought immediate results, although his mistaken conception of the British objectives and strategy caused the loss of valuable time and led to the dispersion of his strength. It is apparent in his letters that he felt all possible places of debarkation along the Gulf had to be secured, that the maintenance of the line of supply through Alabama was crucial, and that British contact with the Creeks had to be frustrated. He was further convinced that any attack on New Orleans would be a flanking movement by way of Mobile overland to Baton Rouge. He failed to take into account the facts that it was easier to move an army by water and that a powerful fleet could be a military asset in an attack on a port. His actions at this juncture reflect the limitations of an inland experience and inland interests. It is almost as if he thought his task were still the protection of Tennessee.

Jackson's arrival at New Orleans in early December did not change his ideas about the British plan of attack. Nevertheless he set about strengthening the city's outlying defenses and, always concerned over intelligence problems, took pains to have all possible approaches covered. In spite of this the British effected a secret landing, and when Jackson first heard of it they were reported only eight miles from the city. The commander at once ordered a surprise attack on the British advance guard. In view of the historians' invidious remarks about Jackson's ignorance of naval matters, it is amusing to notice that his attack by land was in concert with the armed schooner *Caroline*. Indeed, the American naval assistance wrought such havoc that General Pakenham proceeded to waste four days getting up guns to pulverize the American water defense. It was these four days that enabled Jackson to perfect his ramparts; and it was against these that the fatuous Pakenham led his brave men to slaughter on January 8, 1815.

Jackson has been criticized for the slowness with which the military situation dawned on him, his sloth in making entrenchments and rounding up arms, his imperfect arrangements on the west bank of the Mississippi, where the Americans were driven back. We are disposed to believe that for a first battle against trained soldiers the general did not do badly. Certain it is that he was quick to repair mistakes, that he took advice and avoided rash actions. He was lucky in that the foes held him in contempt. He was wise in realizing that with his force well entrenched the terrible fire power of his rifles would make the attackers' bayonets a mere decoration.

The victory at New Orleans was not achieved without serious

collision with the civil power. The Creoles were not too warmly attached to the American cause, and Jackson's herculean efforts to muster an army invited resentment. He accepted the aid of Lafitte's pirates and armed the free Negroes over the inhabitants' protest. On December 28, when told the legislature was about to vote a submission to the enemy, he sent an order to the governor to disperse that body. He imposed the hard restrictions of martial law.

These things the civilians could endure before the battle; they were intolerable afterwards. The general did not relax, for the British were still hovering in the offing. The Frenchmen who, in a panic, had obtained certificates of French citizenship, he banished to Baton Rouge. A death sentence for mutiny imposed on six Tennessee militiamen was reviewed and approved. A newspaper article had precipitated a mutiny of some Louisiana troops. Jackson had the author arrested and court-martialed. Federal Judge Hall, who issued a habeas corpus, was locked up. Jackson refused to submit to the court's authority. In the midst of this uproar, on March 13, came the news of peace. Eight days later Judge Hall issued a summons for the general to show cause why he should not be attached for contempt in refusing to answer the habeas corpus. After days of legal fencing, a fine of $1,000 and costs was imposed, the final tribute of New Orleans to its savior.

If Jackson had been a general in active service for longer than eighteen months, his actions would have been attributed to the effects of militarism. In his later career the six militiamen were to rise up and haunt him, and modern writers have clucked their tongues in disparagement. Admitting the hot temper and talent for controversy which belonged to the man, it may be said in defense of him that the military situation was still precarious. The British still had an army of twelve thousand men and enough warships to blow New Orleans off the map. Their departure from Louisiana had been followed by the capture of Fort Bowyer. Ordinary prudence required the maintenance of discipline and alertness against a new attack. Jackson, used to ruses of the Indians, refused to act on mere rumors of peace. It is difficult not to think he was right.

The conclusion of peace with the British by the Treaty of Ghent in 1814 did not end Jackson's military career. General Jackson continued in the Regular Army, commanding the Southern Division until June 1821. Things at first were quiet enough. But in 1817 controversy broke out with the War Department. The relations of the Secretary to the Army were poorly defined. The practice existed of sending orders directly to officers without notifying the division commander. Jackson had remonstrated against this in 1814, but no attention had been paid to his complaint. In the spring of 1817 an officer especially detailed by Jackson was detached by direct order of the War Department and sent elsewhere. Jackson addressed President Monroe on the matter, and again receiving no answer, issued a division order prohibiting obedience to any order to officers emanating from the War Department "unless coming through him as the proper organ of communication." Two months later a final issue was presented. Jackson again protested, and the matter was ultimately resolved in his favor.

The civilizing effect of military command is apparent in this controversy. The letters to the President were cogent, lawyer-like documents and establish that Jackson understood good administration. His official communications are the more admirable as evidence of self-discipline, for the intensity of Jackson's feelings appears in a letter to General Scott, who had informed Jackson that his division order was mutinous. The reply was long and in Jackson's inimitable seventeenth-century manner. The glove was hurled in a final taunt:

To my government, whenever it may please, I hold myself liable to answer, and to produce the reasons which prompted me to the course I took; and to the *intermeddling pimps and spies* of the War Department, who are in the garb of gentlemen, I hold myself responsible for any grievance they may labor under on my account, with which you have my permission to number yourself.

General Scott declined the challenge.

While this controversy was in its final stages, trouble broke out again with the Indians. There had been difficulties with the

Creeks over the treaty lands, and, as earlier, Florida (still in the hands of the Spanish) had become the seat of incitation of the aborigines. On December 26, 1817, Secretary Calhoun ordered Jackson to the border and directed him to attack the Seminoles, if necessary pursuing them into Florida.

The géneral moved with his usual speed, and within three months the Indians were crushed. From a military point of view the campaign was of no great importance. What lent it significance was, first, the capture, court-martialing, and execution of two Britons, Arbuthnot and Armbrister, who were deep in the counsels of the Indians; and, second, an attack upon and capture of Spanish Pensacola on the pretense that an army of redskins was there assembled. The first episode caused the most intense excitement in England, where Jackson was "exhibited in Placards through the streets of London"—and in Washington produced agitated cabinet meetings. The notion was pressed that Armbrister and Arbuthnot were prisoners of war and that the sentences were unlawful. Actually, as a great international lawyer has remarked, it was the incitement of "an organized system of assassination and rapine, not war" with which Armbrister and Arbuthnot were charged. The record of foreign conspiracy in this matter is too long and too bloody to doubt the political expediency of Jackson's action.

The seizure of Pensacola was an affair of different complexion. At the moment, negotiations for the purchase of Florida were under way, and the news had a painful effect upon the Spanish minister. The instructions which authorized Jackson to pursue the Indians into Florida were no power of attorney to attack the Spaniards. Jackson claimed that President Monroe had indicated his approval in advance, but direct evidence of this is wanting. That the general exceeded his instructions is obvious, and equally obvious is the fact that the gentlemen in Washington were aware both of western feeling about the running sore of the border and of Jackson's nationalism. He was a man whom only a positive negative would restrain from the execution of what he conceived to be his proper mission.

From first to last Jackson was Jackson. To his military career he brought the virtues and faults of maturity. His fortitude was great, for he started his Creek campaign with two bullets freshly in him, and he organized the defense of New Orleans nearly prostrate with dysentery. His courage and boldness endeared him to his soldiers, to the point that they endured even the rigor of his discipline. There is no question that his military experience increased his sense of responsibility; and if it left unchastened his immense confidence in his own judgment, the stumbling of Dearborn, Eustis, Armstrong, and Monroe in the War Department and the relative isolation of his command were justification enough. The posts where Jackson fought demanded a man, and "by the Eternal" that is what they got.

II

The election of John Quincy Adams to the presidency in the election of 1824 confirmed General Jackson in a belief in democracy. Owner of the Hermitage and a famous racing stable, slaveholder and capitalist, ex-judge, ex-military commander, ex-governor of the territory of Florida (acquired partly through his extravagances)—there is little in this catalogue to indicate that the hero of New Orleans would go down in history as the articulate voice of the rising tide of democracy of the 1820s.

But there is another side of the picture. In the background lies Jackson's frontier upbringing, his enlistment as a boy in the cause of the Republic, his youthful ardor for Jeffersonianism (Jackson was one of the twelve members of the House of Representatives in 1796 who voted against a tribute to the outgoing Washington). And more potent as an influence in shaping Jackson's outlook is the record of the relations of Jackson, the general, with the political leaders of the day. His army experiences had bred a deep distrust of the politicians, the men who, holding the reins of civil government, had so often to curb the Covenanter. Deep rancor stirred when he remembered the opposition he had encountered from the civil authorities of New Orleans in January 1815, the lassitude, if not treason, of the legislature. And other scars had accumulated: Monroe's lack of candor, his milk-and-water attitude toward Jackson's invasion of Florida in 1818, Clay's public animadversions on the seizure of Pensacola, and the furor in Congress over his actions as governor of Florida. All these things had nourished in Jackson a contempt for the Washington politician. The people knew no such qualms over the right and wrong of Jackson's actions; unlike the politicians, they drew up no resolutions deprecating his defeat of the British or deploring his triumph over the Spanish. In the eyes of the people, Jackson's achievements justified his methods. To the people, Jackson gave his heart.

And the election of 1824 strengthened Jackson's own convictions. The presidential race had been an open field with four competitors for the "Virginia legacy." In the wave of nationalism that swept the country after the War of 1812, the old party line-up of Jeffersonian Republican versus Federalist was swallowed up and disappeared. New issues and new men were arising; but party combinations had not yet crystallized. The pulsing agrarian West, the burgeoning industrialism of the northeastern and middle states, the rising ascendancy of the cotton economy in the South, all were in conflict. Sectional interests, sectional views on the moot issues of the day (the tariff, internal improvements, the land policy) militated against political fusion and the emergence of new parties. Personalities alone stood out clearly; beneath all other issues boiled the new democracy—the common man, the frontiersman, the small farmer, the worker in town and city, each pressing forward to claim his inheritance.

For the years immediately preceding the election of 1824 had been witnessing a quiet revolution. In almost every state manhood suffrage had been inaugurated. Religious and property qualifications for officeholding were falling. The ranks of elective officials had grown. Electors for the presidency were no longer to be chosen by the select bodies of the state legislatures; nor were nominations to rest uncontested in the hands of the inner ring of the Federal Congress. "King Caucus" was dying—long live the people!

All this was clearly in Jackson's favor. His competitors were able and outstanding men. Each was supported strongly by a particular sectional interest: Henry Clay, the magnetic son of Kentucky, John Quincy Adams, Secretary of State under Monroe, William Crawford of Georgia, the administration men's states'-rights candidate. But the name of Old Hickory was known in every county of the land, a fact keenly appreciated by Jackson's friends, "the Nashville Junto." The other candidates had demonstrated their abilities in public office—in the Cabinet, in Congress, as diplomats at home and abroad. Jackson had proven his qualities on the battlefield. His lesser political experience was to the common man a pledge of integrity, an augury of independence of action. A man who had risked his life for his country—this was a gage that as President he would put his country's interest ahead of special privilege or partisan benefit. This optimistic and trusting faith of the common man in the military hero rose up in a wave of feeling that was eventually to bring Jackson, second in a long line of generals, to the doors of the White House.

Getting under way early in 1822 in Tennessee, the Jackson movement had rapidly gathered strength. Lest he be regarded merely as a western figure, his friends had secured his election to the United States Senate in October 1823. There he conducted himself with dignity. His political pronouncements were few. A qualified stand on the tariff (our American interests must be protected), a willingness to continue to serve the Republic, and a frequently expressed belief in the people—the simple creed of an old soldier that was bound to have a country-wide appeal.

Open campaigning by presidential candidates was not popular at that date, but various expedients provided an adequate substitute. Letters and carefully framed replies were published in partisan newspapers, and a network of committees of "friends" of each candidate was spread over the country. A candidate could grace a public dinner and offer a few remarks

(Henry Clay was outstandingly in demand on these occasions),
and, as toast followed toast, the pulse of enthusiasm be quickened. "Spontaneous" mass meetings were popular, and the
militia muster days became Jackson rallies. It was reported
in North Carolina:

> In almost every Captain's party, the drums were beating and fifes
> whistling for the hero of New Orleans. The officers would treat the men
> . . . and then raise the war whoop for General Jackson. Then the poor
> staggering . . . creatures would sally forth to vote. The result was
> always in favor of Jackson.

It is not surprising, therefore, that the hero of New Orleans
stood highest in 1824 when the electoral vote was counted,
although no candidate received a majority—Jackson 99, Adams
84, Crawford 41, and Clay 37. And Jackson's popular vote
outran Adams' by nearly forty thousand. To Jackson this meant
that he was entitled to the office. Under the terms of our
Constitution, however, the election was thrown into the House
of Representatives, with which body rested the duty of choosing a President from among the three highest candidates. Clay,
thus eliminated from the contest, held in his hands the fateful
decision. He could not be President, but he could be President-
maker. In view of Clay's known dislike of Jackson, his action
could scarcely be in doubt. He threw his influence to Adams,
declaring that he did not believe that the "killing of two thousand five hundred Englishmen at New Orleans qualifies for the
various, difficult, and complicated duties of the chief magistracy." Adams was inaugurated, and the hero of New Orleans
became the indomitable champion of the people.

To Jackson, Adams' election was a willful denial of the
popular intent and "a subversion of the rights of the people."
The cry of a corrupt bargain between Adams and Clay was
raised; suspicion deepened into conviction when Clay became
Secretary of State. Always outspoken, Jackson labeled Clay
the "Judas of the West," and the name stuck. John Randolph
of Roanoke assailed Clay and Adams on the floor of the House
—"the coalition of Blifil and Black George—the combination,

unheard of till then, of the Puritan with the Blackleg"—and the phrase rang through the country. Clay's denials and protests publicized the charges but failed to dispel the haze of distrust and suspicion that hung about the affair.

During the next four years the anti-Adams campaign was waged. Adams, able and incorruptible New Englander, was derided as the rich aristocrat wasting the public money for luxurious furnishings for the White House, a dishonest politician using executive patronage for selfish party considerations. Corruption and reform—the battle cry of the Jackson men was sounded in season and out. Opening in 1825 with the "corrupt bargain" charge, the campaign of 1828 closed in a whirlwind of smear tactics on both sides. The slur of treason was flung at Jackson, friend of Aaron Burr. Indefensibly, the old scandal of Rachel Jackson's divorce and remarriage was unearthed, and Rachel's name (the "My Love" of so many letters through so many years) was again dragged in the mud. But Jackson's military reputation was the chief target of the Adams-Clay men. The specter of a dictator was brandished; the election of a "military chieftain" (Clay's phrase) would endanger our liberties and our republican institutions. "Coffin" handbills were a startling feature of the campaign and were distributed gleefully by the Adams men. "Shot to death by order of General Jackson," rang the heading, while the pictured coffins of the six militiamen executed for desertion at New Orleans in 1815 stood out in black accusation of Jackson's "arbitrary cruelty."

But the Adams-Clay men failed. During all the clamor Jackson was held silent by the advice, entreaty, and direction of his managers. Neither to his private resentments nor to his political views was he permitted to give voice. Secretary of State Clay appeared frequently at public dinners; the activities of Adams' "travelling cabinet" were roundly denounced. Jackson remained in retirement. Save for patriotic appearances at Fourth of July meetings and attendance at one monster celebration of the victory of 1815 at New Orleans, he eschewed the public eye. "I have not gone into the highways and market places to proclaim my opinions and in this feel that I have differed from some," he declared stingingly. His campaign was skillfully conducted. In the dual role of hero and democrat, Old Hickory, the hero of New Orleans, was carried to victory on the shoulders of Van Buren, the "little magician" of New York politics, and of the devoted "Nashville Junto."

III

Jackson has given his name to a decade; "Jacksonian democracy" has become a familiar phrase, synonymous with the rise of the common man, workingmen's parties, locofocoism, and the new era—less kindly described as the "hot air" period of our history. Yet, strange contradiction, his administrations have almost as frequently been dubbed "the Reign of Andrew Jackson." Indeed, "King Andrew" was a favorite gibe flung out by his adversaries, a paradox only to be resolved in terms of the man and his past experiences. Had his political enemies clung to the old epithet military chieftain, they would have come nearer to the truth, for Jackson the general lived on in the presidency. His administrations were to him—and certainly to his opponents—a series of battles in which he exhibited the same qualities that had distinguished his military career. In his own view he fought for the people and the Union as before he had battled for the Republic.

Jackson's first important policy was the inauguration of "reform." The defeat of 1824 had been to him a denial of the people's will; the election of 1828 he termed "a contest between the virtue of the American people and the influence of patronage." He regarded his political opponents, therefore, not only as personal enemies but as enemies of the people. "We have begun reform, and that we are trying to cleans the augean stables, and expose to view the corruption of some of the agents of the late administration," he wrote in May 1829. Characteristically, to Jackson, a man was either friend or foe. His military experience had confirmed this outlook; to some degree this impaired his capacity for office. Convinced that he

was meting out retribution and not retaliation, he opened the
doors of the Federal Government to the spoils system. With
the resolution of a Covenanter and the determination of a
conqueror, he introduced the new democratic principle of "ro-
tation in office" and made the Federal service a party province.
Political supporters were given high office—Van Buren, John
Eaton, and William T. Barry in the Cabinet, Major W. B.
Lewis and Amos Kendall in lesser places. A simple policy of
reward and punishment—to his opponents, "proscription";
to his followers, the division of long-coveted plunder; to Jackson, the vindication of the people's will.

The same dogged determination to stand by a friend and
give battle to a foe vitiated Jackson's judgment in the Eaton
affair. The marriage of Eaton, Secretary of War, to Margaret
Timberlake (the former Peggy O'Neale of romantic but un-
savory reputation) had been undertaken with Jackson's approval, but Washington society was scandalized. Men shook
their heads, and the ladies of the Cabinet organized a social
boycott. As the champion of Peggy Eaton, Jackson plunged
into this "petticoat war." All his chivalrous instincts were
roused. *"I never war against females* and it is only the base
and cowardly that do," he had written in 1827. Two other
considerations actuated him. One was his long-standing friendship for Eaton; the other was the conviction that his political
enemies—first Clay, then Calhoun—were hounding pretty
Peggy Eaton as in the past they had persecuted his Rachel.

From the date of Eaton's appointment until his resignation
in April 1831, the grim old chieftain made the Eatons' cause his
own and fought their battle. He warned that any combination
against Eaton "is an indignity, and insult to myself"; all who
refused to accept Mrs. Eaton felt his displeasure. He abandoned the practice of holding cabinet meetings rather than sit
with men who countenanced Peggy's detractors. He even threatened half his Cabinet with dismissal unless their wives proved
more tractable. "I will not part with Major Eaton from my
cabinet, and those of my cabinet who cannot harmonize with
him had better withdraw, for harmony I must and will have,"

he declared, insensible to the drollery of his pronunciamento. He harried the diplomatic corps, offering to the Dutch minister the choice of accepting his passport or having his wife, Madame Huygens, receive Eaton's wife. He drove from the White House a favorite nephew, Andrew Donelson, and his wife Emily. His heart was shaken, but the fortitude of a soldier sustained him.

Eventually, on April 7, 1831, Eaton resigned, the tension was relieved, and a thorough reorganization of the Cabinet was effected. The battle was over, but the political results were far-reaching. The breach between Calhoun and Jackson became final. Van Buren, the fortunate widower who had remained in the Eaton-Jackson camp, emerged as the favorite. No episode illustrates more clearly the mettle of the "military chieftain," although his strength had been employed in a better cause at New Orleans.

There were many controversies during the eight years of Jackson's administrations and none more absorbing than his struggle against the Second Bank of the United States. Chartered in 1816 for a period of twenty years, this institution was quasi-public, quasi-private in character. Operated as a private corporation for profit, it was linked to the Government by the terms of its incorporation and, in return for the privileges it received, acted as agent for the transfer and custody of government funds. From its inception the Bank had been hated and feared in the western states. Its insistence on sound banking principles irked the state banks; after the panic of 1819, debtor, land speculator, and local banker blamed the institution for the hard times that followed. By constitutional provision or spite taxes, Indiana, Illinois, Georgia, Tennessee, North Carolina, Kentucky, Ohio, and Maryland struck at branches of the Bank operating within their borders. John Marshall twice ruled against the state tax and upheld the expediency and constitutionality of the Bank. The West remained unconvinced and nursed its resentment.

The Bank question in its inception was thus a battle of the West against the East—a cause bound to appeal to Jackson.

The election of 1828, however, focused his attention on the "monster." Charges were freely made that Bank influence had been used in favor of Adams. This was enough to arouse Jackson. Again the people's cause and his own became identical; the Bank was dangerous to the liberties of the people and must go.

Against the advice of his Cabinet, Jackson tendered a gage of battle in the annual message of 1829. Despite congressional approval of the Bank's operation, Old Hickory returned to the fray in successive messages. For two years the skirmishing was inconclusive. Thoughtful men hesitated to destroy an institution so intimately interwoven with the country's whole financial fabric. And the leaders of the Democratic party, apprehensive of the coming election of 1832, shied away from the issue. Moreover, the reorganization of the Cabinet in the spring of 1831 had brought two pro-Bank men close to Jackson —Livingston, Secretary of State, and McLane, Secretary of the Treasury. Nicholas Biddle, president of the Bank, redoubled his efforts at compromise. The rumble of battle died down, and by December 1831 a virtual armistice was reached. Jackson would stay his hand and the Bank would not apply for a renewal of its charter before the election of 1832. In the annual message of that year, therefore, only an echo of the controversy sounded. Close on the heels of his message the Secretary of the Treasury sent a report to Congress upholding the Bank on every score. For the first time in his career, Jackson appeared to be in retreat!

Within a few weeks open combat was renewed. Unexpectedly Henry Clay, Jackson's old adversary, forced the issue. The convention of the National Republican party (risen from the ashes of the Clay-Adams coalition) called for the re-charter of the Bank and the election of Henry Clay. The reluctant Biddle threw his hand in with Clay; in early January 1832 an application for re-charter was sent to Congress. And a few days later a combination of Clay-Calhoun forces triumphantly rejected the nomination of Van Buren, the favorite, as minister to England. Jackson's cup of wrath was filled and overflowing. The

Bank question was no longer merely a sectional or even a party battle. Now it was openly Jackson against Clay—the cause of the people against aristocracy and corruption. In 1826 Jackson had termed Clay "the bases[t], meanest, scoundrel that ever disgraced the image of his God." The years had not changed his opinion.

Throughout the spring of 1832 the Clay and Bank men marshaled their forces. Overconfident, Clay pushed the issue; in July a bill providing for re-charter passed both houses of Congress. Jackson, it was believed, would not dare veto the bill in the face of the impending election. Many an enemy had underestimated Jackson's courage and tenacity; none more fatally for himself than Clay. Regardless of the disapproval of his Cabinet except Postmaster Barry and Roger B. Taney, then Attorney General, Jackson returned a flat veto. "Old Hickory is to his cabinet here what he was to his aids," Francis P. Blair had written months earlier. Jackson, the general, was in the saddle again and was riding hard.

Jackson's veto message holds fresher interest as an exposition of his concept of executive powers than as a statement of his objections to the Bank. The latter were familiar to the people —the charge of unconstitutionality, the diatribe against the Bank as a monopoly in the interests of the few against the many, the fling at the influence of foreign stockholders. But the lines defining the executive power were unexpected—a distillation of Jackson's past experiences. He thundered:

> Each public officer who takes an oath to support the Constitution swears that he will support it as he understands it, and not as it is understood by others. . . . The opinion of the judges has no more authority over Congress than the opinion of Congress has over the judges, and on that point the President is independent of both.

Here speaks the old headstrong Jackson who had issued the ukase of 1817 asserting his powers as commander of the Southern Division of the Army and rebuking a President and Secretary of War. Here is foreshadowed the Jackson who by executive decree was to balk congressional policy.

In November 1832 Jackson (and the people) triumphed with an electoral vote of 219 for Jackson against 49 votes for Clay. Jackson was determined that the victory over the Bank—and Clay—should be complete. "Until I can strangle this hydra of corruption, the Bank, I will not shrink from my duty, or my part," he wrote. In consultation with Taney and the "Kitchen Cabinet," he formulated a decisive blow, "the removal" of deposits. No more government funds should be placed in the Bank lest they be used to corrupt Congress and the people. In the past, Jackson believed, this had been done; "if such corruption exists in the green tree, what will it be in the dry?" he queried.

Again the executive acted with the independence of a daring strategist. Congress expressed confidence in the Bank; Jackson awaited the summer recess. The Cabinet was reshuffled and an obdurate Secretary of the Treasury dismissed. "Nothing is more important in war than unity in command," Napoleon had written. Before Congress reassembled, the "removal" order was issued. Thereafter government funds were to be deposited in state banks only.

No single action of Jackson's created so great a furor. The financial life of the country felt the shock as the Bank, deprived of the stream of government funds, contracted credit. Clay and Calhoun men were transformed into Whigs, united against executive prerogative. "The Bank ought to be kept in the rear; the usurpation in the front," wrote Clay cannily. "It is the usurpation which has convulsed the country." For the first time in our history the Senate of the United States passed a resolution censuring the action of a President. Angered but unshaken, Jackson continued his war in the name of the people, and the people applauded his audacity. The Bank charter was allowed to expire. On July 11, 1836, a final blow, the "Specie Circular," was launched against speculators and "paper money" men. Sponsored by Jackson, Van Buren was elected in 1836, and—final vindication—the resolution of censure was expunged from the Senate Journal on January 16, 1837. The effectiveness of Jackson's strategy is unquestionable, the popularity of his leadership attested by the election returns of 1834 and 1836; the wisdom of that leadership is still open to doubt.

Jackson's belief in the independence of the executive brought him into opposition with the Supreme Court as well as with Congress. The issue arose from a conflict between the state of Georgia and the Federal Government over the regulation of Indian affairs. As early as 1802 the Federal Government had bound itself to secure a cession of the Cherokee Indian lands to Georgia, but the undertaking had not been completed. The Cherokees, reluctant to move westward, had refused to give up their lands and in 1827 set up their own tribal government, claiming the rights of an independent, sovereign nation. Resentful of the Indian oasis within her borders, Georgia peremptorily extended her authority over the Indians and their lands, despite the fact that the Constitution vests in Congress the authority to regulate Indian affairs.

Cases pivoting on the constitutionality of the Georgia legislation were hurried to the Supreme Court; in the most famous of these, *Worcester* vs. *Georgia,* John Marshall flatly held the state laws to be "repugnant to the Constitution, laws and treaties of the United States." There Jackson let the matter rest. Frontiersman and Indian fighter, his sympathies were all with the state. "John Marshall has made his decision—*now let him enforce it"*—the apocryphal comment attributed to him neatly summarizes his attitude. In the face of the Supreme Court's ruling, the executive pursued his own policy, upholding Georgia. Eventually the Indians were forced to set forth on the long pilgrimage west beyond the Mississippi. "I look upon Jackson as a detestable, ignorant, reckless, vain and malignant Tyrant," wrote James Kent furiously; and Kent expressed Marshall's private convictions. But Jackson was unmoved; the executive was more than a match for the judiciary.

One other battle over a domestic policy—the nullification controversy—demonstrates Jackson's qualities, and this time more happily. On no other question did he display more admirably the qualities of a successful general—preconcertion of plan and decisiveness of action, fired by a single-minded patriotism.

For some years before the crisis of 1832, the tariff question had agitated South Carolina. Despite the nationalist stand of Calhoun in his earlier career, rumblings of discontent were stirred in the South by the protective nature of the tariff bill of 1820 and the act of 1824. An agrarian society, courting foreign markets for its cotton and in turn importing therefrom manufactured goods, grew restless. By 1827 the storm was gathering and men inveighed against the "double tax" levied on southern interests in the guise of a national measure. The "Wool and Woolens" bill of 1827, followed by the "Tariff of Abominations" of 1828, brought forth flat remonstrance. The "South Carolina Exposition" (framed but not openly fathered by Calhoun) solemnly set forth the state's position, and the *Crisis,* "the first bugle call in the South to rally," inflamed public sentiment. The protective tariff was denounced as not only injurious to the South but unconstitutional; states' rights must be supported.

Between 1828 and 1832 the clouds darkened. Jackson's stand on the tariff was not clear; his position on state opposition to Federal authority was soon patent. The "nullifiers" of South Carolina nourished hopes that he would treat them with the same leniency that he had shown Georgia. "Look again to Georgia, she has not once but twice vanquished the Federal Government, and so it will be with us," cried one of their leaders at a states'-rights celebration in July 1830.

But the circumstances were dissimilar. In the case of Georgia, Jackson, conqueror of the Creeks, was disinclined to take up the cudgels, even though Federal authority was involved. South Carolina presented the issue of a state in bold opposition to a general Federal law. If not a consistent nationalist, for he adhered to the Democrats' opposition to internal improvements at Federal expense, Jackson was to prove himself an unmistakable Unionist. In January 1830 the Webster-Hayne debate posed the issue. Three months later, at the Jefferson birthday dinner, Jackson announced his stand. "Our Federal

Union—it must be preserved," and the toast rings as forcefully today as it did in the ears of Calhoun and his friends.

Yet the fire of states'-rights feeling was not dampened. In June 1831 Jackson sent a conciliatory letter of warning, urging adherence to the Union. The reply of the state legislature was pregnant of trouble:

"Is this state legislature to be schooled and rated by the President of the United States? Is it to legislate under the sword of the commander in chief?"

Shortly after this, Calhoun openly published his conversion to the states'-rights doctrine; the tariff of 1832 translated local emotion into state action. On November 24, 1832, the nullification ordinance was passed in the South Carolina state convention. The legislature of the state met two days later and after some deliberation on December 20 passed measures implementing the nullification ordinance. Provision was made for exacting an oath of all civil and military officers of the state to support the nullification ordinance. A second act to take effect February 1, 1833, set up the machinery for the recapture of property seized under the "annulled" acts of Congress, and for the protection of persons and property against Federal process. The governor was authorized to use the military force of the state in the event of coercive action by the Federal Government. A final trumpet blast was sounded in a series of resolutions denouncing the President, scoring his inconsistency with reference to Georgia and asserting the right of secession. Jackson thus faced rebellion.

Meanwhile the commander in chief had not been idle. Even before the Nullification Convention assembled at Charleston, Jackson's plans had been perfected. Navy vessels were stationed in Charleston Harbor; General Winfield Scott, commander of the Eastern Division of the Army, was dispatched to Charleston with orders to reinforce Fort Moultrie. "Proceed at once, and execute those views. You have my carte blanche in respect to troops"—here snapped the old Jackson of military renown. And there was no weakening in his stand. Although on December 4 his annual message was couched in conciliatory terms, six days later his famous proclamation, "Disunion by armed force is *treason*," sounded a clear warning. And on December 14 he wrote, "The Union must be preserved, and it will now be tested, by the support I get by the people. I will die with the Union." Early in January 1833 the "force" message called on Congress to empower the use of the armed forces of the United States for the enforcement of the tariff laws in South Carolina.

For weeks a largely oratorical struggle was waged between Unionists and states'-rights men—at Charleston, in the halls of Congress, before the forum of the people. Eventually, in March 1833, the Force bill and Compromise Tariff were enacted simultaneously, and the Ordinance of Nullification repealed. Jackson's stand had upheld the Union and was to furnish a precedent to which the troubled Lincoln was to turn in a later crisis. If other aspects of his administration dim somewhat the luster of his qualities, his defense of the Union burnished anew his laurels.

Jackson's heart and energies were devoted mainly to domestic affairs, and it is primarily as the President at home that he engages our attention. Yet in the field of foreign relations he was by no means a negative figure. On the whole he displayed circumspection and wisdom in his dealings with other countries; and if on occasion he reached for his dueling pistols, in other cases he played the peacemaker. Like his role in domestic policies, his record in foreign relations was mottled with divergent colors; yet, throughout, a thread of personal integrity of intention gave consistency to his actions.

The first problem in foreign relations that confronted the new administration was the prickly question of the United States trade with the British West Indies. In common with other European powers, Great Britain had professed the mercantilist doctrine that the trade of the colonies must be a closed trade reserved to the mother country. Since 1783 successive Presidents and diplomats of the young Republic had sought to break down these trade barriers, but with only limited success. The iron necessities of the wars growing out

of the French Revolution had made breaches in the walls of
every colonial empire, but with the re-establishment of peace
in 1815 Great Britain had reaffirmed her monopoly of the
West Indian colonial commerce.

Between 1816 and the date of Jackson's inauguration, the
opening of the British West Indies had been a major objective
of American foreign policy. First as Secretary of State under
Monroe and then as President, John Quincy Adams had fought
stubbornly for the admission of American traders to the West
Indian ports on the same footing as British vessels. Grudging
concessions offered by the British had failed to satisfy Adams
and led to retaliatory American legislation. By 1826 commerce between the United States and the islands had been
brought to a virtual standstill.

It might have been expected that the hero of New Orleans
would have maintained the Adams anti-British policy. But in
1829 a more immediate animosity dominated Jackson—his
fierce hatred of the Adams-Clay administration. There was no
way in which the triumph of the election of 1828 could be
more strikingly expressed than by a disavowal of Adams'
cherished West Indian diplomacy. The verdict of the people
must be blazoned abroad.

It was this mood which in 1829 dictated Van Buren's instructions to Louis McLane, the newly appointed minister to
Great Britain. The trade proposals which Adams had rejected
would be acceptable to the new regime. The text of Van Buren's
instructions read:

> Their views [i.e., those of the Adams administration] have been sub-
> mitted to the people of the United States, and the counsels by which your
> conduct is now directed are the result of the judgment expressed by the
> only earthly tribunal to which the late administration was amenable for
> its acts.

The tone of the instructions was unprecedented. Rancor
against the Secretary of State rose high at home and further
embittered the Jackson-Clay relations. But Congress sustained
the President in 1830 by legislation designed to secure a re-

opening of the trade on the terms rejected in 1826. In addition to this measure, Jackson applied leverage by threatening that he would seek an embargo on trade with Canada as well as with the West Indies should the British refuse the American overture. By November of the same year an accord was reached. Trade with the West Indies (on the British terms) was resumed. Adams and Clay were rebuked internationally.

Party politics had ruled Jackson in this settlement, and he had consequently shown a surprisingly conciliatory disposition. In the case of our relations with France, however, no such considerations stayed the saber of his will. Here an admixture of national pride, coupled with scorn for a country that failed to carry out its obligations, provoked him to direct and hardhanded action. "There is no character I abhor more than the liar & hypocrite," he had written in 1831. It was a conviction so alien to the spirit of contemporary diplomacy that it might well have touched off the fuse of war.

For some time before Jackson took office the relations between the United States and France had been ruffled by controversies that dated back to the opening years of the nineteenth century. On the one hand, the United States had long pressed for payment of claims arising from infractions of our commercial rights as neutrals during the Napoleonic wars. France, in turn, asserted that the United States had failed to carry out certain articles of the Louisiana Purchase treaty of 1803, and under Charles X and Louis Philippe alike the French monarchy had been loath to acknowledge responsibility for the misdoings of the Empire. Finally, in July 1831, this diplomatic stalemate was ended and happier relations seemed assured. France agreed to pay twenty-five million francs to the United States in satisfaction of the spoliation claims. For its part, the United States promised to pay one and a half million francs in settlement of outstanding French claims, and reciprocal tariff concessions paved the way to better trade relations.

Unfortunately the treaty lacked popular support in France. While the United States promptly fulfilled its side of the bargain, the French Chamber of Deputies repeatedly failed to appropriate funds for the specified payments. Throughout 1833 and 1834 Jackson's ire mounted against this form of double dealing. In December 1834, in his annual message, he called upon Congress to take economic reprisals. "After the delay on the part of France of a quarter of a century in acknowledging these claims by treaty," he stated bluntly, "it is not to be tolerated that another quarter of a century is to be wasted in negotiating about the payment."

The message aroused an international furor and strained relations between the two countries. The President's message was regarded as an affront to the Gallic national honor. Although the United States Senate negatived a proposal to take reprisals, the situation was complicated in May 1835 by the retort of the French Chamber appropriating the requisite funds but making payment dependent upon an apology from President Jackson. As the King's ministers supported this view, matters moved from bad to worse. In the fall of 1835 the American minister left France. "The honor of my country shall never be stained by an apology from me for the statement of truth and the performance of duty," declared Jackson firmly in his message to Congress in December. A month later the French minister to the United States withdrew. Diplomatic relations were broken off, and an impasse was reached. Yet Jackson was unwilling to push matters further and accepted gladly the mediation of Great Britain. In the spring of 1836 the controversy was closed. France, mollified by an "explanation," made the payments; the danger of war was averted. Jackson's procedure may have been rash, but he set an example of open diplomacy and of plain speaking both to the French and the American people that some of his successors might well have emulated.

The third outstanding problem in foreign relations during Jackson's administrations centered in our interest in Texas, in 1829 still a part of Mexico. In the treaty of 1819 with Spain, the United States had by implication waived its claims to the province and had accepted the confining limit of the Sabine

River as our southwestern boundary. The establishment of
the independence of Mexico in 1824, however, had aroused
anew American interest in Texas. Its location on the Gulf of
Mexico, its proximity to the mouth of the Mississippi River
gave it a strategic importance that made its possession by a
weak power dangerous. Fear of British and French intervention in Mexico and possible future designs upon Texas quickened American apprehension. Mexican encouragement of
American immigration and the lure of fresh fields had drawn
a growing tide of Americans across the border, so that American interest in the annexation of Texas grew rapidly. Adams'
attempts to purchase the territory had been rebuffed and
served only to arouse in Mexico a fear of the "colossus of the
North."

When Jackson took office, therefore, the prospects of acquiring the territory were not bright. For once Jackson was in
accord with his predecessor's views. The expansion of the
United States he regarded as a national rather than a party
issue. Attempts to secure the cession of Texas were renewed,
and Jackson even sought to acquire the whole stretch of land
west to San Francisco Bay, a foretaste of the later Manifest
Destiny fever.

The acquisition of Texas was thus a cherished project
throughout Jackson's terms of office. Nevertheless his expansionist ambitions were always held in leash by his sense of
rectitude. When Anthony Butler, United States envoy to
Mexico and hot advocate of annexation, intimated that a
bribe of five hundred thousand dollars "judiciously applied"
would oil the stiff joints of Mexico's resistance, Jackson con-
temptuously rejected the proposal and shortly thereafter recalled the minister. When the Texas revolution broke out in
1835, Jackson's sympathies were all with the insurgents, yet
he made honest efforts to keep the United States neutral, and
General Gaines, in command of the Western Department, was
ordered to prevent armed bodies from crossing into Texas
from this side of the border.

In March 1836 Texas declared its independence; at once

the new republic sought recognition at Washington and annexation to the United States as soon as possible. Popular sentiment was all with the Texans, and during the summer Congress passed a resolution advocating recognition as soon as a *de facto* government should have been established. Throughout the year, Jackson still hung back, unwilling to subject the United States to even a suspicion of dishonorable action, unmoved by the tide of popular opinion. Indeed, when word came that General Gaines had crossed into Texas territory under the delusion that there was danger of a Mexican attack, Jackson at once ordered him to withdraw.

In his annual message, December 1836, the President reiterated the need for caution in recognizing Texas lest wrongful motives of territorial aggression be imputed to us. But a few weeks later the receipt of a report from the United States agent in Texas was made the occasion for a special message (December 22) in which he squarely put up to Congress the responsibility for acting. "It will always be consistent with the spirit of the constitution and most safe that it [i.e., the power of recognition] should be exercised when probably leading to war, with that body by whom war alone can be declared." The Congress was deliberate, and it was not until a few days before Jackson's administration came to an end that a resolution for recognition passed both houses. The first step toward our embroilment in a Mexican war had been taken.

More might be written of Jackson's influence on our foreign policies—his overzealous defense of American rights in the Falkland incident set off against the amenability of his views on the issue of the northeastern boundary. If he was precipitate at times and scandalized diplomats, he achieved results. And always he was ruled by two dominant convictions—his pride in his country, his faith in the people.

And the people quite properly reposed, as the commissions have it, special trust and confidence in his patriotism, valor, and fidelity. No President exercised a more ruthless leadership· few, if any, affected more profoundly the issues of his day or left a deeper impress on our development. As a general he had exhibited independence, fortitude, and rashness. These qualities were native to the man; but his military experience accented the habit of command, and success on the field intensified his belief in his own powers. As general and as President he displayed the same qualities—and held the people's devotion.

VI

General William Henry Harrison

AN OLD PROVERB HAS IT that wheresoever a man dwelleth he shall have a thornbush by his door. Barely had the denizens of the Atlantic seaboard extirpated the British brier when they found springing in their back yard a new and baneful growth. The West with its own political demands threatened the hegemony of the East, and the idiosyncrasies of the newcomers made them repellent. Expedience might dictate the alliance of an Adams with a Clay, of a Van Buren with a Jackson, but to the older civilization the land over the mountains was peopled with Canaanites. From this antipathy was bred the conviction that the West was a region crude, lawless, and inferior. Early travelers like the "learned and virtuous Dr. Dwight" represented this vast domain "as a grand reservoir for the scum of the Atlantic." Lecturers from the hallowed soil of New England perpetuated disdain for trans-Appalachian coonskin culture, and the West itself supplied witnesses for the prosecution in the shape of such characters as the boisterous Colonel Davy Crockett.

Like the tales purveyed by English visitors about the evil-doings in colonial Boston, the picture of the backwoods was a distortion, a flamboyant segment cut from the vast canvas of the peopling of the West in which gentlemen with armorial quarterings as well as commoners with flintlock and hoe had played a part. Every emigrant in his own way was a bearer of eighteenth-century culture to the nineteenth-century West, the carrier of an old heritage to new outposts. The West was to shape this inheritance; wilderness and frontier were to impose a stamp, nationalist, democratic; but old substance was to be worked into the new America—the West of the pioneers. It was a process of transplantation and adaptation that began before the first days of the Republic; it was a process typified in the life of William Henry Harrison, son of the Old Dominion, Log Cabin candidate for the Presidency in 1840.

Born on February 9, 1773, at Berkeley, on the James River, William Henry Harrison was, according to his own testimony, a "child of the Revolution," reared in the traditional Virginia plantation manner. His father Benjamin was a signer of the Declaration of Independence and governor of the state for three terms. At Hampden-Sidney College young Harrison acquired a passion for history and a taste for the classics which he was to cultivate for the rest of his days. Then, at the age of seventeen, he was sent to Richmond to take up the study of medicine. In April of the following year he went up to Philadelphia to continue his studies under the famous Dr. Benjamin Rush. At his father's death Harrison was placed under the guardianship of Robert Morris, financier of the Revolution; without consulting either his guardian or his family, Harrison decided to change his career. Through the influence of Governor Richard Henry Lee he secured a commission as ensign in the First Infantry of the Regular Army on August 16, 1791. Armed with Cicero's *Orations* and Blair's *Lectures,* within a few weeks he turned his face westward.

Harrison thus started his adult life as a professional soldier. For seven years he saw service in the Northwest. These were years of tension, of Indian warfare, and fear of the British still entrenched in the Northwest posts. The year 1790 had been disgraced by General Harmar's defeat. A few weeks before Harrison first reached Fort Washington (Cincinnati), the worsting of St. Clair laid the frontier open. These defeats established certain axioms—the iron necessity of constant vigilance in dealing with the Indians, the unreliability of the valor of ignorance embodied in the militia. It was instruction soon reinforced by the example of an eminent Revolutionary soldier,

"Mad Anthony" Wayne, appointed commander in chief of the expanded Legion of the United States early in 1792.

From Wayne, Harrison learned the art of war as practiced by a veteran—the technique of organizing an army, methods of drill, maneuvers, tactics, the order of march (a slight modification of Steuben's method). For over a year, while the Government sought a peaceful settlement of the Indian troubles by prolonged negotiation, Wayne bent his energies to the task of literally whipping the new army into shape. When the Indians, bolstered by expectation of British aid, rejected American overtures, Wayne was ready to march. From October 1793 until the close of the campaign, Harrison as aide-de-camp was constantly at Wayne's side and concerned with the incredibly difficult problems of assembling supplies, of transportation, and of communication through the wilderness of northern Ohio. On August 20, 1794, but half a mile from a British fort recently erected on the Maumee River within our borders, the Battle of Fallen Timbers was fought. In this battle Harrison won Wayne's commendation. Wayne wrote:

I must add the names of my faithful and gallant Aids-de-camp, Captains De Butt and T. Lewis and Lieutenant Harrison, who, with the Adjutant General, Major Mills, rendered the most essential service by communicating my orders in every direction, and by their conduct and bravery exciting the troops to press for victory.

At Fallen Timbers, where, Harrison said later, he "beheld the indignant eagle frown upon the British lion," the victory was decisive. By the Treaty of Greenville (August 1795) the Indians paid the forfeit of defeat by confinement within certain bounds. South of the treaty line the settler need no longer be "afraid for the terror by night; nor for the arrow that flieth by day." Almost simultaneously the ratification of Jay's Treaty with Britain added to American prestige and diminished British power. For a decade the Northwest knew peace.

Stationed at Fort Washington, Harrison remained in the Army for another three years. The frontier was quiet; life at the post lapsed into a routine pattern. In that period Harrison devoted much of his time to military study—Thomas Simes's *Military Science* and *Military Guide,* Marshal Saxe's *Rêveries,* and Steuben's *Regulations.* Although he was advanced to the rank of captain in 1797, Harrison decided to retire, and his resignation was accepted June 1, 1798. He had married into the prominent Symmes family, and it is possible he felt some tribal pressure. His father-in-law did not think much of an army career, but he was willing to help. As he confided to a friend, "If I knew what to make of Captain Harrison, I could easily take proper arrangements for his family. He can neither bleed, plead, nor preach, and if he could plow I should be satisfied. His best prospect is in the army, he has talents, and if he can dodge well a few years, it is probable he may become conspicuous."

Harrison settled down to be a farmer, but within a few months he was appointed Secretary of the Northwest Territory, and with this office began his political career. In quick succession followed his election as territorial delegate to Congress (1799) and in 1800 his appointment to be governor of the newly created territory of Indiana. It was in this latter capacity that he was to achieve military renown as the hero of Tippecanoe.

II

For years before the outbreak of the War of 1812 the shadow of the British loomed dark in the West. Their hold on the posts within our borders was broken by the Jay Treaty, but their influence over the Indians, checked at Fallen Timbers, did not die. British impressment of our seamen and British infringements of neutral trade might engross the attention of the seaboard; west of the Appalachians, men's eyes were fixed anxiously on Malden and Amherstburg, the British outposts across the river from Detroit. On the fringes of the forest every American settlement was agitated by rumors of British agents filtering among the Indian tribes, inciting attack upon the Americans. In distant Indiana Territory, on the upper Wabash River, Tecumseh, the Shawnee leader, and his brother the Prophet saw visions and dreamed dreams. The strength of the Seventeen Fires (as they called the states) should be quenched and the hunting grounds of their fathers reclaimed. A mystical dream, half religious, half political, that drew the young warriors resentful of the advancing tide of the Americans and spelled disaster to the frontier; a dream which with British aid might become a reality.

This was the menace that troubled the men in the states of Ohio and Kentucky and shook the settlers at the outposts of settlement in the distant territories of Indiana, Illinois, and Missouri. This was the fear that spurred Henry Clay and the War Hawks to aggressive measures against the British in the halls of Congress and gave fervor to their grandiloquence. This was the threat that animated William Henry Harrison, governor of Indiana Territory, at Vincennes, and inspired his resolution to destroy the power of Tecumseh. This it was that resulted in the Battle of Tippecanoe.

Indiana was the focus of discontent, both Indian and white. As governor since 1800, Harrison had perseveringly carried out the policy delineated by Jefferson—the rapid extinction of Indian title to the lands north of the Ohio River. Year by year the resentment of the tribes had mounted as, by cession after cession, millions of acres were wheedled from them. The Treaty of Fort Wayne in 1809 was the match that set off the powder keg. Tecumseh's confederacy, based on the power of the Miamis, supported by the young men of lesser tribes and comforted (if no more) by the sympathy of the British, assumed threatening proportions.

On Harrison, as governor, rested the burden of defending the scattered settlements within the sparsely populated territory. Between 1809 and 1811 fear of Tecumseh's confederacy reached a crescendo; raids on outlying farms and the wild fire of rumor heightened the tension. In the late summer of 1811 permission for a punitive expedition against the Prophet and his followers was finally wrung from the reluctant Administration in Washington. For months diplomatic considerations had restrained President Madison and Secretary of War

Eustis, comfortably distant from the scene. When Harrison received the desired authorization, Tecumseh, leader of the warriors, was absent on a mission among the southern tribes; the time to strike was ripe. A company of Regulars was dispatched to Vincennes, and Harrison was empowered to use force against the Prophet should efforts at pacification prove unavailing.

In October 1811 Harrison set out from Vincennes with his small command—one company of regulars, two companies of militia, and a troop of volunteers led by the dashing Joe Daviess of Kentucky. On November 6 the army encamped within the Indian lands on the banks of Tippecanoe Creek, at the edge of the Prophet's town. There, on November 7, in the dark hours before dawn, the battle was fought. Despite Harrison's awareness of the need for caution, the camp was caught off guard. Aided by the light of scattered campfires, the Indians penetrated the line at one point. The battle, wrote John Tipton in his journal, "lasted 2 hours and 20 minuts of a Continewel firing while maney times mixd among the indians So that we Could not tell them indians and our men apart . . . . we maid a Charge and Drove them out of our timber across the Prairie." The Prophet's town was sacked, and with a battle loss of 179 men dead and wounded, Harrison returned to Vincennes. Not a defeat nor yet a decisive victory.

This was the battle from which was coined the title "Hero of Tippecanoe." Harrison had displayed personal bravery, his line of march had been patterned on Wayne's, his general plan sound. Yet the sixth sense had at the last failed him; his final arrangements lacked prudence. A storm of controversy broke out and raged from the frontier to the seaboard. Conflicting reports represented the battle as an ignominious defeat and a brilliant accomplishment. Echoes of this were to reverberate in the election of 1840. Certain it is that Harrison avoided the pitfalls of Harmar and St. Clair; equally certainly, he fell short of the achievements of Wayne. The Battle of Fallen Timbers had resulted in land cessions and the pacification of the frontier; the Battle of Tippecanoe stimulated the

Indians to vengeance. It was the prelude to the War of 1812.

On June 1, 1812, Madison sent his war message to Congress detailing our grievances against the British; on June 18 Congress declared war. Already General William Hull, aged veteran of the Revolution, had been dispatched to the command of Detroit and the defense of the American frontier. An act had been passed to enlarge the Army—on paper. Without adequate preparation, military or financial, the United States blithely entered upon a war. New England might lag in sullen opposition; the West, confident of victory and boastful in anticipation of the conquest of Canada, was jubilant. At last British foe and Indian ally would be destroyed, an expectation that was to be rudely shaken within a few months by a tale of cowardice, ineptitude, and lack of preparedness at every point along the northern frontier.

In the summer of 1812 Harrison's activities, despite his enthusiasm and ambition, were limited to the command of a volunteer force raised for the defense of the Indiana frontier and to dickering for a larger command. Not until late September (as we have recounted before) did he receive a commission as brigadier general with instructions to retake Detroit and to invade Canada. The situation that confronted him was alarming: Detroit ignominiously surrendered, Fort Dearborn (Chicago) and Mackinac fallen, the northwestern Indians flocking to the British standard, control of Lake Erie in British hands. At every point the northern line lay open. With one voice the West demanded an immediate victory to wipe out the summer's disgrace; and from Washington the Administration, with an eye cocked nervously on the coming election, reinforced that demand. Despite a clear appreciation of the difficulties involved, Harrison yielded to popular pressure and embarked upon an autumn campaign.

On the whole, Harrison's plans for this dubious enterprise were good. But the problems that confronted him were enormous. In the first place he lacked a trained army. With the exception of one regiment of regulars, the force at his disposal (expected to total ten thousand men) consisted entirely of militia and volunteers. This meant a force in a constant flux of comings and goings, since the term of enlistment for the militia was limited to a period of six months. Moreover, the sole military training of most of the militia had consisted in annual appearances on muster days, a time given over (according to Harrison) to "riot and intemperance." These were men familiar with rifle and musket, brave to the point of rashness, but they were innocent of any knowledge of military discipline. When Harrison ordered General James Winchester, commander of the left wing, to proceed down the present Maumee River, the Ohio militia refused to march. "The movement of a force so insubordinate as that every man's will is his law" produced little, wrote Brigadier General Tupper, "but a plentiful harvest of mortification and disgrace." Unlike Wayne or General Winfield Scott, Harrison lacked the iron necessary to hammer the helter-skelter array at his disposal into a disciplined force—an incapacity that won him popularity but more than once proved fatal to his plans.

In the second place, Harrison faced the difficult task of securing supplies. Hundreds of thousands of rations were needed; munitions and artillery had to be secured; blankets, shoes, and warm clothes of all varieties were lacking. In an August heat of enthusiasm the backwoodsmen had rushed to answer the summons to arms, totally unmindful of the exigencies of the winter that awaited them. "I can assure you that in consequence of the sudden and unexpected call there is not one man in twenty who has winter clothing with him," wrote Brigadier General Beall. "Many of my detachment has no socks, and a number entirely barefooted, all dressed in summer clothing." Harrison worked arduously at the problem, but insufficiency of supplies dogged each advance of the army and serves to explain the recurrent threats of mutiny among the militia and their refusal to remain in service beyond their terms of enlistment.

Much of the embarrassment in feeding and clothing the army was due to almost insuperable transportation difficulties. Loss of control of Lake Erie greatly complicated the situation.

Quantities of supplies had to be brought from the East via Pittsburgh down the Ohio, and thence dragged by wagon or oxcart forward to interior supply depots. The task of coming to grips with the enemy was similar to that which had confronted Wayne, but on a larger scale. Roads must be cut, trees felled, streams bridged. Between Winchester's men on the Maumee River (Wayne's old route north to Lake Erie) and the center of the army lay the Black Swamp. In the late fall and early spring the rains made communications and movements virtually impossible; the army was literally stuck in the mud. Indeed, throughout his command, Harrison's most immediate and inveterate enemy was the weather. Unexpected thaws and unseasonal storms impeded him at every turn.

As early as December 1812 Harrison was convinced that the object of his attack must be Malden and Amherstburg, the British posts across the river from Detroit. The latter was not tenable, he wrote; and he indicated that control of Lake Erie was essential for a permanent reoccupation of Detroit and ascendancy in that region. Could this be achieved, a spring campaign against Upper Canada would be assured certain and permanent success.

Nevertheless he continued to push on a winter campaign despite the hazards of such a plan and obviously against his own concept of sound strategy. His persistence, he admitted, was due to "some important political reasons." Pressure from the Administration, impatient for a victory, coupled with the conviction that "my personal fame is materially interested," urged him forward. Wayne's lessons of slow and careful preparation were forgotten, but there were extenuating circumstances. Equally at Washington and in the West was evidenced an irrational conviction that victory must follow a declaration of war regardless of twenty years' neglect of the military. Popular will demanded a triumph, though generals and armies might suffer. Based on an unfounded optimism, it was typically American and was not to be limited to the War of 1812.

Harrison's plan might have met with success had it not been

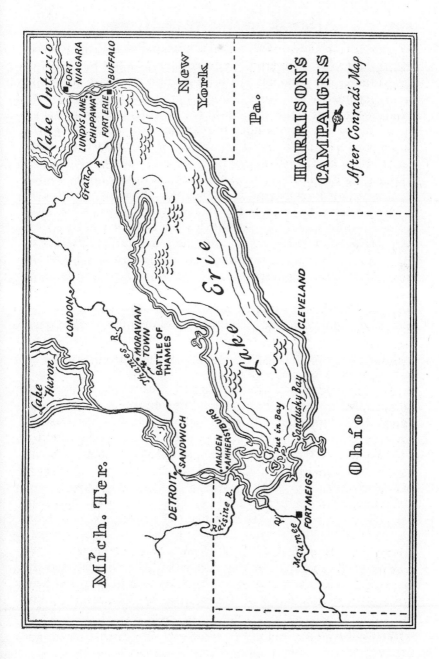

HARRISON'S CAMPAIGNS

After Conrad's Map

for the carelessness of General James Winchester and the troops under his command. Ordered forward to the rapids of the Maumee in January 1813, Winchester moved his force north beyond to the River Raisin. There Winchester's command encountered the devastating defeat and massacre that made the phrase "Remember the Raisin" the battle cry of the West. Harrison, moving forward with a supporting force, was checked by this disaster. With an understandable but not exhilarating caution, he fell back; the next months were passed in establishing Fort Meigs at the Rapids. There the army dug in. A February thaw sealed the fate of any expectation of a successful movement across the ice of Lake Erie. In May, Fort Meigs was besieged and ably defended under Harrison's direction. In the early summer Proctor marshaled his small force of British regulars, Canadian militia, and Indians to threaten once more the northern posts. Except for this diversion, the Northwest Army marked time, and its commander's energies were devoted to the interminable problems of recruiting, supply, and transportation. Harrison had reverted to his original strategical conceptions. Until control of Lake Erie had been secured he would not risk any movement. There were many doubtless who, knowing the general's fondness for Roman analogy, thought that by this time he had surpassed the tardy Fabius. But Harrison had picked another classical prototype, for, urging Governor Shelby to join him in the field, he writes: "Scipio the Conqueror of Carthage did not disdain to act as Lieutenant of his younger and less experienced brother Lucius."

At long last, on September 10, 1813, the naval battle of Lake Erie shattered the British fleet, cleared the enemy from the lake, and laid open the water approach to Canada and to Proctor, the British Antiochus. Perry's ringing message, "We have met the enemy, and they are ours," finally released the energies of Harrison's army. Volunteers and militia had been gathered in anticipation of Perry's success. Governor Shelby and Colonel Richard M. Johnson of Kentucky at the head of a mounted force had joined Harrison but a few days previously. With newly kindled enthusiasm the troops moved up to the shores of Put-in Bay and with Perry's aid were ferried across Lake Erie. The occupation of Malden, Amherstburg, and Detroit (abandoned by Proctor in his inglorious retreat) followed in rapid succession, and the pursuit of the British forces fleeing across the flat stretches of Ontario undertaken. On October 5, 1813, Harrison's army caught up with the British and their Indian allies, drawn up for a final stand at the little missionary settlement of Moraviantown. There occurred the American triumph celebrated as the Battle of the Thames. The Americans surged forward, Colonel Johnson and the mounted Kentuckians plunging hardily against the Indians. In a few hours the fighting was over. The British forces broke and surrendered, Tecumseh, the great chieftain, was killed, and the Indians scattered. Upper Canada was won and the power of the Indians of the Northwest forever shattered. It was a victory greeted deliriously by the American people after months of disaster and defeat, and it insured Harrison a lasting popularity.

For all practical purposes this campaign terminated Harrison's military career. The Kentucky militia returned home; with the remainder of his force Harrison marched on to the Niagara frontier, but he failed to follow up his victory. Granted leave, he proceeded to New York, Philadelphia, and Washington, savoring his triumph. With fine generosity and innocent of irony he offered a volunteer toast at Philadelphia: "The Militia of the United States. They possess the Roman spirit, and when our government shall think proper to give them that organization and discipline of which they are susceptible they will perform deeds that will emulate those of the legions led by Marcellus and Scipio."

Not until January 1814 did Harrison return to Ohio, and never again did he undertake active operations. Irritated by the busybody activities of Secretary of War Armstrong and the unjust criticisms in Congress of his arrangements with contractors of supply, on May 11, 1814, he resigned his command. In the midst of war, Cincinnatus retired to his farm.

III

In the early 1830s General Harrison was living quietly at North Bend, struggling with the routine perplexities of the farmer—how to wring larger profits from stubborn fiel of corn, wheat, and hay. Since his resignation from the Army e had held a variety of public offices: twice representative of Ohio in Congress, then a member of the state legislature, next United States senator. In 1828 he had been appointed United States minister to Colombia, an office from which President Andrew Jackson, shortly after his inauguration, had promptly recalled him. When in 1834 he was appointed clerk of the Court of Common Pleas of Hamilton County, his political career appeared to be ending as a minor figure in a local backwater. In fact it was about to take on national dimensions.

In part Harrison's emergence as a candidate for the presidency in 1836 was a backfire from the Democratic movement in favor of Colonel Richard M. Johnson of Kentucky, then United States senator but still "colonel" in the minds of loyal Kentuckians. An article extolling Johnson as the hero of the Battle of the Thames and the slayer of Tecumseh appeared in the *American Mechanic*. Current verse and drama gave notoriety to the fable. *Tecumseh or the Battle of the Thames*, a "National Drama in Five Acts," played to crowded houses in Washington, Baltimore, and Annapolis. With some reason Harrison's ire was aroused; in turn he took up his pen and entered the fray. In a series of letters he scouted the pretensions put forward by Johnson's partisans and stoutly defended his own record. Once more the interest of the public was focused on the general, and old memories of his services to the West revived. In December 1834 the *Pennsylvania Intelligencer* put forward his name as a presidential candidate. By 1836 he was the foremost opponent of the Democratic ticket.

Political parties during Jackson's second administration were in a state of flux. Resentment at the President's policies was mounting, but it was an opposition springing from myriad discontents. In the Northeast antagonism boiled against the Jack-

son monetary policy. In the South the sediment of the Nullification controversy aligned states'-rights men against Jackson's Union measures. In the West the proponents of internal
improvements had been aroused by the Maysville veto. National
Republicans, Anti-Masons, Anti-Van Buren Democrats were
in revolt. United by a common anti-Jackson animus, they were
not yet fused into one party, nor could agreement on a single
candidate be reached. As a result four candidates contended
against Van Buren: Harrison of Ohio, Daniel Webster of
Massachusetts, Willie P. Mangum of South Carolina, and
Hugh L. White of Tennessee. Van Buren was elected, but
Harrison outran the other candidates. Van Buren received
170 electoral votes, Harrison 73, White 26, Webster 14, and
Mangum 11. The popular vote, however, showed that in many
states Harrison ran close on Van Buren's heels. And more
significant than the election returns was the wide currency of
the sobriquet "Old Tip," the popularity of celebrations honor-
ing his military victories, and the affectionate and enthusiastic
response evoked by his appearance in public. The election of
1836 was, in effect, a dress rehearsal for the coming Whig
campaign. General Harrison was to be a "candidate by continuation."

The panic of 1837 doomed Van Buren politically. Scarcely
had the luckless President been inaugurated when the storm of
protest evoked by the depression burst upon him, and the inglorious and expensive Seminole War did nothing to appease
public resentment. Farmers evicted from their lands and
workers tramping the city streets alike held him responsible
for their troubles; the panic gave a popular basis to existing
anti-Democratic sentiment. Whig prospects grew brighter, and
Harrison's chances for the nomination in 1840 increased, for
astute politicians like Thurlow Weed were convinced that a
candidate with popular appeal was needed. Webster was passed
over, General Winfield Scott considered and rejected, Henry
Clay, the most outstanding aspirant, blocked. Assembling at
Harrisburg in December 1839 in their first national convention, Whig delegates, held in line by the need for unity, agreed

on a ticket—Harrison for President and John Tyler of Virginia for second place. No platform was adopted, for none could be framed that would be acceptable to the heterogeneous elements united under the Whig banner. Only a common purpose bound them together, the determination to overthrow Van Buren and the long-entrenched Democratic administration. Even Henry Clay, smarting with humiliation, swallowed his resentment and supported the ticket, although his adherents secretly agreed with Senator Benton's quip that "availability was the only ability sought by the Whigs."

The campaign of 1840 was epoch-making. "Give him a barrel of cider and a pension of two thousand a year, and our word for it, he will sit by the side of a sea coal fire and study moral philosophy," sneered the Baltimore *Republican,* a leading Democratic paper, when the Whig ticket was published. The remark was a boomerang, for the phrase caught the popular imagination and spread like wildfire. The Log Cabin campaign was on.

The nationalist appeal of the old soldier, the glamour of the Indian fighter who had saved the West, the simplicity of the frontiersman, all were embodied in the slogan, "Old Tip—the Log Cabin Candidate." A delirium of enthusiasm for Harrison swept the country. Old battlefields—Tippecanoe, Fallen Timbers, the site of Fort Meigs—were put to the new uses of political conventions. Celebrations of military victories starred the campaign; barbecues and "monster rallies" became political camp meetings with all the old-time fervor of a frontier religious revival. No aspect of dramatic appeal was neglected. Processions of veterans bearing transparencies of the Battle of Tippecanoe or the "Hero of the Thames," groups of trappers carrying a canoe, speeches, bands, and campaign songs, and inevitably a keg of hard cider, drew crowds waving banners, shouting, screaming for "Tippecanoe and Tyler too." Sixty thousand people assembled at the Whig rally on the battlefield of Tippecanoe in June 1840, thirty-five thousand at Fort Meigs in Ohio. The flood of democracy that had lifted Old Hickory in 1828 now reached its crest.

No feat of political prestidigitation ever surpassed in art-
fulness the campaign portrayal of Harrison. The urbane and
cultivated gentleman farmer of North Bend whose speeches
in Congress and out were saturated with illusions drawn from
his wide reading in the classics was transmogrified (as the
westerners had it) into a resemblance of Davy Crockett's self-
portrait:

> Fresh from the backwoods, half-horse, half-alligator, a little touched
> with the snapping turtle; can wade the Mississippi, leap the Ohio, ride
> upon a streak of lightening, and slip without a scratch down a honey
> locust; can whip my weight in wild cats—hug a bear too close for
> comfort.

The response of the West was immediate, and excitement
ran eastward along the National Pike. Uncle Joe Cannon,
then a little boy on the road to Indiana, remembered how even
his Quaker family caught the infection of enthusiasm, for
Harrison was "the great Commoner to the people of that
section." It was not long before the East succumbed to the
hospitable campaign and to the Philadelphia product bottled
in log cabins and labeled "E. C. Booz Old Cabin Whiskey."

Whig politicians, amazed and delighted, turned their batteries against Van Buren, the eastern aristocrat, lolling in
luxury, born with a golden spoon. Newspapers sprang up;
pamphlets, campaign lines, and song books spread the theme:

> Van Buren cannot be the working man's friend
>   He has left us nothing to do
> But to starve or to beg, his country defend
>   And to work for Old Tippecanoe.
> So I'll shoulder my flail, pack up for North Bend
>   Where I'll thresh for Old Tippecanoe.
>
> The President boasts of his Palace and "chink"
>   And says a Log Cabin won't do,
> And sticks up his nose when Hard Cider we drink
>   To the health of Old Tippecanoe.
> But like the British Proctor will run at the wink
>   Of the eye of Old Tippecanoe.

And from the West to the East roared a chorus:

> For Tippecanoe and Tyler Too, Tippecanoe and Tyler Too
> And with them we'll beat little Van, Van, Van,
>   Van is a used up man,
> And with them we'll beat little Van.

Democrats, furious at the reversal of roles of the Democratic and Whig parties, tried in vain to stem the current by attacks upon Harrison's military record. Every contemporary criticism of his strategy was revived, every unfriendly rumor and political canard was dragged out. Joe Daviess of Kentucky had been sacrificed at Tippecanoe; Winchester had been the victim of Harrison's jealousy in 1813; the ladies of Chillicothe had presented the general with a petticoat after he had ordered young George Croghan to fall back from Fort Stephenson in the summer of 1813; Shelby had planned and forced an unwilling Harrison forward to battle at the Thames; Richard M. Johnson had won that battle. Speeches in Congress and letters in newspapers called forth acrimonious retort and sturdy defense by old soldiers who had served with Harrison. The total result was to further publicize his record and insure his victory. In the election Harrison received 234 electoral votes, Van Buren 60.

So loosely jointed were the Whigs as a party that the post-election period might well have been spent in sober reflection upon means of consolidation. To a certain extent the assignment of rewards had this in view, but two important allies, the Anti-Masons in Pennsylvania and the "Conservative Democrats," were passed over. There were fears expressed that the old general might fall into the wrong hands, but as the Cabinet was finally constituted, Harrison demonstrated his sense by choosing outstanding personalities and representatives of different sectional interests. The office of Secretary of State, first tendered to Henry Clay, was awarded to Daniel Webster, then at the zenith of his powers. John J. Crittenden of Kentucky was made Attorney General; Thomas Ewing of Ohio, Secretary of the Treasury; George E. Badger of North Carolina, Secretary of the Navy; John Bell of Tennessee, Secretary of War; and Francis Granger of New York, Postmaster General.

In February 1841 Harrison journeyed to Washington, and his reception there took on the aspect of an ancient triumph. The story is told that Webster had prepared an inaugural but Harrison refused to use it, as people would know it was not his own composition. The "Godlike Daniel" had to content himself with some additions and emendations and, as he boasted jocularly to Mrs. Seaton, killing "seventeen Roman proconsuls as dead as smelts, every one of them."

Harrison was inaugurated on a cold and miserable March 4, and a month later he was dead. Yet his policies were already delineated by his earlier record, affirmed in campaign speeches and letters, amplified in his inaugural address. In general, he stood for a sound unionism tempered by some regard for states' rights. As a soldier he had served his country, as a representative he had voted for Federal internal improvements and later advocated distribution of Federal funds therefor. He had favored a protective tariff and the "American system." He was willing, he said, to accept a bank if the public interest demanded it, and deplored the results of Jackson's monetary policy. He had consistently decried a standing army and had advocated a plan for the improvement of the militia, making military training a required branch of education throughout the country. A citizen soldiery was his ideal, modeled on the example of the ancient republics; "the glory that was Greece and the grandeur that was Rome" he attributed to the participation of the citizenry in the defense of the state. His was the old republican ideal of the responsibility of the citizen, reflective of the enthusiasm for the Greek Revival of the early nineteenth century.

In addition, Harrison pointedly expressed the Whigs' faith in a limited executive and in the virtues of representative government:

. . . I have never regarded the office of Chief Magistrate as conferring upon the incumbent the power of mastery over the popular will, but as granting him the power to execute the properly expressed will of the people and not resist it. . . . The people are the best guardians of their own rights and it is the duty of their executive to abstain from interfering in or thwarting the sacred exercise of the lawmaking functions of their government.

The President should thus be the agent, not the principal, of the Government.

Against the memory of Andrew Jackson's imperious leadership and the Democrats' use of Federal patronage, Harrison had declaimed at length:

Should I ever be placed. in the Chief Magistrate's seat, I will carry out the principles of Jefferson, and never permit the interference of office-holders in the elections. . . . Cherish not the man, then, who, under the guise and name of Democracy, tries to overthrow the principles of Republicanism. . . .

And in his inaugural address, replete with allusions to Greece and Rome, Harrison again pledged obedience to the people's will, as exemplified in Congress, and his intention to serve but a single term.

Had Harrison lived, it is probable that his course as President would have been largely guided by the strong personalities with whom he had surrounded himself, for he was old and his vigor greatly impaired. As a general, Harrison had shown himself sensitive to the popular will, responsive to popular expectations; as a President, his conduct would undoubtedly have been consistent with his past record, nationalist in outlook, amiable in execution.

All these considerations indicate that his death on April 4, 1841, and the succession of the Vice-President, "His Accidency" John Tyler, Virginian champion of states' rights, profoundly affected our history. Within six months every member of the Cabinet except Webster had resigned, and Webster remained in office only until the ticklish question of the northeastern boundary was amicably settled with Great Britain. The Whig program was wrecked by the integrity or the obstinacy of one man, nominated for the office of Vice-President solely on grounds of political expediency. The project of a new Bank of the United States and Clay's pet scheme for a higher tariff coupled with a distribution of the proceeds of land sales alike failed. Tyler, elected as a Whig, was literally read out of the party, and built his administration on the states'-rights wing of the Democratic party. One can only speculate as to what Harrison would have accomplished, holding in remembrance his last cryptic words as he lay dying:

"Sir, I wish you to understand the true principles of the government. I wish them carried out. I ask nothing more."

VII

General Taylor

DURING THE YEARS that James Fenimore Cooper was creating the romantic redskins of the Leatherstocking Tales, his contemporary, Zachary Taylor, was confronting the Indians of pitiless reality. Taylor cut his niche in history by his successes in the Mexican War, but most of his forty years in the Army were spent on the frontier fighting the savages or at some distant post keeping the ceaseless vigil against hostile outbreaks.

Born in Virginia (1784), Zachary Taylor was taken to Kentucky when an infant. His father was a Revolutionary veteran and became a figure of some local prominence in the new state, sufficiently so that when Congress provided for new infantry regiments in 1808, the Kentucky congressional delegation secured a commission in the Seventh Regiment for young Taylor. In the Army he remained except for a few brief months after the War of 1812, when he resigned because, like others, his rank had been reduced in the peacetime establishment. Rank restored, he returned and slowly trudged up the road of promotion by seniority.

The story of Taylor's adult life is chiefly the story of the Regular Army on the border. And the story of the Regular Army there is essentially the dispiriting saga of the execution of our Indian policy. It has already been remarked upon how vigorously the cession of Indian lands was pressed. In combination was pursued the policy of removing the aborigines to western lands for the purpose of giving elbow room to the rapidly expanding white population. We have come to deprecate the shifting of peoples to suit the convenience of a dominant majority. But in the nineteenth century we were unregenerate and remorselessly transported the savages from the lands of their fathers to places where they did not want to go. The Army's task was to see that the Indians remained within bounds, and if they revolted to suppress them.

Zachary Taylor participated in three of the great Indian wars. In September 1812 he bravely defended Fort Harrison, a little outpost on the Wabash, holding the blockhouse with a handful of men against the fierce onslaught of Tecumseh's warriors. This exploit won him renown and a brevet majority, and showed him to be a cool and levelheaded commander. His second war was the Black Hawk affair in 1832, when he participated in the final action at Bad Axe. But as he served under an indifferent commander who dithered interminably and at the crucial moment was fooled by an Indian ruse, no new laurels were garnered. Five years later Taylor, at length a colonel, was pulled out of the West to head an expedition against the Seminoles in Florida, recalcitrant against the Jackson removal policy.

The Seminole War had been a badly mismanaged and expensive enterprise at which four generals had tried their hands with virtually no results. Taylor, with some eight hundred men, the largest force he had yet commanded, made a difficult march from Tampa Bay to Lake Okeechobee, where on Christmas Day, 1837, he routed a small army of "hostiles." He exhibited good but not brilliant generalship and was presently brevetted brigadier.

Although Taylor had had a few tours of duty in civilized places, a large part of his service was in dreary posts where the routine of drill was supplemented by the monotony of road or fort building and occasionally by the somewhat more enlivening show of force against some restless tribe. This experience stood him in good stead when he set about systematically to purge the middle of Florida of Seminoles and runaway Negro slaves. He reported in June 1839 that "fifty-three new posts have been established, eight hundred and forty-eight miles of wagon road, three thousand six hundred and forty-three feet of causeway and bridges opened and constructed," and that all the country between Fort Mellon and Tallahassee had been diligently scoured. Here was care and thoroughness, an example of army achievement for which no medals were given and little acknowledgment ever made.

The arrival in Florida of General in Chief Alexander Macomb and his reversion to previous unsuccessful tactics moved Taylor to request a transfer in 1840. This was granted, and he was assigned command of the Second Department of the Western Division with headquarters at Fort Smith, Arkansas. Here he remained until June 1844, when he was put in command of the First Department and stationed at Fort Jesup, Louisiana, close to the Texas border.

Meantime the events that were to precipitate the Mexican War and to make Taylor a celebrity were hurrying to a crisis. In 1835 the revolt of Texas had raised a fresh issue in American politics. From the moment recognition of the new republic was extended in 1837, demand grew for annexation. "Manifest Destiny," a vague but emergent conviction that our borders must be expanded to the Pacific, was whipped to a fever by the lust of slaveholding planters for new cotton fields. In 1844 the Democratic party boldly announced its stand for "reannexation" of Texas and for the reoccupation of Oregon. On this platform James K. Polk was elected. Just before he took office his predecessor, John Tyler, signed a joint resolution of Congress providing for negotiation of the annexation of Texas.

Pursuant to a promise to protect the borders of Texas pending consummation of the projected espousal, General Taylor had been ordered to proceed with troops to a point selected by the American chargé d'affaires at Austin. Corpus Christi was chosen, and here Taylor and his army debarked at the end of July 1845. A camp was established west of the river Nueces, and the American army was rapidly being whipped into shape when on December 29, 1845, by joint resolution, the Lone Star State was admitted to the Union.

Relations with Mexico, already strained, definitely worsened.

When Polk, in January 1846, disregarding Mexican contentions that the Nueces marked the boundary of the ex-republic, ordered the United States Army to proceed to the Rio Grande, hostilities became inevitable. Taylor moved his men across country and, fixing his base of supplies at Point Isabel on the coast, took a position opposite Matamoros, some twenty miles away. In co-operation with the Navy, a blockade of the Rio Grande was instituted.

A considerable army of Mexican soldiers was stationed at Matamoros, and the bottling of the river, which cut off supplies, was regarded, not unnaturally, as a warlike act. A small body of Mexicans finally crossed the Rio Grande on April 24, 1846, and the ensuing clash with an American scouting party was made the occasion of Polk's war message of May 11.

Taylor was busy constructing a fort opposite Matamoros when news came that the Mexicans were crossing the Rio in force to the south, apparently designing to cut him off from his base at Point Isabel. Thinking to intercept the enemy, the general with some two thousand men set out May 1. Without encountering the Mexicans he reached Point Isabel. Here he remained, strengthening the fortifications until the Navy landed some sailors and marines to assist in the defense. Meantime part of the Mexican army was besieging the American works across from Matamoros. Taylor, hearing the noise of the bombardment, and his scouts reporting that the main Mexican army lay across the road just traversed, determined to retrace his march. It was on this return journey that the two actions at Palo Alto and Resaca de la Palma were fought. At the first the Mexicans retired, and at the second they were routed. Both affairs were celebrated as famous victories. Years later, after the bloody Battle of the Wilderness, General Grant remarked to his staff:

"While we were engaged in the Wilderness I could not keep from thinking of the first fight I ever saw—the battle of Palo Alto. As I looked at the long line of battle, consisting of three thousand men, I felt that General Taylor had such a fearful responsibility resting upon him that I wondered how he ever had the nerve to assume it; and when after the fight the casualties were reported and the losses ascertained to be nearly sixty in killed, wounded, and missing, the engagement assu..ned a magnitude in my eyes which was positively startling. When the news of the victory reached the States the windows of every household were illuminated and it was largely instrumental in making General Taylor President of the United States. Now such an affair would scarcely be deemed important enough to report to headquarters."

If Taylor had crossed immediately to Matamoros he could without doubt have captured the opposing army entire. But he was a deliberate man and spent better than a week making preparations. Finally, on May 18, 1846, the crossing was made. The Mexican army had fled, and Matamoros was occupied without bloodshed. During all this time General Taylor was virtually without instructions. He had suggested operations against Monterrey, but before a reply was received, a note from Secretary of War Marcy advised him "to prosecute the war with vigor in the manner you deem most effective."

Up to this moment the Administration had done little war planning. The President and his advisers were ignorant of the topography and climate of Mexico, and their political misgivings about General in Chief Winfield Scott were not calculated to speed any competent strategical decisions. Obviously, some general plans at least had to be concerted. Accordingly, soon after giving Taylor carte blanche, another letter (June 8) was dispatched requesting his "views and suggestions." Taylor's answer was eminently sensible. He explained that the chief problems were those of logistics, that he proposed to deposit his volunteers in camps of instruction, and since an expedition from Matamoros to Mexico City was not feasible, he proposed to use his army to cut off the northern Mexican departments.

Polk and his Cabinet were devoted adherents of the principle (later the maxim of Clemenceau) that war is too serious a business to be trusted to generals. A variety of plans were hatched, the most brilliant of which was to facilitate General Santa Anna's return to Mexico from his Cuban exile in the hope that, once re-established in power, he would negotiate peace. We shall see in a moment how Santa Anna deserved the

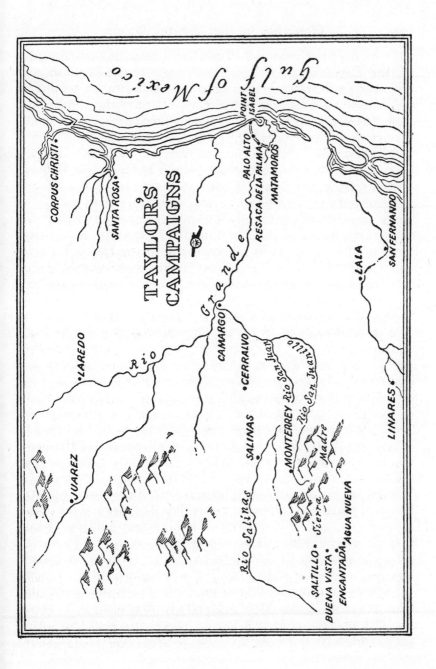

TAYLOR'S CAMPAIGNS

Gulf of Mexico

CORPUS CHRISTI.

SANTA ROSA.

POINT ISABEL

PALO ALTO
RESACA DE LA PALMA
MATAMOROS

SAN FERNANDO

LALA

Rio Grande

LAREDO

Rio

CAMARGO.

CERRALVO.

SALINAS

MONTERREY Rio San Juan

Rio San Juan

JUAREZ

LINARES.

Sierra Madre

Rio Salinas

SALTILLO.
BUENA VISTA.
ENCANTADA. AGUA NUEVA

trust of his Washington patrons. As a part of this romantic scheme Taylor was instructed to intimate to the Mexican generals the peaceful intentions of America and to try to induce the separate Mexican departments to declare their independence. "Policy and force are to be combined; the fruits of the former will be prized as highly as those of the latter."

Meantime at Matamoros had arrived news of Taylor's promotion to major general as well as orders from General Scott directing an advance. Taylor, overwhelmed with a volume of volunteers far beyond his wants, was temporarily incapable of making any move. In July, however, he started dispatching various regiments up the Rio Grande to Camargo, and finally, sensible of criticism at his delay, began the march to Monterrey. On September 19, 1846, his army, amounting to about three thousand regulars and three thousand volunteers, encamped on the outskirts of that city. Here he divided his forces, sending General Worth to attack the western side of the city and to take two commanding heights while his own division approached from the east. Taylor has been criticized for splitting his forces in defiance of a Napoleonic maxim, but he had already discovered the caliber of his opponent, and his success is justification enough.

The fight began on September 21, and it was a bloody one. Taylor made two mistakes. He failed to make preliminary experimental attacks on the barricades at the east of the town and lost heavily as a result. When he had hacked his way into the town and was but a square from the plaza, he withdrew his men to prepare for a general assault in concert with Worth, who had taken the heights and was tunneling toward the plaza from the west. If he had persisted in his advance, it is probable that the enemy would have been crushed.

In the morning of September 24, before a general assault was begun, General Ampudia, in command of the Mexican army, made a proposal that he be allowed to evacuate the city, taking men and arms. After protracted discussion it was agreed that city and citadel be evacuated; that the Mexican army, with arms and accouterments and one battery, retire beyond an agreed line which neither party was to cross for eight weeks or until orders from the respective governments were received.

News of the capture of Monterrey reached Washington on October 11, 1846. Taylor's name was already being boomed for the presidency. The congressional elections were at hand. Polk and his Cabinet were naturally displeased, both with the victory and with the terms given to General Ampudia. Forgetful of the discretion vested in Taylor and the advice to regard policy as much as fighting, Polk records in his diary that there had been a violation of express orders. A barely veiled reprimand was issued, and Taylor was ordered to terminate the armistice.

Taylor's reasons for his generous terms were originally stated to be the gallant defense of the Mexicans (the ideal of chivalry in war was not yet extinguished) and his conviction that the Mexicans were preparing to treat for peace. He later explained to the War Department that his army was simply not prepared to move forward. The armistice consequently paralyzed the enemy at a moment when the supply problem had literally halted his own army. Lieutenant George Gordon Meade wrote his wife: "I approve General Taylor's course," and added the interesting details that the regulars were crippled to inefficiency and the volunteers no longer to be depended upon.

It should be remarked that General Taylor's tactics and his political strategy were projections of Indian war experience. His advances, his methods of protecting communications, and his safeguards lest a defeat of his army mean a general rising in the enemy country were patterned on his Seminole campaign. Typical also of Indian warfare was the practice of trying to negotiate after a military success. Hidalgos the opposing generals may have been, but an old frontiersman would be hard put to distinguish the Mexican soldiery from Cherokees or Creeks, and their guerrilla tactics were cut from the same pattern.

Polk at length convinced himself that Taylor was a "narrow-minded bigotted partisan, without resources, and wholly unqualified for the command he holds." A reconciliation had just been effected with General Winfield Scott, who was to head the new blow through Vera Cruz. For this expedition the general in chief, who had observed his own political capital waning while Taylor's was steadily waxing, proposed to detach most of Taylor's veterans and leave Taylor with only enough troops to remain on the defensive. This was a form of political sterilization the humor of which the anxious Democrats could thoroughly appreciate. The troops were transferred to Scott, and much to his rage, Taylor was left a force of some five thousand men, only 453 of whom were regulars.

Taylor had meantime taken Saltillo, capital of Coahuila, despite instructions cautioning him against further advances. He did this because he regarded Secretary Marcy's letter to be mere advice, and because he thought Saltillo essential to a defensive line. This line he proposed to run from Parras through Saltillo, Monterrey, and Victoria to Tampico. The last place was occupied by American troops, but after moving into Victoria, Taylor resolved to abandon the place owing to difficulties of supply. Scott requested the abandonment even of Saltillo, but Taylor, convinced of its defensive usefulness, grimly hung on and established a camp some seventeen miles south of the town. There, in February 1847, occurred an event Homeric in quality.

General Santa Anna, having been bowed back into Mexico by the Polk administration, had secured his election as President and set about to prosecute the war. An army was collected at San Luis Potosí which the new President, goaded by the press, himself led forth before it was prepared. By a series of forced marches this army was pushed against Taylor. The latter fell back from his camp some twelve miles to the hacienda of Buena Vista, where the terrain favored defense. On the morning of February 22 Santa Anna, announcing, "You are surrounded by twenty thousand men," demanded surrender. Taylor replied, "I beg leave to say I decline acceding to your request." There ensued some skirmishing and jockeying for position. The next day occurred the battle of Buena Vista.

Military men, and particularly the devotees of Jomini, have been free in criticisms of Taylor. His left was broken and driven in, but by timely reinforcement with Jefferson Davis' Mississippi Rifles and by virtue of good artillery support, the Mexican right gave way. At evening the two armies were about on the same ground occupied the night before. Then, during the night, Santa Anna and the remnants of his vaunted twenty thousand slipped away to make an inglorious and devastating retreat.

The effect of Taylor's victory was stunning. Polk scolded in his diary that if the general had obeyed orders and stayed in Monterrey the severe loss of life would have been avoided. Taylor himself believed that "the battle of Buena Vista opened the road to the city of Mexico and the halls of Montezumas, that others might revel in them." The American people needed no reassurances. Here was something for the book. Volunteers had thrashed an enemy more than three times their number, and they had been led by a general whom the soldiers prized. Old Rough and Ready had been made to walk the plank by the Washington pirates, but he had come up with a bag of guineas.

For all his successes, it cannot be said that Zachary Taylor was more than a middling general. His ideas of strategy never advanced beyond his Indian war schooling, and his tactics were of the simplest variety. He does not seem to have planned ahead much, but was willing to meet emergencies as they came up. This was not according to the rules, and the correctness of such generalship can be tested only by results. He had great personal bravery and even greater confidence, for he frequently took risks in putting himself far from his base. Against this is to be balanced his prudence in attending to proper supplies and in seeing to it that recruits were trained before he led them into danger. He was not without political shrewdness, but his long life in lonely outposts gave him little opportunity for developing the sort of political foresight that a great commander must possess.

Without doubt the most valuable asset which General Taylor

possessed was his astonishing capacity of inspiring confidence in his men. He had done this as a tyro at Fort Harrison in 1812. His accomplishment at Buena Vista was a repetition on a grand and almost miraculous scale. Contemptuous of uniforms and military pomp, Taylor went about in a straw hat, checked gingham coat, and a pair of blue trousers without braid. To all outward appearances he was only an elderly edition of the farmer boys in the ranks. His coolness under fire was the steadying example of a parent to the young. He was a plain American leading a lot of other plain Americans.

It has become the mode to deride the military capacities of Taylor. Ulysses Grant, a not incompetent witness, deserves therefore to be heard:

No soldier could face either danger or responsibility more calmly than he. These are qualities more rarely found than genius or physical courage. . . . General Taylor never wore uniform, but dressed himself entirely for comfort. He moved about the field in which he was operating to see through his own eyes the situation. Often he would be without staff officers, and when he was accompanied by them there was no prescribed order in which they followed. He was very much given to sit his horse side-ways—with both feet on one side—particularly on the battle field. . . . Taylor was not a conversationalist, but on paper he could put his meaning so plainly that there could be no mistaking it. He knew how to express what he wanted to say in the fewest well-chosen words, but would not sacrifice meaning to the construction of high-sounding sentences.

Comparing Taylor and Scott, Grant goes on to say:

But with their opposite characteristics both were great and successful soldiers; both were true, patriotic and upright in all their dealings. Both were pleasant to serve under—Taylor was pleasant to serve with.

II

Credit for promoting General Taylor as a candidate for the presidency has been claimed by Thurlow Weed, the benign-appearing and astute Whig politician of Albany, New York. He tells the story of meeting the general's brother two or three weeks after Resaca de la Palma. Weed was informed, no doubt to his horror, that Zachary Taylor had no politics. But he discovered that the redoubtable soldier admired Clay, disliked Jackson, and was prejudiced against foreign manufactures. Weed remarked that "his *prejudices* were quite as important and practical as *principles,*" and told the astonished Taylor that his brother, the general, would be the next President. The Albany king-maker, anxious to keep his candidate from making any rash commitments, imparted a message for the general amounting to the famous counsel of Br'er Rabbit to "lay low and say nuffin." Shortly afterward Weed began a campaign of suggestion in his Albany newspaper.

General Taylor's first reaction was very stand-offish, but although he continued to write like a reluctant bride, it is hard to doubt that Weed's suggestion gradually gripped him. His private letters disclose a real nostalgia for retirement to his Louisiana plantation and an old age dedicated to farming, the avocation to which he had devoted all of his earlier leaves and in which he was passionately interested. But the presidential virus is a strong and insidious infection. In Taylor's case, natural resistance was weakened by rage over the rape of his army by the pushing Scott, a professed aspirant for the nomination.

The victory at Monterrey gave tremendous impetus to the Taylor movement. The problem of the Whig protagonists was to keep this a Whig movement, for Taylor's lack of political "principles" made lively the danger that the Democrats would persuade him to their bosoms. Two of the Whig leaders, Henry Clay and Daniel Webster, were so prominent in the public mind and had such powerful support that the greatest finesse was needed to build up Taylor without knocking down too many political fences. The promotion was done steadily and consistently in the papers. In January 1847 Taylor wrote to Senator John J. Crittenden, the Kentucky leader, that he would not refuse if the "good people of the country should be so indiscreet as to confer that high station on me." But even before this letter was received Crittenden had addressed the Senate in defense of the Monterrey armistice, describing Taylor as a man "above all party" who desired only the approbation of his country. Crittenden had not yet deserted Clay, but he was soon to do so.

Buena Vista supplied fresh kindling to the fire. Taylor meetings became the mode, and at both public meetings and state conventions Old Rough and Ready was acclaimed the Whig candidate. At a convention in Harrodsburg, Kentucky, in the fall of 1847, he was called the "people's candidate . . . from the circumstance that he has been entirely aloof from the party conflicts of the country, has formed no 'entangling alliances' with intruding politicians or wire-workers; and if elected would have no debts to pay with the offices and money of the people for partizan electioneering services." This declaration was symptomatic of a general and bewildering popular fever. The people were sick of politicians and were looking for someone worthy of both trust and affection.

While the country was agitating itself, General Taylor remained at Monterrey until November 1847. His letters to his son-in-law, Dr. Wood, reflect the color of his political thinking. In June he describes himself as "a democrat of the Jeffersonian school, which embodies very many of the principles of the whigs of the present day." In July he writes that he will enter into "no explanations as to my politics or creed" or give any pledges as to what he will do. He still hopes someone else will be elected, but "I would undergo political martyrdom rather than see Gen'l Scott or Cass elected." By August the effects of home happenings are evident. He has no wish to be "the exclusive candidate of the whig party," and this remark he repeats six weeks later:

The whigs as party, between ourselves, I look upon as doomed; the democrats greatly out maneuvering them—I am gratified I took the position I did, which was not to be the exclusive candidate of any party; & if I am elected at all it will be by a union of a portion of whigs Democrats & native votes . . .

For all that Taylor was a political novice, he was gifted with prophetic insight. As a candidate he was much too skittish a colt for any political stable unless the owner was Thurlow

Weed. The latter comprehended both the scruples of Taylor and the present mood of the voters. Taylor's nomination was procured at the Whig convention in June 1848. Abbot Lawrence, a textile manufacturer of Massachusetts, was proposed for Vice-President, but the anti-Taylor Whigs would not "have King Cotton both ends of the ticket," and Millard Fillmore, a party wheel horse from Buffalo, was picked. No platform was put forth, for none could have been agreed upon by the variety of elements that made up the Whig party. In any event, a people's candidate did not need one. Besides there was no assurance that Old Zach would stand on one if it had been adopted.

At Baltimore the Democrats had already nominated Lewis Cass of Michigan and William O. Butler of Kentucky, a political general of Polk's creation. Cass, when a militia colonel, had been taken prisoner outside Detroit when General Hull capitulated in the War of 1812, and had broken his sword rather than surrender it to the British. Exchanged, he had been made brigadier general in the United States Volunteers and had been with Harrison at the Battle of the Thames. In his subsequent civil career he had been governor of Michigan Territory, Secretary of War under Jackson, minister to France, and United States senator. He had been warm for the Mexican War. A platform was adopted repeating the resolutions of 1844 and adding an endorsement of the Polk administration, a claim of credit for winning the war, and some chauvinistic resolutions acclaiming the revolutions then going on in Europe.

The anti-slavery groups in the North, disgusted with both conventions which had evaded the burning issue—should there be slavery in the newly won territories?—held their own tea party in August 1848. Out of these deliberations emerged the Free Soil party with a ticket headed by ex-President Martin Van Buren. On his banners were inscribed the ever useful alliterative Four Freedoms, this time in the form of Free Soil, Free Speech, Free Labor, and Free Men.

The campaign was extremely diverting. As it was still not *au fait* for the presidential candidate to take the stump, General

Taylor indulged in writing what Seward called "inappropriate and unreasonable letters" raising some question as to whether or not he was a proper Whig. He went so far even as to send a written expression of gratification over a "nomination" by a Democratic assemblage in South Carolina. Many assiduous Whigs were alienated. Daniel Webster, addressing his neighbors at Marshfield, Massachusetts, expressed his disapproval of the nomination, but grudgingly admitted that as between Cass, a warmonger, and Taylor, who had fought but disapproved of the Mexican War, he would support Taylor.

Party leaders had become greatly alarmed. They concocted a communication which the general was induced to send out early in September, explaining that he was a true Whig, but that he was not partisan in the sense that he would lay hands indiscriminately on public officers or force Congress by the coercion of the veto "to pass laws to suit me or pass none." It was embarrassing to politicians to have a candidate who expected to guide the nation by the Constitution alone. But they were not sufficiently embarrassed to tell the people party purpose respecting slavery.

The Taylor campaign took on some of the military splash that had carried Harrison to victory. A Taylor anecdote book related the general's quaint ways and repeated his pungent sayings like his remark at Buena Vista to artillery captain Bragg, "A little more grape, Mr. Bragg." Taylor speakers found it difficult to conclude orations when the crowd roared, "Give us some more grape." On their part the Democrats assailed Taylor's military achievements and sought to build up General Cass as a military hero. But they had picked the wrong war and a veteran bare of heroism. Abraham Lincoln, speaking in Congress, was derisive:

"In the days of the Black Hawk War I fought, bled and came away. Speaking of General Cass's career reminds me of my own. I was not at Stillman's defeat but I was about as near it as Cass was to Hull's surrender. . . . I did not break my sword, for I had none to break, but I bent a musket pretty badly on one occasion. If Cass broke his sword, the idea is he broke it in desperation; I bent the musket by accident. If General Cass went in advance of me in picking huckleberries, I surpassed him in charges upon wild onions. . . ."

When the shouting was over and the votes were counted, Taylor emerged with 163 electoral votes, and Cass with 127. The Whigs had won their last presidential election, and they had stepped into a brawl of major political dimensions. The issue—should slavery be extended to the lands acquired from Mexico?—might be evaded in the campaign, but the outgoing Congress when it assembled in December 1848 could not dodge it. At the very opening of the war a rider had been offered to an army appropriation bill providing that neither slavery nor involuntary servitude should exist in any territory acquired by treaty. This was the famous Wilmot Proviso. It had passed the House but was lost in the Senate and at the next session of Congress was shelved. Nevertheless it remained, a tattered banner of the anti-slavery forces. During the session of 1848–49, the Congress strove for a solution of the territorial controversy, but the strong Whig and northern Democrat coalition in the House could make no progress against the Senate.

President Taylor's inaugural threw no light upon the course this slaveholding Louisianian proposed. He announced that his chief guide would be the Constitution and that his exemplar was George Washington. He declared for an efficient army and navy, a foreign policy of non-intervention and settlement of international questions by negotiation. He announced that honesty, capacity, and fidelity were his criteria for officeholding and intimated that he regarded strict separation of government functions as desirable. He was prepared to recommend measures to Congress, "but it is for the wisdom of Congress itself, in which all legislative powers are vested by the Constitution, to regulate these and other matters of domestic policy." This body he expected would adopt measures of conciliation to harmonize conflicting interests and perpetuate the Union. Since the new Congress was not to meet for eight months, there was plenty of time to ponder the implications of these words.

Taylor's baptism of fire was in the patronage battle. Whigs

regarded his Cabinet with satisfaction, but his reluctance as the people's choice to indulge in the usual purge aroused misgivings. Postmaster General Jacob Collamer, described as "too tender for progress," at first held his hand, but soon went to work with a will in changing postmasters. It is probable that Thurlow Weed induced the President to see light. He relates that Taylor became convinced that the "patriotic movement" which overthrew Democratic supremacy meant more than election of a Whig President and choice of a Whig Cabinet. Taylor is quoted as remarking, "I did not think it either wise or just to kick away the ladder by which I ascended to the presidency; colonels, majors, captains, lieutenants, sergeants and corporals are just as necessary to success in politics as they are to discipline and efficiency of an army."

General Taylor, having made a strategic retreat from one position announced in his inaugural, nevertheless stood firm on his promised foreign policy. Here he found himself on the advanced ground of Polk's expansionist program with some action essential in Central America, where the British were attempting to shoulder a bit more of the white man's burden. Encroachments upon the so-called Mosquito territory (Nicaragua) had taken place, and there were reports concerning British intentions to build a canal across Nicaragua. This brought the white man's burden in direct conflict with Manifest Destiny.

The United States had dreamed about an isthmian canal as early as 1826, when Secretary of State Henry Clay had written instructions for our delegates to the Panama Congress. In 1846 a treaty had been concluded with New Granada (later Colombia), wherein the latter had guaranteed our right of passage across Panama Isthmus, and in return we had guaranteed the neutrality of the isthmus and New Granada's sovereignty there. The acquisition of California and the discovery of its gold which caused an impetuous rush of prospectors to the Pacific suddenly dramatized the importance of a short route to our new possession.

The Polk administration had sent to Nicaragua a chargé

d'affaires, Elijah Hise, who, without instructions, concluded a treaty (June 21, 1849) by which Nicaragua granted the exclusive right of constructing a canal or railroad, and in return received a guarantee of possessions by the United States. Before this document reached Washington the Taylor administration promised Nicaragua its good offices in the matter of the Mosquito controversy with Britain. At the same time Hise was recalled and Ephraim Squier sent in his place. The latter in turn concluded a commercial treaty (September 3, 1849) containing a clause respecting a canal, likewise with a territorial guarantee.

Some aces having been collected to play against the British kings, the game between the two foreign offices began. When the Hise Convention arrived, Secretary of State Clayton told Crampton, the British minister, that this treaty was not approved but that great caution would be necessary on both sides to prevent collision over the Mosquito controversy. The position of our Department of State was essentially that announced by Clay in 1826—that the benefits of any canal ought not to be exclusively appropriated to any one nation but should be extended to all parts of the globe upon the basis of fair tolls. This principle had been approved by the Senate in 1835 and by the House in 1839.

It is to the credit of the new administration that in the face of the strongly chauvinistic temper of the country it took a stand of such moderation. There is little doubt that General Taylor was responsible. He was present at an interview between Clayton and Crampton at which the latter was told that the Hise Convention would be adopted only as a measure of self-defense. He approved the suggestion that Britain and the United States make treaties with Nicaragua giving no exclusive rights to either, and that all powers making similar treaties should have equal privileges.

In the midst of these negotiations arrived the Squier treaty with Nicaragua, and another agreement which Squier had concluded with Honduras ceding Tigre Island for eighteen months. This island the British promptly seized with an armed force.

The receipt of this explosive news made necessary a request for a disavowal from England. Lord Palmerston was slow in giving the required assurances, but nevertheless negotiations were resumed in Washington with a new British representative, Sir Henry Bulwer. The fruit of these conversations was the celebrated Clayton-Bulwer Treaty of April 19, 1850.

The treaty was based on the principle of neutralization, and its object was to settle the views and intentions of both countries regarding a Nicaraguan canal. Both contractants agreed to protect the canal, to guarantee its neutrality so that it might "forever be open and free," and to invite other powers to enter into similar stipulations. In addition, the instrument established the general principle that both parties agreed to extend their protection by treaty to any other practicable communications by railway or canal across the isthmus, especially the communications then projected by way of Tehuantepec and Panama. On the second underlying issue, the Mosquito coast, it was agreed that neither party would "occupy or fortify or colonize or assume any dominion over Nicaragua, Costa Rica, the Mosquito coast or any part of Central America," nor would either make use of any protection or any alliance for the purpose of occupying, fortifying, or colonizing any of those parts.

Few treaties ever involved more intricate subsequent negotiations or were more violently criticized. It took another ten years before the British gave up their Mosquito claim, and it was another fifty years before the shackles on our freedom of action for an isthmian canal were removed. Taylor and Clayton had remained true to the policy of the great Whig Clay and were the readier to compromise as the shadow of the slavery controversy lay black across the path of domestic policy.

General Taylor's pacific course in the British negotiation stemmed from his magnanimity, already exhibited at Monterrey in his dealings with General Ampudia. He obviously hoped that the slavery question at home could be handled with temperance and good will, and he expressed himself to this effect in his first annual message. Congress was informed that California had already called a constitutional convention and would shortly apply for admission as a state, and that the people of New Mexico likewise would probably soon present themselves for admission. The President recommended abstention from "those exciting topics of a sectional character that have hitherto produced painful apprehensions in the public mind." In a concluding paragraph he proclaimed his attachment to the Union and pledged himself to maintain it to the full extent of "the powers conferred upon me by the Constitution." Whatever comfort the pro-slavery men may have taken from his declared belief in the legislative supremacy of Congress and his antipathy to the veto was rudely shattered by his conclusion.

It should be observed that during a military career in places where responsibility for independent decision had been forced upon him either by events or the absence of instructions, General Taylor was perforce a believer in the power of the *fait accompli*. Shortly after his inauguration he had sent an agent to California to investigate the situation there, and it is probable that Taylor's plan for an immediate formation of a state government, skipping the interim of territorial status, was imparted. In any event the Californians held their constitutional convention and adopted a fundamental law in which slavery was prohibited. This had been approved by the people in November 1849.

Taylor's scheme, in which both Seward and Secretary Clayton probably had a hand, was much too simple a solution of the problem. In January 1850 Congress called for an explanation of the cryptic references to the territories in the President's annual message. This was furnished, coupled with an earnest plea for the right of self-government which Taylor thought would be infringed should Congress see fit to attach any conditions to admission. The questions exciting the country would be "settled by the silent effect of causes independent of the action of Congress," and consequently the President recommended awaiting the salutary operation of those causes.

The wild and tossing seas of petitions, memorials, resolutions, and bills dealing with the territories were not oiled to calmness by the explanations of the Administration. The ultras on both sides were equally enraged. On the night of the day the House received Taylor's message, the rivals Clay and Webster met and consummated an understanding over a compromise which the Kentucky senator hoped would settle things.

The resolutions embodying the compromise were introduced by Clay on January 26, 1850, and embodied the following points: (1) California to be admitted at once without restriction; (2) territorial government to be established in the remainder of the Mexican Cession without restriction as to slavery; (3) Texas' western boundary to be fixed, excluding any New Mexican territory; (4) the United States to assume Texas' pre-annexation debt; (5) slave trade to be prohibited in the District of Columbia in slaves brought in from the outside; (6) an effective fugitive slave law to be enacted.

Secession sentiment had waxed so greatly in strength that Clay's plan was unacceptable to the intransigent southerners. The mere idea of a fugitive slave law was anathema to northern radicals. The President himself was strongly opposed, as he thought the admission of California should be unconditional. For three weeks tension grew, and at the height of the excitement Robert Toombs, Thomas Clingman, and Alexander Stephens called on the President. Thurlow Weed met them on his way to the White House. When he entered Taylor's room he discovered the old general pacing the floor. "Did you," said Taylor with an oath, "did you meet those traitors?" He then explained that his recent visitors had threatened secession, to which he had answered that if necessary to execute the laws he would take command of the Army, and if they were "taken in rebellion against the Union" he would hang them "with less reluctance" than he had "hung spies and deserters in Mexico."

In the course of senatorial debate all the great figures had their say. Clay had opened the battle. On March 4 Calhoun's last formal speech was delivered for him by Senator Mason. Three days later, the "Godlike Daniel" rallied in support of Clay, calling down on his head the curses of Horace Mann, of Theodore Parker, and the poet John Greenleaf Whittier. Then Seward, in opposition of compromise, made the celebrated "higher law" speech which earned him the taunt of treason to the Constitution.

The reference of Clay's resolutions to a committee brought forth in May 1850 three bills. The first provided for admission of California on the basis of the constitution adopted by her people, for territorial organization of New Mexico and Utah without any restriction as to slavery, and fixed the Texas boundary. The second bill was a sharp-toothed fugitive slave law. The third bill abolished the slave trade in the District of Columbia.

In the ensuing struggle President Taylor stood firm upon his policy of immediate admission of California and of postponing consideration of the other territories. The alarums from the South were such as to harden the resolution of this stanch Union man. The much-touted Nashville Convention of southern delegates was commonly believed to be a move towards disunion, and although its meeting in June produced nothing of the sort, rumors that the Texans were prepared to settle their boundary troubles by force aroused the general's ire. He began the preparation of a special message to Congress when suddenly death intervened. He was taken ill after the Washington Monument cornerstone ceremonies on July 4. Two days later he was dead. His successor, Millard Fillmore, an accomplished trimmer, reversed the policy of resistance to Clay's plan, and by the end of September Congress had enacted a series of laws embodying the compromise. The settlement was hailed with relief, but the statutes might properly have been preambled with the bitter words of Rumour:

> I speak of peace, while covert enmity
> Under the smile of safety wounds the world.

The political talents of Taylor's Congress were so considerable, and their vociferation so brilliant—and so redundant— that the firmness and decision of the President have seemed almost ingenuous. Believing that he held a mandate from the people and that the Constitution was guide enough, he had little sympathy with the fanciful glosses which politicians deemed essential to make the organic law workable. In trying to imitate Washington and put the chief magistracy above party, Taylor set himself a task impossible for the times, but it was his accustomed role as commander in lonely posts or in the field. When one reads the pages of the *Congressional Globe* engorged with hot and disputatious words, and when one recalls how Representative McClernand of Illinois went armed with a bowie knife and how others also equipped themselves against violence in the legislative halls, one is led to wonder whether or not the old general remembered long and endless palavers with Indian tribes, where the white man's resolution and imperviousness inevitably triumphed. The British negotiations revealed he was capable of compromise. The slavery men made the mistake of threatening him. They would have been well advised to read the Taylor anecdote book. The general had an answer to attack—"a little more grape." Ultimately this was to be the solution.

VIII

General Pierce

It has been a merit of our military system that, no matter how briefly or how obscurely a citizen soldier may have worn the insignia of rank, he usually has acquired a bonus of political prestige. The grant of titles of nobility is forbidden in the Constitution, but from the labels not outlawed—the General, Colonel, Judge, and even the ambiguous "Honorable"—we have compiled a Debrett of democracy indispensable for the fabrication of a party ticket.

By the time he was forty Franklin Pierce had acquired a variety of titles of honor in the politicians' handbook. The son of a revolutionary veteran twice governor of New Hampshire, Pierce had served both in the House of Representatives and in the Senate of the United States, and by virtue of an appointment in 1831 as military aide to the then governor of New Hampshire could claim with "the Honorable" of legislative service the no less pre-eminent "Colonel," *honoris causa*. But there was greater distinction in store for him. As one of President Polk's political generals he was to gain stature in his party quite disproportionate to his actual achievements in the field. On the strength of the bays won in battle this small-town lawyer was to be presented to the electorate as the reincarnation of Old Hickory, and in this refurbished uniform was to vanquish the leading soldier of his day.

When the war with Mexico broke out, Pierce was practicing law at Concord, New Hampshire. In May 1846 he volunteered, and with fellow citizens drilled as a private in the ranks. His hopes were undoubtedly higher. Polk had appointed him United States attorney for his district and in August 1846 had invited him to be Attorney General. This flattering offer Pierce declined, explaining his reluctance to leave his practice and his family, "except at the call of my country in time of war." He did not have long to wait.

In February 1847 Congress authorized the creation of new regiments in the Regular Army to serve for the duration, and in one of these Pierce was commissioned colonel. As soon as a supplemental bill providing for general officers was enacted, Polk forthwith named his friend Pierce to a brigadier generalship. As a matter of military economy this legislation was quite remarkable. No Regular Army officer could afford to take a commission in the new regiments, for these were to be liquidated at the war's end, and any officers transferred would be in danger of being thrown out of the Army. An opportune occasion for an extension of the spoils system was thus brought into being. "As a consequence of this policy," wrote General Upton, "inexperienced colonels and ignorant captains led the new regiments to battle, while in the old battalions the future commanders of our armies were trudging as file closers in the rear of their companies."

Although the War Department issued orders in March intended to hasten the dispatch of the new levies, things in New England were bogged down because of the difficulty of filling the local quota. Recruiting faced the double obstacle of sectional antipathy to the war and the perennial American preference for commissions over service in the ranks. After considerable effort the companies were filled, and on May 27 Pierce and his troops set sail for Mexico.

The arrival of reinforcements had been impatiently awaited by General Winfield Scott. Vera Cruz had capitulated March 27, and the action at Cerro Gordo had been victoriously fought. Unhappily for Scott's plans, however, the enlistments of a large number of his volunteers had run out and most of the men refused to re-engage. The march to Mexico City was stalled at Puebla, where Scott whiled away the time trying to purchase a peace and quarreling savagely with Nicholas P. Trist, chief clerk of the State Department, who had been sent down to negotiate a treaty. Early in July new regiments to the number of three thousand men arrived, but as Scott's total army even then numbered only some eight thousand men, it was determined to postpone the advance until Pierce brought up his troops from Vera Cruz.

Pierce had landed on June 27 and, discovering that yellow fever was raging in town, pitched camp on the beach three miles away. The immediate problem was transportation, and to this end two thousand wild mules had been collected. On the very day of debarkation the harassments of command broke upon the new brigadier, for some fifteen hundred of these unpredictable beasts stampeded and were lost. The next weeks were devoted to the assembly of a new pack train. It was too hot for much drill, and except for occasional alarms on account of guerrillas the energies of the invaders were concentrated upon inuring the wild mules and mustangs to the amenities of harness.

The first detachments of Pierce's 2,500-man force started inland on July 14, and the general himself broke camp two days later. Puebla lay in the mountains one hundred and fifty miles away, and the going was hard. The column came under fire by guerrillas on July 19, but the enemy was dispersed with ease, and after the second such brush the general appears to have acquired a contempt for his foe—"the nearer you get to these people in fight the safer."

It took three weeks to reach Puebla, where Pierce received the felicitations of General Scott. It was a creditable first performance and perhaps owed something to the fact that three Regular Army officers were on Pierce's staff. The general's journal of his experiences is more illuminating as an exhibit on the pervasive flowering of New England than on his own blooming as a commander. It has the high-toned literary style then favored: comments on scenery, the moral qualities of Mexicans, self-conscious reflections about "conquering a peace," and a pinch of Yankee boasting. We cannot find that the route was effectively scouted, for the appearance of partisans was usually unexpected, and proper precautions against straggling were not enforced.

At Puebla, Pierce's brigade was incorporated in the third division, commanded by Major General Gideon Pillow, the President's former law partner. On August 17 the army started for Mexico City; communications with the base at Vera Cruz had been severed by the removal of the garrison at Jalapa. The wiseacres in Europe were amazed and predicted that Scott was doomed. But Santa Anna, for all his gaudy uniforms and the plethora of generals at his command, did not see fit to defend the passes in the perimeter of mountains surrounding the plateau on which the Mexican capital is situated. The American army moved on to this plateau without opposition.

After careful reconnaissance it was determined to approach the city from the south. There were two available roads. On the first the enemy occupied a strong position, on their left Lake Xochimilco and on their right the *Pedregal,* an apparently impassable lava field. Scott determined to flank this position by proceeding up the second road to the west of the lava field, passing across a corner of it. On August 19 General Pillow was ordered to make a practicable road. Before this job was done Pillow discovered that further work brought his men within range of Mexican batteries strongly entrenched near Contreras. Although he had but two guns Pillow ordered an attack. Pierce had barely gotten into motion when his horse took fright; the general was thrown against the pommel and received a painful blow in the groin. The horse went down, and Pierce fell off in a faint. When he revived he discovered his knee was badly wrenched, but obtaining another mount he observed the repulse of the assault.

The attack was badly managed. The incredible Pillow had sent Riley's brigade to the rear of the Mexican position. These men were isolated by the failure of the frontal assault and faced extermination by reinforcements hurried up by Santa Anna. The battle broke off at night amid torrential rain. While the Mexicans celebrated a victory the unhappy Pierce lay suffering in an ammunition wagon. Luckily, reinforcements reached Riley, a way was found to approach the Mexi-

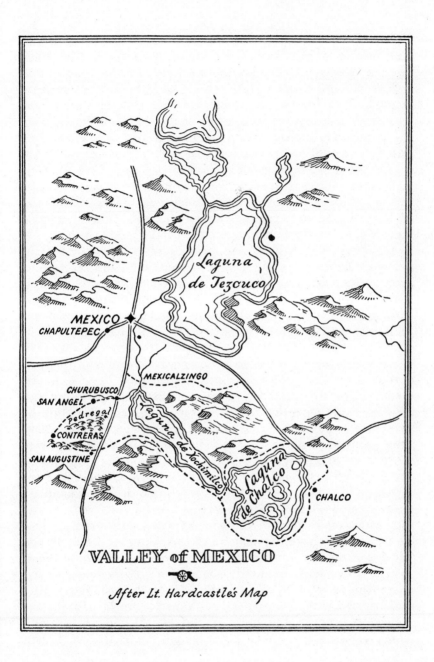

Laguna de Tezcuco

MEXICO

CHAPULTEPEC

MEXICALZINGO

CHURUBUSCO

SAN ANGEL

Pedregal

Laguna de Xochimilco

CONTRERAS

SAN AUGUSTINE

Laguna de Chalco

CHALCO

VALLEY of MEXICO

After Lt. Hardcastle's Map

can position from the rear, and at dawn Riley's men stormed the camp and routed the enemy in seventeen minutes.

Scott lost no time. The retreating Mexicans were followed along both roads to Churubusco. There the core of the defense was a strong bridgehead on the south bank of the river of that name. Against this General Worth's division was ordered, and Pillow was directed to support on the left. Hawthorne tells an affecting story of Pierce's bedraggled arrival at headquarters for orders. Scott demurred at letting him go in. "For God's sake, General," exclaimed Pierce, "don't say that, this is the last great battle and I must lead my brigade!" Scott yielded and again Pierce rode forth.

The way lay through cornfields and then some marshy ground. Pierce was obliged to dismount, and struggling through the marsh in the face of enemy fire, he again severely wrenched his injured knee and fell a second time in a faint. The battle was won elsewhere on the line, and Pierce's men achieved small renown, for they were badly led and received rough treatment at the hands of Santa Anna's reserves.

Although the way to Mexico City was now open, Scott permitted himself to be beguiled into an armistice, the enemy pretending a desire for peace. Pierce was among three generals chosen to arrange the terms. After a night's wrangling an agreement was made from which the Americans received no profit, but which gave Santa Anna a much desired respite to reorganize his army. The peace negotiations failed, and on September 6 Scott informed his division commanders of the fact. The bloody and useless fight at Molino del Rey took place on September 8, but Pierce's men were not ordered in until the battle was over. Nor did the unfortunate general, dogged by a malignant fate, participate in the taking of Chapultepec. Weakened by his injuries and by persistent dysentery, Pierce collapsed and was confined to bed for thirty-six hours. Early on the morning of the 14th, the day of the scheduled entry into Mexico City, Pierce dragged himself into his clothes and joined his brigade. But the expected assault was never made. The City Council sent out a white flag—the battles were over.

Pierce remained in Mexico City until December, when he was finally permitted to return home. After reporting to Polk he was given leave, and he resigned his commission shortly, upon the submission of the peace treaty to the Senate in February 1848. New Hampshire received Pierce as a hero. But by any standard more exiguous than the mere faithful performance of duty, Pierce can scarcely be said to have attained such stature. He was not lacking in personal courage, but neither physically nor by disposition was he cut to the pattern of good military leadership. He possessed the regard of his men, yet except for the episode of the march from Vera Cruz to Puebla he gave small signs of a capacity for command. His friend Hawthorne, however, could spin about Pierce's military career a warm web of words that transformed his deeds from dull soldiery to noble knighthood:

The valor that wins our battles is not the trained hardihood of veterans, but a native and spontaneous fire; and there is surely a chivalrous beauty in the devotion of the citizen soldier to his country's cause, which the man who makes arms his profession and is but doing his duty cannot pretend to rival.

What better voucher of the American tradition and the general's share in it? What words more comforting for memories of past misadventure?

II

When the presidential campaign of 1852 opened there was but one domestic question of lively concern—should the Compromise of 1850 be maintained? After the two major parties had held their conventions this problem had vanished from the political scene. Both parties adopted "finality" planks. Citizens North and South breathed easier, and discovered that as far as platform principles were concerned they faced a choice no more exciting than picking between two railroads to Washington. Only a handful of irreconcilables, abolitionists and anti-slavery men in revolt against the Fugitive Slave Act of 1850, at odds with the mood of the country, clung to the

Free Soil banner and demanded repeal of the Compromise, renewal of the fight for freedom.

Since Whig and Democratic leaders, sensitive to the aspirations of the great body of voters, had determined that agitation over slavery was to be banned, interest in the election focused mainly upon the candidates—Brigadier General Franklin Pierce, the Democratic nominee, and Major General Winfield Scott, Whig opponent. Politicians were cannily aware of the tradition of success of the military hero. The War of 1812 had spawned two presidents; as much might be hoped from the Mexican adventure. Citizen soldier matched against professional soldier, political general against army veteran—for each, the laurels of military renown were claimed.

In the case of the Democrats, the nomination of the military hero had been an accident of circumstance. Throughout the spring of 1852 General Pillow, ex-Brigadier General Caleb Cushing, and a clique of political-minded Mexican War officers had cherished hopes of promoting the candidacy of their brother-in-arms Franklin Pierce, who had been hovering on the edges of political life while pursuing the prosaic practice of law in Concord, New Hampshire, since the close of his military episode. Yet when the Democratic convention assembled at Baltimore June 1, 1852, there had been little expectation of success. Four outstanding leaders dominated the delegates. Lewis Cass, defeated candidate in 1848, led the field. James Buchanan, Polk's Secretary of State; Stephen Douglas, rising star of western democracy; and William L. Marcy, former governor of New York State and cabinet officer, each counted a stubborn following. Each outranked Pierce in ability and in political service; each failed to command the two-thirds vote requisite for nomination. Days of balloting resulted in deadlock. On the thirty-fifth ballot Pierce's name was for the first time put before the convention; on the forty-ninth ballot the exhausted delegates stampeded for the dark horse. Obscurity spelled availability. To the surprise of the Democratic party and to the stupefaction of the incredulous candidate, the nomination was tossed to Franklin Pierce.

Along with thousands of other Americans, Major Jack Downing's mythical Uncle Joshua shared the general amazement. "Major, who is General Pierce? It ain't a *fictious* name is it?" With rude gusto the Whigs repeated the query, secure in the knowledge that General Scott, hero of Chippawa and Lundy's Lane, of Cerro Gordo, Churubusco, and Chapultepec, was known from West to East. The Democrats worked manfully to concoct a convincing answer. The campaign biography was assigned to Nathaniel Hawthorne, renowned for his recent *Scarlet Letter,* but the artist proved to be happier with the sins of Hester Prynne than with the virtues of his friend Frank. For the persuasion of the rank and file who expected some dash to an election, the astute directors of the campaign turned confidently to the well-tried political elixir and muscle builder successfully used with Polk. Pierce was put forward as "Young Hickory of the Granite Hills." The obvious parallels were all present: lawyer, representative, senator, soldier. There was lacking only the divine spark. But the Democrats made up in clamor what they lacked in vendible quality.

The Whigs leveled their attacks at Pierce's military record and derided the "fainting general." In the West, where the traditions of the War of 1812 still had vitality, Chippawa Clubs were formed in emphasis of Scott's long-standing renown. The military motif was trumpeted in the verse:

> Damn the locos,
> Kill 'em—slay 'em.
> Give 'em hell
> With Scott and Graham.

The Democrats countered by a pamphlet in which their candidate's brother soldiers defended his record. "Young Hickory" and "Granite Clubs" were organized, and campaign songs whipped up a synthetic enthusiasm:

> Come, brave Locos,
> Gallant men and true,
> The Whigs were Polked in '44
> We'll Pierce in '52.

If Pierce's fame was too little, General Scott's was too abundant, for it embraced episodes which raised doubts as to his fitness for civil office. Since the War of 1812 he had been almost as renowned for his fights with superiors and associates as for his military triumphs. Each controversy—with Monroe, Jackson, Wilkinson, Gaines, Marcy, Trist, Pillow—had been blazoned abroad in letters whose lack of restraint and vitriolic language betrayed the choleric tone of the general's temper. Democratic journals and broadsides made merry over the record of "Old Fuss and Feathers," and certain phrases culled from his letters were bandied hilariously. "A hasty plate of soup" (picked from a letter to Marcy) inexplicably convulsed the country. "Shot in the rear" (a capsulated version of his "fire upon my rear" protest) was twisted by innuendo to locate a wound received at Lundy's Lane and thus make of Scott a figure as laughable as Falstaff.

Nor did Scott's conduct during the campaign retrieve him. In July a celebration staged at Niagara Falls in honor of the victory of Lundy's Lane (which had occurred across the river on Canadian soil) failed dismally to awaken enthusiasm. The Whig managers, discouraged by the lack of popular response, fearful that the Free Soil party would drain away many of Scott's northern supporters, decided to risk infraction of the unwritten rule that forbade open electioneering by a candidate. Under pretext of inspecting sites for an old soldiers' home, Scott unblushingly turned a tour of duty into a political jaunt. From Washington through New York the itinerary ran. "He says he is traveling for the purpose of selecting a site for a Military Hospital; from present indications Scott ought to be the first candidate for admission," jeered a Democratic broadside. Anxious to defend himself against the insinuations of aristocratic and nativist prejudices, Scott's overnumerous speeches were mainly panegyrics on the old soldier and the "sons of Erin," coupled with lamentations that the poor people assembled to hear him must stand in the rain while he rode in a "warm covered carriage." Even by the standards of stump

speaking, it was not oratory of a high order. The trip won
him few friends. The hastily donned habiliments of democracy
were grotesque on the aristocratic warrior notorious for his
gaudy uniforms.

Meanwhile Pierce remained quietly at Concord in New
Hampshire and delegated to his managers the business of the
campaign. To the scurrilous charges of the Whigs he made
no reply, leaving to his friends refutation of the accusations
of drunkenness, abolitionism, and cowardice that were leveled
at him. If he remained obscure, he remained dignified. If the
enthusiasm of the "Young Hickory" and "Granite Clubs" was
forced, the party organization was well knit. In November
Pierce received 252 electoral votes, Scott 42. Inferior in military ability, Pierce had shown greater political sagacity; subordinate in the field, he had routed his old commander.

The election of 1852 was more than a victory of Democrat
over Whig, of Pierce over Scott. Its true significance lay in
the triumph of moderate over extremist. Nearly three million
people voted the Democratic and Whig tickets, both pledged
to the Compromise of 1850, 1,601,274 votes for Pierce,
1,386,580 for Scott. The Free Soilers dwindled to 155,825—
only half the number polled in 1848. The election was thus a
ratification of the final settlement of the slavery controversy,
a gauge of popular opinion, popular expectation. On this question Pierce could count the country united.

It was inevitable that in his inaugural address Pierce should
declare his adherence to the people's decision. What he offered
to the country as the dominant theme of his administration
was the triumphant invocation of Manifest Destiny. He
trumpeted:

> . . . The policy of my Administration will not be controlled by any
> timid forebodings of evil from expansion. Indeed it is not to be disguised
> that our attitude as a nation and our position on the globe render the
> acquisition of certain possessions not within our jurisdiction eminently
> important for our protection, if not in the future essential for the preser-
> vation of the rights of commerce and the peace of the world. . . . if
> your past is limited, your future is boundless.

Nor was Pierce's vision of expansion limited to territorial acquisitions. American commerce should expand; new channels of trade be opened, new outlets be sought for the bounding prosperity of the United States. Throughout the world American influence must be felt, American rights be asserted. The citizen, he declared, ". . . must realize that upon every sea and on every soil where our enterprise may rightfully seek the protection of our flag American citizenship is an inviolable panoply for the security of American rights."

It was a bracing message, a call to arms to American enterprise. It was a public avowal of the program of "Young America." The address, declared Jefferson Davis, "was worthy of the patriot who uttered it, becoming the power of the people for whom he spoke and required by the history of recent events. . . . I thought of the respect which would follow the annunciation 'I am American' and compared it with that which attached of old to the cry, 'I am a Roman citizen.'"

The personnel of the Pierce administration gave promise that the President's words would rapidly be converted into deeds. Pierce himself had entered the Mexican War a believer in Manifest Destiny; nine months as brigadier general had confirmed his faith. The march from Vera Cruz to Mexico City had bred in his mind a conviction of the superiority of the Americans, a contempt for the Mexicans. "No trust is to be placed in this people," he had observed in his journal in July 1847, noting the absence of "New England enterprise and thrift." The Treaty of Guadalupe Hidalgo had opened new vistas of potential wealth; on either side of the United States stretched a road to the "boundless future." Pierce was happily convinced of the greatness of his country; the law of progress exemplified by its past was, in his eyes, prophetic of its future. "Heretofore our system of government has worked on what may be termed a miniature scale in comparison with the development which it must assume within a future so near at hand as scarcely to be beyond the present of the existing generation," he declared enthusiastically in December 1853.

William L. Marcy, Secretary of State, was equally an advocate of expansion. His knowledge of foreign affairs, moreover, had been gained as Secretary of War under Polk, a service which had given him intimate acquaintance with designs for the acquisition of territory. Jefferson Davis, Secretary of War, had been trained at West Point and had fought with Taylor at Buena Vista. Caleb Cushing, the Attorney General and promoter of Pierce's candidacy, had served as envoy to China and had been a brigadier general in the Mexican War. These men, with Pierce, were the policy-makers. With the President, they gloried in the new-found strength of the Republic, shared the intoxicating vision of the United States as a great power, its web of empire stretching from Cuba in the Caribbean to Hawaii in the mid-Pacific. If American leaders earlier had exalted the republican virtues of Rome, Pierce and his advisers were enthralled by Rome the empire. "The American Union must infederate into its political pale all the countries with which it is brought into social contact," ran the text of *The New Rome or the United States of the World,* a panegyric on the mission of America published in 1853, "Respectfully Dedicated [to Franklin Pierce], Being a Guess at the Spirit in which he was elected." It was a theme that recurred frequently in the speeches of the leaders of the Administration in justification of the expansionist program. The United States was to be the modern Rome, matching the destiny of the ancient empire. Their enthusiasm aroused Whig opposition and evoked the satire of Major Jack Downing. Jeered the "Downingville" oracle, following one of Caleb Cushing's addresses:

That speech came over Cousin Sargent Joel like a streak of lightning. He went right to work and scoured up his old fire-lock as bright as a pewter-platter. And now, from mornin' till night, with his fire-lock on his shoulder, he marches about the house and round the barn in a military step, sayin' to himself as he goes, "March, march, march; we are the men of modern Rome! March, march, march; annexin' day is close at hand! March, march, march!"

Nevertheless, at the moment America was in an ebullient mood. The Mexican adventure had stirred a vernal restlessness, a discontent with the hermitic existence ordained by the diplomacy of non-intervention and isolation. The European revolutions of 1848 had given fresh vigor to the hardy American belief in the mission of democracy. Cheated of converts by the collapse of the German and Hungarian uprisings, public enthusiasm had been sustained by the stream of political refugees and had reached a high state upon the visit of Kossuth, the Hungarian patriot. Lush oratory and testy diplomatic notes characterized official sentiments in the capital. In other quarters more practical-minded citizens like General Quitman, governor of Mississippi, and John L. O'Sullivan, inventor of the Manifest Destiny cliché, implemented the missionary spirit by conniving in filibustering expeditions. It needed only the Roman analogy and the benison of President Pierce to effect a fusion of prevailing sentiments—of American mission and American destiny—into a gusty plan of empire.

With zeal and spirit the great design was initiated, and not unnaturally the war veterans in the Cabinet first turned their attention to Mexico. The relations with this country were not happy. Difficulties over definition of the boundaries stipulated in the peace treaty, over Indian depredations, and over filibustering required settlement. The United States was already committed to a policy of acquiring transit rights across the Isthmus of Tehuantepec, and the promoters of a southern railroad route to the Pacific were anxious to secure additional cessions of Mexican territory, in particular the Gila River Valley, with its snow-free passes to the Pacific. It is not insignificant that Secretary of War Davis, when senator from Mississippi, had moved an amendment to the Treaty of Guadalupe Hidalgo that called for the cession of vast reaches of northern Mexico.

In May 1853 James Gadsden was dispatched to our sister republic and instructed to treat for the purchase of territory and to settle outstanding claims. A few months later he was authorized to offer $50,000,000 for a large slice of northern Mexico, and Lower California as well. Whatever Mr. Gadsden's talents may have been, he was not an astute trader. The result of his mission was a treaty (finally confirmed in June 1854) by which we acquired for the sum of $10,000,000 a strip of desert which included the desired route, quittance of claims against our citizens, and preferential transit rights across the Isthmus of Tehuantepec, rights of which no use was ever made, but which at the time seemed precious. Trans-isthmian communication was the door to California, the link of future empire.

It was in the year 1854, however, that a combination of circumstances accelerated the pace of Pierce's foreign policy. The Administration had not been unaware of British resistance to American expansion at the expense of Mexico and of British suspicion of American designs in Central America, the Caribbean generally, and Cuba in particular. In the last month of Fillmore's presidency, the Department of State had firmly rejected a French and British proposal to guarantee Spain's possession of Cuba, but the outgoing President himself had advised Congress that the United States entertained no designs upon the island. This policy the Pierce administration at first professed to follow, although the President's inaugural pronouncement had roused a buzz of speculation. Two events in the early months of 1854 changed the picture. In February the seizure of the cargo of the *Black Warrior* (flying the American flag) by the Spanish authorities at Havana precipitated the Cuban question; in March the entry of France and England into the Crimean War produced a radical change in the diplomatic situation and gave the United States a free hand in the Western world.

Interest in the annexation of Cuba was not new. ". . . If an apple, severed by the tempest from its native tree, can not choose but fall to the ground, Cuba . . . can gravitate only towards the North American Union," John Quincy Adams had prophesied in 1823. By the mid-century, strategic considerations and commercial interest had been reinforced by the anxiety of slaveholders over the slave population of Cuba; in 1848 the United States had even offered to purchase the island for $100,000,000. Since that date, filibustering expeditions based in the United States, strangely compounded of republican quixoticism and self-seeking adventure, had stimulated American interest, aggravated Spanish resentment. Punitive action taken in retaliation by the Spanish authorities in Cuba and restrictions imposed on American trade with the island increased American irritation and lent strength to the intention—

> That the Antilles Flower—the Key of the Gulf
> Shall be plucked from the crown of the Old Spanish Wolf.

The *Black Warrior* incident naturally aroused a popular outcry and furnished the Administration the occasion for a bold declaration of policy. In a message to the House of Representatives on March 15, 1854, Pierce rattled the sword, warning Congress that peaceful relations with Spain were imperiled. "There have been in the course of a few years past many other instances of aggression upon our commerce, violations of the rights of American citizens, and insults to the national flag by the Spanish authorities in Cuba," he said. The proximity of Cuba, its relations "to our commercial and other interests" made it impossible to expect that the Spanish policy could "long consist with peaceful relations." And he ended significantly:

> In case the measures taken for amicable adjustment of our difficulties with Spain should, unfortunately, fail, I shall not hesitate to use the authority and means which Congress may grant to insure the observance of our just rights, to obtain redress for injuries received, and to vindicate the honor of our flag.

A few weeks later, in April, Soulé, the American minister to Spain, was ordered to attempt again the purchase of Cuba. In the same month the scope of the Administration's ambition was delineated. Instructions were issued to the American minister in Hawaii to negotiate a treaty for the annexation of these islands, precious as an entrepôt for the trade of the Pacific, a stepping-stone to the Far East. The Russian minister was sounded out on the subject of the sale of Alaska to the United States. A project for the lease of a coaling and naval

station at Samaná Bay in the Dominican Republic was inaugurated. The great design of empire was begun.

It was a "spirited policy"; yet in spite of the grandiose plans
initiated in the spring of 1854 little was brought to completion
during Pierce's term of office. Throughout the summer of 1854
the President sought to marshal congressional backing for an
aggressive Cuban policy, but northern senators, agitated by
the passage of the Kansas-Nebraska Act on May 30, regarded
the President's overtures with suspicion. In October the three
American diplomats, Buchanan, minister to England, Mason,
minister to France, and Soulé, minister to Spain, met at Ostend
on the Belgian coast to consult on the Cuban question. Out of
this conference came the famous report popularly known as
the "Ostend Manifesto." It was the publication of this document that killed Pierce's cherished plan. In the somewhat gar-
bled version that appeared in the press, the three ministers
recommended the purchase of Cuba for $120,000,000; should
Spain refuse to sell, it was implied that the United States
should consider the use of force to acquire the island. To the
North, the report was fresh proof of the President's desire
to extend slave territory, his subservience to the slavocracy.
Despite Marcy's disavowal of the "robber doctrine" and
Soulé's resignation, the damage was done. The North repudiated annexation; Cuba remained in the hands of Spain.

Nor were the other projects of empire more successful. The
Hawaiian treaty proved unsatisfactory in certain provisions.
Returned to the islands in an amended form, it was dropped
by a new monarch opposed to annexation. The treaty for the
lease of Samaná Bay was never ratified by the Dominican
Republic; Mexico (as has been said) refused to cede Lower
California; Russia was disinclined to consider the Alaskan
proposal.

In another diplomatic quarter Pierce gained an empty victory. This was the attempted settlement of the Central American question, a problem inherited from the previous administration. Despite the stipulations of the Clayton-Bulwer
Treaty, British-American friction in that area had continued.

Under color of the treaty, Great Britain claimed control of the Bay Islands, was maintaining a protectorate over the Mosquito Indians along the eastern coast of Nicaragua, and had proclaimed the town of Greytown, at the mouth of the San Juan River, an independent government. While the design of empire was brewing, Buchanan, in London, was instructed to controvert these pretensions and secure a treaty delimiting British aggression, a task that was to occupy years of fruitless negotiation.

While diplomatic discussions dragged along abroad, sporadic attempts—both official and unauthorized—were made this side of the Atlantic to reinforce the American position in Central America. In the spring of 1854 an attack was made at Greytown on the property of the Accessory Transit Company (owned by American citizens), and indignities were shown the American minister to Central America. Captain Hollins was dispatched by Pierce's orders in command of the U.S.S. *Cyane* to secure reparations; in July 1854 the overzealous commander bombarded and burned the town. In the face of protests against this action both at home and abroad, Pierce vigorously defended the naval officer's course in his annual message of that year. Meantime filibustering activities were again set in motion; Nicaragua was now to be the goal. Despite the Administration's disavowal of the "colonizing" schemes, William Walker slipped away from California in 1855 to set up a puppet government in the sister republic. The words of the President's inaugural address, his prophecy in his first annual message of "the probable accession of the populations already existing in other parts of our hemisphere," his defense of the attack on Greytown—all gave color to the charge that the Administration was planning further annexations. Although Pierce withheld recognition of the Walker-Rivas government during 1855, the collapse of Buchanan's negotiations with the British early in 1856 led the President (against Marcy's advice) to change his course. This recognition of Walker proved fruitless as well as unpopular. The puppet government collapsed, the half-acknowledged scheme of promoting Amer-

ican influence in Central America failed. Walker, escaping to
the United States on an American naval vessel, was ultimately
to meet defeat and death in Nicaragua. Eight days after
Pierce left the presidency, the Dallas-Clarendon Convention,
limiting British influence in Central America, passed the United
States Senate, only to be rejected by Great Britain. The ambitions of 1854 again proved to be more flash than fire.

In his efforts for the promotion of American commerce
Pierce achieved greater success. If his dream of empire was
hemispheric, his view of commercial expansion was global. An
outstanding achievement was the Marcy-Elgin Treaty of 1854
providing for tariff reciprocity with Canada, opening the
northeastern fisheries to Americans, and granting mutual freedom of navigation on Lake Michigan and the St. Lawrence
River. During 1853–54 the Administration spared neither
effort nor expense in securing the success of the treaty. A special secret agent in Canada disbursed government funds liber-
ally in order to create a favorable opinion in the Canadian provinces; in the United States the President's championship of
the Kansas-Nebraska bill was the bait used to snare the
support of southern senators to a measure so obviously designed in the interest of the "down-Easters." It was a triumph
of diplomacy, but, as events at home were to prove, it was not
achieved without cost. In South America our diplomacy was
directed to the opening of the Amazon River to American
traders, to securing more liberal commercial privileges in the
La Plata region, to the defending of American rights in guano
islands. In the European field, Marcy made strenuous efforts
to obtain the abolition of the Danish Sound dues, a lingering
remnant of medieval shackles on trade. Finally, in the Far East
the treaty of 1854, the result of Commodore Perry's mission,
pried open Japan. Like the Caleb Cushing treaty with China
of 1844, it paved the way for future concessions and marked
a milestone in the penetration of the East by the West.

There may have been cynics who viewed the militant foreign policy of Pierce as an unconscious reaction to the slurs
on his career as a general, but no one could deny that in every

facet it sparkled with Americanism. At home and abroad American rights were asserted. Crampton, British minister to the United States, was given his passport because of his implication in the enlistment of men for the British army, an infringement of American neutrality. Koszta, Austrian refugee, sought and received the protection of the American flag in far-off Turkey. It was a diplomacy expressive of the frontier spirit, the self-confidence engendered by the conquest of a continent, the homespun quality of pugnacious democracy. The "Dress Circular of 1853," with its injunctions of sartorial republicanism, was a blazoning of American simplicity to the effete capitals of Europe, a symbol of the superiority of the republican over the monarchical tradition.

In foreign relations Pierce caught the dominant strains of the day; in domestic affairs he was less happily apperceptive. So enthralled was his administration with the prospect of the outside world that it failed to gauge the intensity of the fire it had kindled at home. For it was during this administration that the slavery controversy burst out anew; the tinder of the Kansas-Nebraska bill of 1854 lighted the way to the Civil War. Although neither Pierce nor any member of his Cabinet had a hand in the inception of the measure, on them rests a large share of the responsibility for its final provisions and for its passage. Kansas-Nebraska was the price paid for a dream of empire.

Since the acquisition of the Pacific frontier, schemes for the building of a transcontinental railroad had been constantly agitated. In 1853 surveys of possible routes had been undertaken by the United States Army at the order of Secretary of War Davis; in his annual message of that year, Pierce endorsed the construction of a line as a measure of national defense. The location of the railroad was both economically and politically critical, since population movements would follow construction. A southern route would make accessible territory open to slavery; a northern route would eventually mean additions to the free states. Every plan for the organization of new territorial or state governments was thus inextricably bound up with the railroad project; every plan for a railroad affected the problem of future political development. It was against this background of sectional conflict over the future of the West that the "little Giant," Senator Stephen Douglas, chairman of the Committee on Territories, early in January 1854 introduced his report on the organization of Nebraska territory.

Douglas' report proposed that the northern section of the Louisiana Purchase, long closed to slavery by the Missouri Compromise, should be organized as the new territory of Nebraska. With ambiguous phrases, the bill was framed to reopen the region to the slaveholder by incorporating the principle of "squatter sovereignty," a feature of the Compromise of 1850. The organization of the territory would enhance the possibilities of a selection of a northern route for the transcontinental railroad; the opening of the territory to slavery would appease southern opposition; the emphasis on self-determination would appeal to the democratic West. It must have seemed to Douglas the perfection of political wisdom. Designed to unite faction, it was destined to split the country apart.

At once the Senate was in an uproar. Pro-slavery men supported a demand for an explicit repeal of the Missouri Compromise; anti-slavery men, led by Charles Sumner, rallied to the free-soil principle. For days the final form the bill would take remained uncertain. It was Pierce who made the decision —the territory must be open to slavery. Pressed for support by Douglas, guided by Jefferson Davis and Caleb Cushing, the President wrote the fatal declaration that "the Missouri Compromise was superseded by the principles of the legislation of 1850 . . . and is hereby declared inoperative and void—and the people perfectly free to form and regulate their domestic institutions in their own way." And it was Pierce who used the patronage to whip recalcitrant Democrats into line, Pierce who signed the Kansas-Nebraska Act in its final form on May 30, 1854.

The President's motives are by no means obscure. In the

interval between his inauguration and the convening of Congress, the first steps in his ambitious foreign policy had been undertaken, and in this same period his appointment policy and distribution of the spoils had offended virtually every faction of his party. In his desire to please all, he had succeeded in pleasing none. The very amiability that had endeared him to fellow officers during the Mexican War (despite his lack of military glory) proved now to be his undoing. Pierce faced his first Congress in the unprecedented and precarious position of a President with a well-defined program but without party support. Command of the Senate was essential for the achievement of his projected foreign policy; command of the party essential for renomination in 1856. Furthermore, Pierce held strong convictions of strict construction of the Constitution and a respect for states' rights which he consistently adhered to until his death. "Popular sovereignty" (Douglas' term) was in accord with the pattern of his ideas, a logical part of his dogma, although obviously restricted to the geographical limits of the United States. To this confusion of ambition and principle he sacrificed the peace of the country, hard won in 1850, ratified by the election of 1852, avowed in his own inaugural address.

The Kansas-Nebraska Act was the opening of Pandora's box. For this measure unlocked all the furies of sectional conflict that had been temporarily sealed by the Compromise of 1850. Anti-slavery sentiment again swept the people of the North, aroused by a measure which they regarded as a betrayal of the solemn pledge of 1850.

"The crime is committed," wrote Thurlow Weed in May 1854, "the work of Monroe, Madison and Jefferson is undone. The wall they erected to guard the domain of liberty is flung down by the hands of an American Congress, and slavery crawls like a slimy reptile over the ruins." Out of this gust of anger the Republican party was born, made up of anti-slavery men of various political complexions, dedicated to a crusade against the spread of human servitude. Southerners, both Democrat and Whig, united in defense of the new principle of "popular sovereignty," of states' rights and the slaveholder.

It took nearly two years for the drama on the Kansas prairie to unfold to a climax. Within a few months of the passage of the act, the struggle for the physical possession of Kansas territory had been initiated. Pro-slavery men and border ruffians from Missouri surged into the new lands; "Free Soilers" assisted by the Emigrant Aid Society of Massachusetts moved grimly west. By the close of the year 1855 the rival groups, territorial pro-slave and "free state" anti-slavery men, were engaged in a bitter contest for political control of the territory, each clamoring for recognition as the rightful government.

In 1856 civil war tore "Bleeding Kansas." Early in the year, alarmed by the increasing violence and pressed by the territorial governor for support, Pierce issued a proclamation against "unlawful combinations," "attempted insurrection," or "aggressive intrusion" into the territory. Furthermore, the territorial governor was authorized to call to his aid the Regular Army forces stationed at the frontier posts, Forts Leavenworth and Riley, should the situation become critical.

In May sporadic violence flared into open warfare. The sacking of the "free state" town of Lawrence by pro-slavery men on the twenty-first of that month was avenged two days later by the massacre at Pottawatomie Creek, the fanatical exploit of John Brown and his sons. The first affray at Osawatomie and the battle at Black Jack followed in quick succession. The war of "popular sovereignty" was on.

Echoes of the conflict reverberated in the halls of Congress and smote the conscience of the people. On May 19 and 20 Charles Sumner delivered his scorching philippic, "The Crime against Kansas," in the United States Senate; two days later he suffered a brutal beating at the hands of Preston Brooks, nephew of Butler, the South Carolinian senator, whom Sumner had castigated in his speech. During the summer violence

continued in Kansas, controversy raged throughout the country. Not until the early fall was a semblance of peace established in Kansas with the aid of the United States military;
but the political struggle continued unabated in Congress and
before the forum of the people. The prologue to the Civil
War had been spoken.

Throughout these months of controversy Pierce vigorously
defended the validity of the Kansas-Nebraska Act and the
operation of the principle of popular sovereignty. The Missouri Compromise, he declared, had been clearly unconstitutional, an unwarranted abuse of the powers of Congress. It
was a "dead letter in law before its repeal." On the anti-slavery
men he laid the responsibility for the evils of Kansas, scoring
the northerners as agitators, aggressors, attackers of the Constitution. From this stand he never retreated. In his last annual
message to Congress, in December 1856, the President could
congratulate the country on "the establishment of constitutional order and tranquillity throughout the Union." The verdict of history belies his words.

In 1852 Pierce had received the largest electoral vote of
any presidential candidate since the election of President Monroe in 1820. Four years later he failed to obtain renomination
from his own party. "Pierce died of Jefferson Davis and Cushing," wrote Bancroft. Entranced by the vistas opened by the
Mexican War, intoxicated by the picture of an expanding
and pulsating America, the General-President had staked all
on his foreign policy and had reaped emptiness. The Kansas-
Nebraska bill had proved to be a boomerang fatal to all his
ambitions. Blind to the true significance of the slavery question, the outgoing President could not foresee the tragic years
of civil war ahead or know the bitter and lonely road that he
would walk. He had shown courage in Mexico; he was never
to be more courageous than in these last years of ostracism.
An empire builder, born out of time, a States' Righter, cling-
ing to his principles of government, a Copperhead, implacably
opposed to the War of the Rebellion, he was to hold his convictions until death. "Some men are so constituted that they

do not incline to bow before a storm," he said in his last public speech. These are the words of a man of principle from whom ambition had fled. Against Pierce the President, history lodges a severe indictment; clemency for Pierce the man must temper final judgment.

IX

General Grant

———◆◆———

WE TAKE THE UNION FOR GRANTED NOW. The ardors of those hot years when it came so near to dissolution are but cold embers in the ashes of textbooks. To make room for the "currents" and "forces" of the new history, the stalwart figures who carried the flag have been banished one by one. Their military triumph settled the issue of disunion; their deeds may now rest with their bones. What an irony! Ulysses Grant laboriously setting down the last words of his memoirs under the whip of a fatal malady, living again the four years of battles, how could he be uncertain of the interest of history or doubt its verdict? How could he foresee that newspapers which had alternately extolled and abused him would be the oracles of another generation? How could he guess that the printed papers of adversaries like Gideon Welles and Charles Sumner could give an easier yield than *The War of the Rebellion—Official Records*, ". . . black mummy cases Embalming the long forgotten . . ."? Poor Grant. The Union he had helped to save hurrying on to new destiny; only the sons of his former foes remindful of the deeds of their fathers' old commanders, investing the gray of the Confederacy with the glamour of a lost cause, the blue of the Yankees growing shabbier with the years. In the dourness of defeat the Scots made imperishable the romance of Bonnie Prince Charlie; the exploits of Union men are smothered in crinoline and the scent of southern roses.

Grant himself remains, impenetrable, a tragic figure in our history. Prey of the journalists while living, prey of the historians when dead, his career has been cleaved as if he had been two persons—a general successful because he sacrificed his men, a President failing because he was incompetent. Only soldiers, who value knowledge over opinion, have sensed his genius, have known him for one of the great captains of modern times and esteemed him a great person. But the soldiers take leave of him at Appomattox, for what he did thereafter is no concern of theirs.

It could only have happened in America, an obscure citizen of the Republic by the power of his personality, his fortitude, and his good sense slowly rising above surrounding mediocrities, meeting and defeating the best the enemy could pit against him until he encountered and conquered the almost incomparable Lee. There were few signposts in Grant's earlier life to point the way he would travel, except the courage he displayed in the bloody fight at Monterrey, the doggedness with which he got his regiment across the Isthmus of Panama in 1852. If the later interim of failure in civil life shows anything, it was an imperviousness to adversity.

As we have indicated, the peculiar military policy of the United States in 1861 not only facilitated Grant's first commissions but gave him opportunity to exercise his capacities. There was at the moment no centralized direction of the war effort. Washington was concerned over its own safety, and since the country was divided into military departments, the activity of the departments in the West was to a great extent the affair of the western states. The panorama of authority in these quarters is constantly bewildering in the early war years, with the boundary of state and Federal control of troops often blurred; alternate indifference and pressure from Washington; generals moving on their own initiative; the Secretary of War detaching officers without advising department commanders; operations begun and abandoned because of some emergent interest like the President's championing of the loyal eastern Tennesseans; settlement upon a single grand strategy for the great western theater upset by episodes like Lincoln's plan to put McClernand in charge of the Vicksburg campaign while Grant was kept in ignorance.

Ulysses Grant's progress in learning the business of generalship was deliberate and had to be keyed to the shifts and winds of official tergiversation. Back of it all, popular clamor, abolitionist, moderate, Copperhead; a feebly muzzled press goading, deriding, and seldom praising. In front, the enemy, committed to a strategy of defense, their offensive thrusts in the eighteenth-century tradition of capital capture—decisions that catalyzed the North's eastern strategy, and so made of the West a seeming minor theater.

The first stage of the western war was the rescue of the border states. This was the political goal that underlay the strategy of Grant's seizure of Paducah, Forts Henry and Donelson, and the South's fruitless retort at Shiloh. It is difficult to be certain that at the start Grant saw his first problems in other than their immediate military dimensions. Kentucky had declared its neutrality, but southern troops were moving in. Grant telegraphed his superior, General Frémont (September 5, 1861), that he was going to move on Paducah, which dominated the exits of the Tennessee and Cumberland rivers. Receiving no answer, he advanced and occupied the place, a move which compelled hasty and extensive Confederate withdrawals. Grant's political naïveté led him to explain his operations to the Kentucky legislature, an act for which he was reprimanded. But the legislature at once passed resolutions favorable to the Union.

Grant spent the next two months organizing his forces and on November 7, 1861, fought a small battle at Belmont at which he proved himself as inexpert as his men were green, but he learned that when neither party is disciplined, nothing is gained by delay. This was the beginning of the terrible and nearly unrelenting drive southward along the great western rivers.

Two days after Belmont, General Halleck superseded Frémont as Grant's superior. We have seen how Halleck fitted General Palmer's equation of generalship. An unknown variant was to be discovered by subordinates—the jealousy for glory. It was jealousy of Buell in an adjoining department that moved "Old Brains," as the soldiers called Halleck, finally to consent to Grant's importunities for an attack on Fort Henry. The purpose of this operation and of the succeeding one against Fort Donelson was to secure command of the Tennessee and Cumberland rivers, a strategy which involved the control of western Tennessee, chiefly because these important arteries of commerce would be in Union hands, and at the same time force the withdrawal of the Confederate van at Bowling Green. The success of the Fort Henry venture was largely due to the co-operation of navy gunboats, but the succeeding operation against Fort Donelson was Grant's own achievement. Here for the first time he exhibited his uncanny divination of what the enemy was about; here in the moment of crisis his gift of infusing confidence into disordered troops was first displayed. " 'Fill your cartridge-boxes, quick, and get into line; the enemy is trying to escape and he must not be permitted to do so.' This acted like a charm," wrote Grant. "The men only wanted someone to give them a command." Modest to the point of shyness, he makes the magic of leadership simple, matter-of-fact.

Donelson surrendered on February 16, 1862, and the country was electrified. Not so, Halleck. The correspondence between his department and Washington and his own letters to Grant are classics of pettiness. Charging Grant with insubordination (because he had gone to confer with Buell, commanding the adjoining Ohio Department), Halleck relieved him of command. Eight days later Grant was restored. There had been a new shuffle and Halleck had been dealt the command of all the western armies. In restoring Grant, "Old Brains" blamed the suspension on Washington and failed to tell his subordinate how he had intrigued against him. Grant, master of the stratagems of war, was a guileless and trusting person. It was not in him to believe evil of those with whom he dealt. He writes of the episode: "I felt very grateful to him and supposed it was his interposition which set me right with the government. I never knew the truth until General Badeau unearthed the facts in his researches for his history of my campaigns."

Every operation in which Grant had thus far participated had taught him something of generalship. He was on the verge of learning something more. At Pittsburgh Landing, on the Tennessee, he had been collecting troops preparatory to an attack on Albert Sidney Johnston. He neglected entrenching his position, his mind being fixed on the offensive he was about. His headquarters were down the river at Savannah. At dawn on April 6, 1862, the Confederates struck at Shiloh, a few miles from Pittsburgh Landing, where Sherman held the key to the Union position. When Grant arrived at 6 A.M., a scene of the greatest confusion greeted him. Here was a situation that called forth the strange quality of his fortitude—the effect of disaster to evoke the reserves of his dauntlessness. The result of his prompt measures was apparent when, on the second day, the southern army withdrew. It was a costly victory, but the cost would have been smaller had Grant been prepared to pursue. He was to remember that for such an operation there must be preparation.

This battle of Shiloh was destined in its aftermath once more to test Grant's fortitude. The initial exultation of the press was followed by screams that there had been a surprise, and ugly charges of drunkenness and incapacity were leveled at Grant. Halleck, anxious to reap what profit he could, arrived upon the scene. Grant was put second in command and was treated so intolerably that he asked to be relieved of his duties in the field. He withdrew to Memphis, where he established his headquarters. Here, as he tells us, he learned how a southern city demeaned itself under military occupation and experienced the mutual irritations of conquest. Here he may have pondered why, as Badeau tells us, "his superiors made their plans invariably without consulting him and his subordinates sometimes sought to carry out their own campaigns in opposition or indifference to his orders." This was a condition which afflicted many Union commanders, but none did it visit more sorely than Grant. The preliminaries of the Vicksburg campaign are an example.

Halleck became general in chief in July 1862, and Grant again was in charge in western Tennessee. In the fall of that year his subordinate, General McClernand, secured from President Lincoln permission to organize the troops remaining in Indiana, Illinois, and Iowa and to command an expedition against Vicksburg. Grant was not consulted, nor did Halleck inform him. Lincoln's order is dated October 21, 1862. At what time rumors of this project reached Grant is not clear, but it is certain that on November 2 he began to move down the Mississippi Central Railroad and ten days later received Halleck's order, "You have command of all troops sent to your department, and have permission to fight the enemy when you please."

No matter from what angle this episode is examined, lies the ugly shadow of the double-cross. Grant's own conduct has an aspect of deviousness which seems out of character; actually it was completely characteristic of this blunt and resolute man, incapable of self-assertion except through action. He believed McClernand incompetent and that raw levies were incapable of the intended operation. Prudence demanded it be forestalled. This quality of keeping his own counsel and fixing his course by his own lights was lacking in political sensitivity. Such calculation he did not possess, and when in later years he attempted to cultivate it, his failure was dismal.

The Vicksburg campaign is one of the epics of our history. The fortress stood on a bluff, frustrating Federal control of the Mississippi, the surrounding terrain a jungle of bayous, cypress swamps, and impenetrable tangles of cane and vine. For months Grant maneuvered about this Gibraltar. His superior, Halleck, was an exponent of taking places; Grant was a believer in taking armies. Grant's problem was to satisfy the Washington objective while accomplishing his own. The winter was spent in a struggle to come to grips with the fortress itself. Then, with the subsidence of flood, came the succession of brilliant moves: Grant's decision to cut loose from his base of supplies and to destroy the rebel forces in the rear of Vicksburg; the crossing of the Mississippi below Vicksburg; the blows at Joseph Johnston while Pemberton, the commander at Vicksburg, was maneuvering against Grant's non-existent lines of communication; the swift turning upon and defeat of Pemberton at Champion's Hill; and finally the investment of the stronghold and its surrender.

A military leader is not great unless he possesses a grasp of the political implications of what he is engaged upon. Grant from the beginning had comprehended the signal strategic importance of controlling the Mississippi Valley, both in dividing the South and in uniting the West. Artery of commerce, the Mississippi still constituted a strategic life line— for the Middle West a road to the sea, for the Confederacy a link of sections. To secure control of the river was a political as well as a military triumph. The capitulation of July 4, 1863, gives us further insight and measure of Grant's capacities. All through the winter there had been animadversions in the press and elsewhere upon his competence. The "unconditional surrender" message at the taking of Fort Donelson had captivated the public fancy in 1862, and at Vicksburg the opportunity to restore his credit by a similar gesture was at hand. When the white flags went up on July 3, Grant's initial reply to Pemberton was in the unconditional surrender vein. This Pemberton rejected at their conference. Then Grant, noticing among the Confederate staff a disposition to surrender, agreed to send in final terms that night. He held his one and only council of war, and against the advice of all but one general offered to parole the prisoners. These terms were accepted. Grant explains his action by referring to the difficulty and expense of transporting the prisoners, and General Badeau adds that he hoped to demoralize the whole interior country "by spreading this dispirited mass of men among the yet unconquered remainder." Unquestionably, too, the political effect in the North of a Fourth of July surrender—a consideration upon which Pemberton calculated—weighed more with Grant than a perpetuation of the sobriquet acquired at Donelson.

Grant's growth with his job is apparent in his next strategical suggestion, an attack upon Mobile, the only Gulf port then closed to Federal ships, a move which if successful would have hastened the reduction of the deep South. The President, however, was intent upon operations in western Texas because of Mexico, where war was in progress following a joint intervention of England, France, and Spain, at least two of which were dallying with the Confederacy. Furthermore, the Administration was bent upon opening up trade in the conquered Mississippi Valley, and to this end mopping-up operations were essential. Grant was opposed to an immediate opening of trade. His recent experiences had convinced him that a war of attrition would hasten subjugation. He wrote strongly to Secretary Chase, and his concluding words deserve notice, as they express a characteristic attitude: "No theory of my own will ever stand in the way of my executing in good faith any order I may receive from those in authority over me." This was no way to get the politicos on the Potomac around to his views. His great army was dispersed and Grant was sent to the relief of Chattanooga.

While the high command at Washington was persisting in its views of the war as a series of detached operations, Grant had obviously grasped the wholeness of the design and was moving mentally toward an integrated solution. When he was summoned in March 1864 to supreme command, "the armies of the East and West," as he later reported, "acted independently and without concert like a balky team, no two pulling together." In the vortex facing an enemy safeguarded by strongly fortified lines was Meade and the Army of the Potomac, with Federal forces on either flank that did not act in conjunction with him. The Army of the Cumberland lay near Chattanooga, and part of Sherman's Vicksburg army was on its way to that place. Schofield, with the old Army of the Ohio, was holding Longstreet. Across the Mississippi three columns were moving away from the principal theater. All this Grant undertook to correct. In his masterly letters to Sherman (April 4, 1864) and Meade (April 9, 1864), he

sketches the strategy—"to work all parts of the army together, and somewhat toward a common centre." Sherman is
to move against Johnston, break up his army, and get in the
interior, "inflicting all the damage you can against their war
resources. I do not propose to lay down for you a plan
of campaign but simply lay down the work it is desirable to
have done and leave you free to execute it in your own way."
Meade he tells, "Lee's army will be your objective point.
Wherever Lee goes there you will go also." The strategy of
place-taking was displaced by the strategy of army-taking.

To read Grant's letters and orders of this period and not
admire the breadth and sagacity of his plans is impossible.
Unity of strategical direction was the cornerstone. A strangle
hold was to be kept on Lee, while Sherman concentrated against
his rear.

In their initial stages the blows against Lee were animated
by urgency of a decision before the presidential election, a
political consideration of which Grant was entirely aware. It
was this urgency that forced the terrible trilogy, Wilderness,
Spotsylvania, and Cold Harbor, and the intermediate actions
from which the tragic poets of the press created the legend of
Grant, the butcher, the black shadow which has since enveloped
his fame. The injustice of this should have been dispelled by
the exhaustive studies of Colonel Livermore in 1900, whose
figures deserve attention. Grant's losses in killed and wounded
at Donelson, Shiloh, Corinth, Champion's Hill, Vicksburg, and
Chattanooga averaged 10.03 per cent. His losses from Wilderness to Appomattox ran 10.42 per cent. The highest incidence
was Wilderness and Spotsylvania, where losses ran 29.6 per
cent. At Cold Harbor they were 11.1. The figures of Lee's
losses are wanting, but it is worth noticing that at Antietam,
Confederate losses had been 22.6 per cent; at Chancellorsville
18.7 per cent, and at Gettysburg 30.1 per cent. In Grant's Virginia battles the Union army was the attacker, and it is well
known that the attacker loses men in higher proportion than the
defender. The northern public was unused to fighting with the
consistency and pertinacity that marked the operations from

May 5 to June 3. "He pushed his army," says Badeau, "through such a month of ceaseless and seemingly resultless battle as the world has hardly ever seen, dealing, however, as he knew the blows from which his antagonist would never recover. In the Wilderness the rebellion received its death stroke."

During the Virginia campaign of 1864, Grant's plans frequently miscarried because of his subordinates. General Benjamin F. Butler allowed himself to be boxed at Bermuda Hundred, Sigel proved incompetent, and even the able Meade blundered at Spotsylvania over Sheridan's orders. Grant's arrangements for command were defective to this extent, that by leaving Meade as commander of the Army of the Potomac and himself assuming an over-all status, there was a dual command over the main instrument of attack. He is reported by General Porter to have justified Meade's command by remarking that he and Meade were in close contact, that the latter was capable and subordinate, "and by attending to the details relieves me of unnecessary work and gives me more time to think and to mature my general plans." Curiously enough, Grant was reluctant to advise removals. He had been very patient with McClernand before he dismissed him at Vicksburg. It was upon Halleck's importunities that he superseded Sigel, and it was only after Butler's fiasco at Fort Fisher that this worthy was relieved.

Grant's own judgment in selection was generally excellent, although he set a higher premium upon personal loyalty than he should have. This quality he possessed himself in a marked degree. Nothing was more characteristic of this than Grant's story about his reaction to reports that Sherman had spoken slightingly of him in his *Memoirs*. He purchased the book and slowly plowed through it.

During these weeks I did not see Sherman, and I am glad I did not. My mind was so set by Boynton's extracts that I should certainly have been cold to him. But when I finished the book I found that I approved every word. . . . You cannot imagine how pleased I was, for my respect and affection for Sherman were so great that I look on the three weeks as among the most painful in my remembrance.

Grant's loyalty and expectation of reciprocation were of a part with the stubbornness of his make-up. As one of his staff once wrote:

Having determined in a matter that required irreversible decision he never reversed nor even misgave but was steadily loyal to himself and his plans. This absolute and implicit faith was, however, as far as possible from conceit or enthusiasm; it was simply a consciousness or conviction, rather, which brought the very strength it believed in; which was itself strength and which inspired others with a trust in him because he was able thus to trust himself.

This quality, which in later years was to play him false, carried Grant over the James to Petersburg, through his war on Lee's communications, patiently holding the great Confederate leader while Sherman hammered his way through Georgia, until all was ready for the final great maneuver. It is in the climax of this campaign at Appomattox that this stubby middle westerner, so matter-of-fact, so impervious, and outwardly so ordinary, shows the flash of the nobility that men expect in the great. As he pens the terms of capitulation in McLean's house in April 1865, he looks up and notices the glittering of Lee's sword. This suggests an addition that officers should retain their side arms, horses, and personal property. Lee is greatly affected and then asks if the men can keep their animals. Grant demurs and then replies that he cannot change the terms, but the South is impoverished and "I will instruct the officers I shall appoint to receive the paroles to let all the men who claim or own a horse or mule take the animals home with them to work their little farms."

When Grant returns to his lines, he hears the firing of salutes and orders it stopped. "The war is over, the rebels are our countrymen again and the best sign of rejoicing after the victory will be to abstain from all demonstrations in the field." His first order in the war had been in a response to cries for a speech from the turbulent 21st Illinois: "Go to your quarters." Equally matter-of-fact is his order on the day of surrender. The job he had undertaken is done. He is not conscious of nobility or of generosity. He is just General Grant giving another order.

II

Slowly, after Appomattox, the long lines of soldiers, the blue and the gray, returned to their homes North and South, but the work of the Army was not done. South of Texas, across the Rio Grande, lay Maximilian's Mexican Empire, a refuge for ex-Confederates and a potential threat to the security of the border. In the trans-Mississippi West among the tribes of the plains, Indian raids and military vengeance punctuated the postwar years. But it was the pacification of the devastated southern states, turbulent with paroled veterans and newly freed slaves, that absorbed Grant in the months following the surrender. There an army of occupation had to be stationed until the readmission of the states to the Union should finally have put a period to the War of the Rebellion. These were the military problems of peace with which the Army soberly wrestled while political leaders wrangled over policies and formulated new lines of division.

In July 1866 Grant was raised to the rank of General of the Army in recognition of his services—the first man since Washington to be so honored. His popularity was unbounded; a grateful people showered him with gifts—houses in Philadelphia and Galena, a purse of money from the citizens of New York, a library from Boston. In strange medley the thank offerings poured in—cigars, portraits, and horses. Political leaders, both Democrats and Republicans, pondered his possibilities as a "vote catcher," but he refused to take sides on the great issue of the day—what was to be done with the South. Politicians and friends alike sought to fathom his silence and failed. Grant did "not think it proper for an army officer, particularly the army commander, to take part in elections." During the months of controversy over the southern policy he maintained a complete reserve. The Army did its work and awaited events.

The problem of the treatment that should be meted the conquered states and their reconstruction was from the northern point of view purely a political and not an economic issue. During the war Lincoln, using his war powers as commander in chief, had attempted "Executive Reconstruction," the restoration of civil government in the parts of the Confederate States occupied by Union troops, and their rapid readmission to the Union. Congress had regarded this action as an encroachment upon its powers and had refused to recognize Lincoln's "states." Before the war closed it had been made plain that Congress intended to keep in its own hands the reconstruction of the South. Disregarding this factor, Andrew Johnson, Lincoln's successor, had undertaken during the summer of 1865 to regulate the terms of the readmission of the rebel states by executive authority. His plan was essentially Lincoln's, exacting from the southern states only the repeal of the secession ordinances and emancipation of the slaves by ratification of the Thirteenth Amendment and increasing somewhat the categories of disfranchised leaders. No attempt was made to grapple with the problem of representation created by emancipation, a course that aroused a storm of opposition. By December 1865 the South had complied with Johnson's conditions, but his insistence on executive power had been ill-advised. Representatives of the southern states were refused admission by an angered Congress. The war was over, but the fate of the South was yet to be settled. The battle between Executive and Congress had only begun.

During these months Grant's attitude was one of moderation. Toward individual southerners he displayed great magnanimity; he favored a middle-of-the-road policy. In November 1865 he made a short trip to the South and reported his impressions to Johnson in early December. "The mass of thinking men of the South accept the present situation of affairs in good faith," he wrote. ". . . My observations lead me to the conclusion that the citizens of the Southern States are anxious to return to self-government within the Union as soon as possible." But, he went on, four years of war had bequeathed a legacy of lawlessness. Garrisons of Federal troops must be maintained until civil authority was completely established. "I did not meet anyone, either those holding places under the government or citizens of the Southern States who think it practicable to withdraw the military from the South at present . . . the white and black mutually require the protection of the general government."

Nevertheless Grant recognized that the use of colored troops in the South was a source of friction. Only white troops, he recommended, should be employed in the interior country areas. Colored troops should be restricted to the ports and must be kept in bodies large enough to protect themselves. In addition, his report dealt with the moot question of the Freedmen's Bureau. This agency was a center of controversy. Southerners bitterly resented its work for the education of the Negro and blamed its agents for the freedman's refusal to work while he waited for the Federal Government to give him the expected "forty acres and a mule." Grant recognized the economic and social problems created by emancipation and admitted that agents of the bureau had made mistakes. But its work should be continued, he reported, until "civil law is established and enforced, securing to the freedmen their rights and privileges." He recommended, however, that the work of the bureau should in the future be carried out by the Army. This would be economical and would secure uniformity both of policy and execution. He would, he stated, have "every officer on duty with the troops in the Southern States as an agent of the Freedmen's Bureau, and then have all orders from the Bureau sent through department commanders."

From this report it is clear that Grant was favorably disposed toward Johnson's policy of restoring state government, but believed that some degree of Federal intervention was necessary. During the year 1866 a variety of factors induced the general to favor stronger measures. Grant's change of attitude has been ascribed frequently to a budding political ambition centered on the presidential nomination of 1868. This facile interpretation lacks substance. It was the events of the years 1866–68 that shaped the general's course. Throughout 1866 continuing lawlessness was reported by military subordinates stationed in the southern states. Additional troops had to be dispatched to quell the riots at Norfolk (April), Memphis (May), and at New Orleans (August)—highlights of violence. Washington seethed with rumors. Southern leaders and Johnson men declared that the Radical Republicans had instigated the trouble; the Radicals screamed that it was due to the plots of pardoned rebels and of the President. Grant, hedged by silence, said nothing; but it was Grant who received the telegrams and letters from the commanding officers detailed to restore order. "It was no riot," read a dispatch from General Sheridan, in command at New Orleans, "it was an absolute massacre by the police. . . ." This factor weighed with Grant. Between the general and his officers four years of war had forged bonds of mutual trust and affection. Their reports of riot and turmoil seemed to Grant clear proof of a new contagion of rebellion in the South. On him lay the burden of responsibility for the preservation of order lest the fruits of victory be imperiled.

In addition, the development of the struggle between President and Congress weakened Grant's confidence in Johnson. Tension mounted throughout the spring of 1866. Johnson unwisely vetoed each congressional proposal, publicly attacking the leaders with headstrong passion. Outstanding Radicals—the embittered Thaddeus Stevens, the ideologue Charles Sumner, the "transcendental red Republican" Carl Schurz—pushed their plans for the protection of the freedman, the humiliation of Johnson and the South. Rooted in idealism, engrafted with lust for vengeance, nurtured by political passion, perfected by private greed, the congressional program took shape. Over the President's veto, the Freedmen's Bureau bill and the Civil Rights Act were passed. The Fourteenth Amendment (making all persons born in the United States citizens thereof, including thereby the Negro, decreasing the representation of the southern states unless Negro suffrage were granted, disavowing Confederate debts) was drawn up and ratification thereof made a condition precedent to readmission to the Union. Enmeshed in the contest of President and Congress were two fundamental constitutional issues—the balance of power between executive and legislative, the definition of Federal versus state authority.

Grant began to share the Radical's suspicions of Johnson's intentions and fear the growth of executive power.

The results of the congressional elections in the autumn of 1866 finally determined Grant's attitude. The issue had been clearly put to the people. Vote for Johnson men or endorse the Radicals. In the weeks preceding the elections Grant had reluctantly accompanied Johnson on his "swing around the circle"—a political traveling circus with Grant and Admiral Farragut "tame lions harnessed to the President's car." Ostensibly Johnson's trip to the West was to attend the laying of the cornerstone of the Chicago monument to Stephen A. Douglas. But the real intent of influencing the coming elections was patent. The tour was undertaken, jeered Petroleum V. Nasby, self-appointed "Chaplin to the Expedishn," "for the purpose uv arousin the masses uv the West to a sense uv the danger which was threatenin uv them in case they persisted in centralizin the power uv the Government into the hands uv a Congress, instid uv diffusin it through out the hands uv one man, wich is Johnson." The tour was not a success. Everywhere the crowds cheered Grant, but Johnson was received coldly and even with animosity. Only the Copperheads greeted him with enthusiasm. "There is a kinder feeling among Republicans towards beaten Rebels than towards Copperheads," noted Gideon Welles. "But these last pay court to the President in the absence of the greater part of the Republicans, who have become Radicals." It was not a circumstance calculated to secure Grant's attachment, and the President's lack of restraint must have belittled him in Grant's eyes. The elections were a Radical landslide. The North had given its answer; the South was to be punished.

By October, Grant was convinced that Johnson no longer deserved either the people's confidence or Grant's. No one had influence with the President, he wrote—

unless they join in a crusade against Congress and declare their acts, the principal ones, illegal, unconstitutional, and revolutionary. Commanders in Southern States will have to take great care to see, if a crisis does come, that no armed headway can be made against the Union.

The general's suspicions were sharpened when the President sought to get him away from Washington by requesting him to go as a superior courier with a diplomatic mission to Mexico. This Grant refused to do, as the assignment was of a civilian and not military nature. General William T. Sherman wrote to his brother John in October 1866:

> On my arrival I found out that the President was aiming to get Grant out of the way, and me in, not only as Secretary of War but to command the army, on the supposition that I would be more friendly to him than Grant. Grant was willing that I should be Secretary of War but I was not. . . . Both Grant and I desire to keep plainly and strictly to our duty in the Army, and not to be construed as partisans.

Yet Grant still hoped for the speedy readmission of the southern states and with prescience urged on the southern leaders a speedy ratification of the Fourteenth Amendment, lest more stringent measures be adopted. Recklessly the South rejected the amendment. Within another two months Grant's prophecy was fulfilled. By a vote of 138 to 51 in the House and of 35 to 11 in the Senate, in March 1867, Congress with brutal thoroughness undertook "reconstruction."

Under the congressional plan, the state governments that had been set up by Johnson's authority were completely wiped out. Two years after Appomattox, the South was to be treated as conquered territory. The "rebel states" (save Tennessee, readmitted to the Union in July 1866) were divided into five military districts under military commanders. Stringent conditions for the restoration of state governments and readmission to the Union were imposed: disfranchisement of a large body of whites, enfranchisement of the Negro, and ratification of the Fourteenth Amendment. Until this should be accomplished, military government was to endure.

On Grant, as General of the Army, fell the task of putting the whole program into execution. Fearful of disloyalty in the South, distrustful of the President, Grant favored the congressional scheme and had conferred thereon with Radical leaders. By an amendment to the Army Appropriation Bill, Congress expressly stipulated that every order relating to the Army, whether issued by the President or the Secretary of War, must be sent out through the General of the Army. The President, under the Constitution Grant's commander in chief, was bitterly opposed to every step; the Secretary of War, Stanton, Grant's immediate superior, was hand in glove with the Radicals. Grant walked the tightrope of duty, balancing precariously on a strict execution of the law. Publicly he still refused to take sides, but privately to his old friend Washburne he defined his position: "Whilst there is an antagonism between the executive and legislative branches of government, I feel the same obligation to stand at my post that I did whilst there were rebel armies in the field to contend with."

In August 1867 Grant's responsibilities became even more complicated. To his duties as General of the Army were added those of head of the War Department. In the face of the Tenure of Office Act (passed over the President's veto in March 1867), Johnson, resentful of Stanton's intrigues and galled by congressional encroachment on the executive power, suspended Stanton from office. In his place he assigned Grant as Secretary of War *ad interim*, a duty which Grant accepted reluctantly with the brief statement that he "always obeyed orders." Nor was Grant's acceptance disingenuous. Five years earlier, when his actions as military commander were under fire, he had stated his philosophy succinctly. He had written in March 1862:

> So long as I hold a commission in the army I have no views of my own to carry out. Whatever may be the orders of my superiors and law I will execute. No man can be efficient as a commander who sets his own notions above law and those whom he has sworn to obey. When Congress enacts anything too odious for me to execute, I will resign.

It was under this conviction that Grant acted both as general and as Secretary of War. Grimly and tenaciously he pushed the execution of the congressional policy.

At no time were Johnson and his coadjutor Welles under any illusions as to Grant's convictions that the acts of Congress must be executed. The general repeatedly stated this belief and resisted the arguments and entreaties of Secrtary Welles. Under the circumstances the divergence of outlook between President and Secretary-General became progressively more obvious. Temperamentally they were opposed. Johnson was indecisive, emotional, and passionate; Grant was silent, imperturbable, and rocklike. Their political philosophies were poles apart. Influenced by his Secretary of the Navy, Gideon Welles, Johnson adopted the old Jacksonian position—that the President was free to refuse to execute a law which he believed to be "palpably unconstitutional." Grant viewed a law in the light of a military order—once issued, it must be obeyed. His concepts were simple, long and deeply founded. Congress had enacted laws; it was the duty of the President to execute them. Only the Supreme Court, said Grant sturdily, could decide on the constitutionality of a law. "The will of the people is the law in this country, and the representatives of the people made the laws." A "political ignoramus," snorted Gideon Welles, pained "to see how little he [Grant] understood of the fundamental principles and structure of our government, and of the Constitution itself." In this Welles was mistaken. Grant understood the text of the Constitution; he did not understand political interpretation thereof.

With this philosophical difference of attitude toward the law, with sharply variant feelings toward the South, friction between Johnson and Grant over the execution of congressional reconstruction was inevitable. The President's removal of the hard-bitten Generals Sheridan and Sickles, despite Grant's protests brought the Secretary-General to the edge of rebellion. The final rupture of their relations took place in January 1868, when the Senate, under color of the Tenure of Office Act, by a vote of 35 to 6 refused to concur in Stanton's suspension and notified Grant of its action. This at once changed Grant's status. Continuance in the office of the Secretary of War would have been a direct violation of Section 5 of the Tenure of Office Act and would have made Grant liable to a fine not exceeding ten thousand dollars or imprisonment for not longer than five

years. At such a prospect the general balked. Two days before
the Senate had acted, he had informed the President of his un-
willingness to continue in office should Stanton be reinstated.
Despite Johnson's entreaties and hysterical offer "to undergo
the whole imprisonment and fine himself," Grant surrendered
the key of the War Department to the Adjutant General and
notified the President of his action. This prompt surrender of
the office and the failure of the General of the Army to deliver
the office key into the President's own hands aroused Johnson's
wrath. In a rage he publicly accused the general of duplicity and
misrepresentation. Grant retorted in kind, the controversy
boiled into the open, and the break was final.

It was this that precipitated Johnson's impeachment; it was
this that made Grant an open enemy; it was this that fired
Grant's political ambition and made him the nominee of the
Radical Republicans. Jubilant at Grant's break with Johnson,
the Radicals, cool and hesitant throughout the previous months,
adopted him as their own. "He is a bolder man than I thought
him," Thaddeus Stevens gloated; "now we will let him into
the church." At the Republican convention on May 16,1868,
Grant was nominated unanimously on the first ballot. Two
weeks later he formally acknowledged the nomination, closing
his letter of acceptance with the words, "Let us have peace."
What this phrase meant no one knew, but the words swept a
country wearied of war and of the unseemly struggle of President and Congress. Politicians promoted his candidacy intent
on saving the Republican party. The people, remembering that
he had won peace in 1865, hopeful that he would establish
peace in 1869, responded to Miles O'Reilly's song:

> So boys! a final bumper
> While we all in chorus chant,
> For next President we nominate
> Our own Ulysses Grant;
> And if asked what state he hails from,
> This, our sole reply shall be,
> From near Appomattox Court House,
> With its famous apple tree.

In any presidential campaign it is difficult to disentangle enthusiasm for the candidate from endorsement of the platform —in none more so than in the 1868 election. Newly enfranchised Negroes, led by their patrons, the carpetbaggers, carried the South for Grant. In the North old abolitionists and anti-slavery men hailed the Republican ticket; business and banking interests backed a platform of "sound money" and tariff protection. In the West men voted for Grant for any or none of these reasons, but everywhere a current of public favor and high expectation ran for the hero of Appomattox. In November, Grant secured 280 votes to Seymour's 80. Historians might later attribute his success to the Negro vote; in Grant's eyes, he owed his election to the whole people.

When Grant took office on March 4, 1869, his position was unprecedented. No man (unless it was Taylor) since the rise of parties in the United States had entered the office as un-trammeled by party commitments or party affiliations. "I am not the representative of a political party though a party voted for me," he told a Republican politician bluntly a few weeks before his inauguration, thus setting party circles awhirl. Eastern Brahmins were to find him coarse and lacking in cultivation —he smoked cigars. An army colonel had summed him up with more perspicacity: "He is an odd combination; there is one good thing, at any rate—he is the concentration of all that is American. He talks bad grammar, but he talks it naturally, as much as to say, 'I was so brought up and, if I try fine phrases, I shall only appear silly.' . . . In fact, he has such an easy and straightforward way that you almost think that he must be right and you wrong, in these little matters of elegance." Here lies the key to the puzzle of Grant as President. Politician and scholar alike had expected him to change in office. To them he was a disappointment; Grant remained Grant.

Grant's first difficulty in office—one that was to affect his career throughout eight years as President—arose from the divergence of his view of himself as the agent of the people and the politician's view of him as the agent of the Republican party. Even before his inauguration, his failure to consult party leaders as to the composition of his Cabinet or the text of his inaugural address had aroused a buzz of opposition. Yet this was consistent with Grant the commander, silently making his own decisions without consulting his generals, laboriously writing out his orders by hand.

When Grant submitted his list of cabinet names to the Senate, the storm broke. The announcement acted on the Senate, said Welles, as a "cold water bath." Grant's was a personal, not a party, Cabinet. He had offended against the canons of party custom and party expectation. From this dates the charge of "Grantism"—the bogey of personal government. In his lesser appointments Grant occasionally disregarded the unwritten rule that the Federal service was a party province, spoils to be apportioned by the senators and congressmen of each state. Garfield was to nurse resentment for a decade because Grant, without consultation, appointed a postmistress in Garfield's district. Plums handed out to old army friends and Grant's use of his former military staff, Badeau, Porter, Babcock, and Dent, aroused violent opposition. There was open muttering at the "military ring enthroned in the White House."

Historians generally have condemned Grant's appointments with as little discrimination as his contemporaries exercised. Some were bad; some were bizarre; but a great many were good. In assaying Grant's appointments the standards of political morality of 1868 must be considered. "These Post Offices should be filled by men who are competent to run the Party machine in their vicinity," wrote Postmaster Keyes, chairman of the Republican state central committee in Wisconsin, and Keyes's outlook was not unusual. It had been shared by Lincoln and was the devout conviction of most of the men in public life. The exploitation of patronage and the assessment of officeholders for election funds constituted the sinews of the party organism. "Senatorial courtesy" and the prerogatives of representatives thus formed a solid barrier in the way of the reform of the public service.

To this spoils system Grant surrendered, but not without protest. During his first administration he was willing if not eager to try the experiment advocated by Jenckes, the father of the civil-service movement. Beginning in 1870, in each annual message he earnestly urged civil-service reform in Congress. He discussed cogently the "arduous and thankless labor" of appointments and pointedly attacked the evils of the current system which did "not secure the best men and often not even fit men" for public office. In 1871 he appointed an excellent committee, headed by George William Curtis, to investigate and frame rules for civil service, and made an effort to put these into effect. Congress responded by cutting out the appropriation for the commission's work.

In 1874 Grant made a last effort. In his message to Congress he firmly stated that he would abandon the movement unless Congress gave him support. This was never forthcoming. After his retirement Grant frankly stated his position. The reformers he had found to be "as anxious for patronage as others." Grant had decided that party patronage was a "condition of our representative form of government" on which senators and representatives were dependent for re-election. "Civil service reform rests entirely with Congress," he declared. ". . . The President very rarely appoints, he merely registers the appointments of members of Congress." This was an accurate description of party government in the seventies. The worst that can be said of Grant was that he was no better than the people's representatives in Congress.

With more justice, Grant was blamed for treating his Cabinet with the brusqueness of a general towards his staff. "If I mistake not, he designs to let his Cabinet perform each his own work, like department military commanders," observed Welles. With superb incomprehension of political usage Grant appointed and dismissed cabinet members without consulting anyone, even the person in question. Here was the general of whom Lincoln had said: "He hasn't told me what his plans are. I don't know and I don't want to know. I am glad to find a man that can go ahead without me." Yet, unlike Andrew Jackson, Grant frequently consulted his Cabinet, as Hamilton Fish's diary reveals. On many questions he yielded to his

Secretary of State. There remained, however, always an element of the unpredictable in his actions. It was this quality that created uneasiness in friend and foe alike.

Grant's career as President was for many a tale of Great Expectations and subsequent disillusionment. "By instinct if not by reason, all the world united on Grant," wrote Henry Adams. In common with other reformers, Adams had expected Grant to demonstrate the qualities of a great commander, to restore "moral and mechanical order to administration," to quell the Senate and to curb the House. Laboring under an illusion, they had voted for "the Man on Horseback"; having expected a Napoleon, they were to recoil in bitter disappointment from a constitutionalist.

As President, Grant followed a policy, once adopted, with the same doggedness as he had exhibited in military affairs. The powers and prerogatives of Congress were explicitly granted by the Constitution; in matters within the legislative sphere Grant was therefore ruled by his democratic dogma— the will of the people. He conceived of Congress as the policy-making branch of government. The battle between Johnson and the Radicals had pivoted on this issue, and Congress had triumphed. Grant's administration marks the initiation of "congressional government," or as Lowell termed it, "government by declamation."

No one, I take it for granted, is disposed to disallow the principle that the representatives of the people are the proper ultimate authority in all matters of government, and that administration is merely the clerical part of government. Legislation is the originating force. It determines what shall be done; and the President, if he cannot or will not stay legislation by the use of his extraordinary power as a branch of the legislature, is plainly bound in duty to render unquestioning obedience to Congress.

So Woodrow Wilson was to write as a young student of government in 1885. It was this philosophy that Grant exemplified.

This is particularly shown in Grant's policy towards the southern states. By the opening of Grant's first administration, congressional reconstruction was in full swing. Until his resignation from the Army on the very date of his inauguration as President, Grant, General of the Army, had been personally charged with the execution of that policy. He had said, "Let us have peace." To Grant (as he stated in 1871) this meant acquiescence by North and South in the results of the conflict. Peace he coupled with "cheerful obedience to law." He endorsed the Fifteenth Amendment safeguarding Negro suffrage, he urged the restoration of the Confederate states still lingering under military government. He expected the South to accept the new order which Republican leaders—Stanton, Sumner, Schurz, Stevens, Butler, and Boutwell, reformer and spoilsman alike—had erected. Confronted with the problems inherent in any attempt to force alien social concepts on a conquered people, he sought steadily to give reality to the platform on which he had been elected and to carry out party pledges. "He habitually wears an expression as if he had determined to drive his head through a brick wall, and was about to do it," had been said of Grant in 1864. Five years later, only the terrain, not Grant, had changed.

By the end of Grant's first year in office, outwardly the fabric of the Union had been repaired. But the South remained in a turmoil. In every ex-Confederate state the carpetbagger government was stained with corruption. Mutinous whites, stripped of control, had resorted to the weapons of terrorization and violence. Ku Klux Klansmen, Knights of the White Camellia, and "rifle clubs" ranged the counties. Elections were marked by fraud, riot, and death. In the face of this situation Grant advocated stern Federal measures to make the Constitution effective.

Swayed by a variety of motives, Congress embarked on the second phase of congressional reconstruction. By large majorities the Enforcement Acts of May 31, 1870, and February 28, 1871, were passed, designed to safeguard the freedman's rights and to maintain the Republican party. These provided for the supervision of all elections, exacted severe penalties, vested jurisdiction in Federal courts and authorized, if necessary,

the use of Federal troops to insure a faithful observance of
the Fourteenth and Fifteenth amendments. The more sweeping
Ku Klux Klan Act, enacted April 20, 1871, made it "lawful for
the President, and it shall be his duty" to use Federal troops to
suppress any domestic violence or conspiracies. In addition, he
was empowered to suspend the writ of habeas corpus in any
region where "unlawful combinations" were depriving citizens
of any of their constitutional rights and privileges.

This was done by the people of the United States through
their representatives. It was under these mandates that Grant
intervened in unhappy South Carolina, in malodorous Louisiana, and in lawless Arkansas. In 1871 nine counties in South
Carolina were put under martial law; Federal troops were
repeatedly used at elections for the support of the carpetbagger
regime. Similarly, in Louisiana a Republican administration
was maintained by application of the Enforcement Acts from
the election of 1872 until 1877. Grant made no attempt to
justify these governments. He stigmatized the Louisiana election of 1872 as a "gigantic fraud" and repeatedly asked Congress to frame a policy for the direction of the executive in
these cases. This Congress failed to do.

"I cannot but think that its inaction has produced great
evils," Grant stated in January 1875. The majority in Congress,
unwilling to lose the Republican Negro vote, sidestepped the
issue. "Social equality is not a subject to be legislated upon,"
declared Grant bluntly. In the face of this dictum, Congress
passed the Civil Rights Act of 1875, designed to confer social
rights on the Negro, a final tribute to Charles Sumner and the
New England conscience. Political craftiness governed their
policy; it was wise to make a noble flourish and let Grant, the
executor of their laws, bear the odium.

Congressional weaseling was the more reprehensible in the
face of Grant's frank statement of his position: "While I remain Executive all the laws of Congress and the provisions of
the Constitution, including the recent amendments added
thereto, will be enforced with rigor, but with regret that they
should have added one jot or tittle to the executive duties or

powers." And he pointed out clearly that, without Federal interference, "the whole scheme of colored enfranchisement is worse than mockery and little better than a crime." As general, Grant had demanded strict execution of orders; as President, he imposed on himself the same meticulous discharge of the law. "I know no method to secure the repeal of bad or obnoxious laws so effective as their stringent execution," he had stated in his inaugural address. It was the guiding principle of his southern policy.

In retrospect, it is easy to judge Grant harshly and to accept without question the attacks of such an opponent as Horace Greeley, that weather vane of political opinion. Had Grant been a greater statesman, he might have openly denounced the Radical program as impossible of execution at that date. Had he been more of a politician, he might have acquiesced in the moderates' tacit and disingenuous renunciation of the freedman's rights. Grant, as general, had never known how to conduct the strategy of retreat; his obstinacy and concept of duty alike forced him to "fight it out on this line."

Corruption in government during the postwar years was not restricted to the South. The carpetbagger of South Carolina had his prototype in Democrat Boss Tweed of New York City, in a governor in Nebraska, in a treasurer in Pennsylvania, for greed recognized neither geographical nor party boundaries. The profiteering, "fixing," and swindling of the Government which had been rife during the war years had promoted a full tide of speculation and money grabbing. It was the gilded age of bonanza mines, gushing oil wells, railroad building, watered stock, and business expansion. Socially, it was the era of red plush and gilt mirrors, of flowing champagne and parvenu vulgarities. The times were high, wide, and handsome. Political morality was at the ebb in city, state, and Federal government. The scandals of the Grant administration were the muddy residuum.

The one scandal that directly involved Grant was the famous "Black Friday" panic of September 24, 1869. In this drama the President played the role of a country jay outsmarted by city slickers. The crisis in the New York gold market was caused by a corner on gold, run by Jay Gould and "Jubilee Jim" Fiske, the two most notorious speculators of the day. For the success of their operations it was imperative that treasury gold be kept off the market. For months the partners schemed. Corbin, Grant's brother-in-law, was drawn into the plot. Grant's friendship was cultivated; the President naïvely accepted dinners, appeared at "Jubilee Jim's" private theater, traveled in the plotters' company. Grant's weakness for wealth was his Achilles' heel, a reflex from a poverty-shadowed youth and his own failure as a money-maker. His honesty made him vulnerable; he was incapable of suspecting a friend. Unwittingly he became a dupe, persuaded by the smooth Gould that a premium on gold would stimulate the export of crops and thus help the western farmer. In September, by Grant's order, the monthly sale of government gold was suspended. Gould, Fiske, and Corbin spread the rumor that the President and his wife were involved in the speculation. Gold leaped to 162, and hundreds were ruined in the frenzied market before Grant awoke to the true situation. A congressional committee exonerated him, but public confidence was shaken. At best, his conduct had been lacking in prudence and good taste.

This smirch on Grant's reputation was doubly unfortunate in view of the avalanche of political scandals that overwhelmed Washington during his administrations. For none of these was Grant responsible except to the degree that his subordinates were involved. In many cases the corrupt practices antedated his inauguration; the canker was deep-rooted in every branch of the body politic. In 1871 the New York City customhouse was exposed as "a party engine," riddled with graft. The following year the *Crédit Mobilier* scandal erupted, involving Schuyler Colfax, Vice-President of the United States, and eleven members of Congress, all of whom in 1867 and 1868 had accepted gifts of shares in the construction company of the Union Pacific Railroad, then recipient of public land grants, Federal loans, and other privileges. Congress sank lower in the public estimation when the Pacific Mail Company investigation revealed that the steamship line's lobby had distributed large sums of money to the House postmaster and members of Congress. In 1874 the "Sanborn Contracts" forced Richardson, Secretary of the Treasury, to resign; in the same year Washington rocked with the disclosures of "Boss Shepherd's" mal-administration of the District of Columbia.

The climax came in 1875 with the unearthing in the Bureau of Internal Revenue of the "Whisky Ring," a group whose activities dated back to Andrew Johnson's administration. General Orville E. Babcock, Grant's private secretary, was shown to be deeply implicated, an unhappy circumstance for Grant. Under the illusion that Babcock was the victim of political persecution, Grant made a deposition expressing his confidence in his secretary and even offered to testify in person at his trial. Hot on the heels of the "Whisky Ring" trials came the Belknap Scandal, involving the administration of Indian agencies. It was charged that Belknap, Secretary of War, had taken bribes of nearly $40,000 from the trader at Fort Sill for the privilege of keeping that concession. Grant accepted Belknap's resignation in the morning of the very day on which articles of impeachment were framed against the Secretary of War!

Small wonder that in the Centennial Year 1876 James Russell Lowell marveled at "such advance in one poor hundred years." Small wonder that the brunt of the blame was heaped on Grant. He was betrayed by his most endearing qualities—his dogged faithfulness to his friends and his trust in them. In his attempts to protect Babcock and Belknap, Grant was culpable. Some of his appointments, as that of Tom Murphy (protégé of Senator Conkling of New York) to the New York customhouse, had been weak and indefensible. But the real culprit at the bar is the age in which Grant lived. Legislator, administrator, and citizen alike, made cynical by materialism, stand convicted.

On the credit side of Grant's record stands his sound-money policy, a redemption of the Republican pledge of 1868. The greenback issue stemmed from the Civil War when the Government, forced to suspend specie payments, had resorted to the expedient of issuing treasury notes. After the war a feeble attempt to contract the greenbacks was soon halted by the outcry of inflationists. The "Ohio Idea"—a redemption of United States bonds in paper money—swept the West. Backed by the Democratic party, it was a major issue in the election of 1868. The Republican victory killed this proposal. Within two years of Grant's inauguration, a law for the funding of the national debt was enacted with specific provision for the payment of all Federal bonds in coin.

The real crisis in the money question came in Grant's second administration. The panic of 1873 raised a desperate cry for more currency. Agrarian unrest was at its peak in the Middle West. Farmers, battling savagely for state granger laws, demanded greenbacks as a panacea for their troubles. A sound-money policy, cried "Rise Up" William Allen, governor of Ohio, was "a d——d barren ideality." The crusade for cheap money had started.

In the following year Congress made the first move to open the floodgates of inflation, passing a bill for the permanent increase of greenbacks to $400,000,000. Although the President had uniformly supported a sound-money policy, the bill found him undecided. The country was in the grip of black depression, and the temptation to "prime the pump" with cheap money was great. Furthermore, Grant's philosophy of government inclined him to follow rather than to lead Congress; he had previously restricted himself to the veto of such unimportant items as private claims bills. Every ounce of party pressure was exercised to secure his approval. Every consideration of political expediency urged an acceptance of the bill. For some days Grant hesitated. First he framed a careful message approving the bill, and then in disgust threw it aside. In its place he sent a strong veto. "I could not stand my own arguments," he said. ". . . When the Cabinet met, my message was written. I did not intend asking the advice of the Cabinet, as I knew a majority would oppose the veto. I never allowed the Cabinet to interfere when my mind was made up, and on this question it was inflexibly made up." Only one change was made in the message before it was sent to Congress—the deletion of the phrase "patent medicine." This omission Grant regretted. "The country might have accepted the word as a true definition of the inflation scheme," he remarked later.

Even without this phrase it was a "memorable" message. The veto marked a definite check to the greenback agitation. Early in 1875 the Resumption Act was passed, providing for resumption of specie payment on January 1, 1879, for reduction of greenbacks to $300,000,000, and for a guarded increase in the currency through the safe medium of national bank notes. Grant's veto stands out as a monument of courage and common sense. Here he had acted the commander.

On only one other question did Grant essay a decisive leadership. This was in the field of foreign affairs. Since the days of Washington the shaping of foreign policies had rested in the executive's hands; the Constitution and custom alike had tended to strengthen presidential powers in this sphere. It was not, therefore, contrary either to precedent or to his own political tenets that here Grant sought to take a leading role.

Grant's policy was in general premised on two guiding principles. In the first place, he shared the mid-nineteenth-century conviction of the mission of America, an anticipation of the "spread-eagle rapture" of later years. "It is my firm conviction that the civilized world is tending towards republicanism, or government by the people through their chosen representatives, and that our own great Republic is destined to be the guiding star to all others," he declared in 1872. At the close of the Civil War this belief had colored his attitude toward the establishment of Maximilian's empire in Mexico, buttressed by French arms. While still a general in the Army, he had urged armed intervention in favor of Juarez and the Mexican Republican forces, and had regarded Seward's Fabian policy as a betrayal of the Monroe Doctrine. This same impulse determined his attitude toward the Cuban revolt of 1868. In common with the American public, Grant was hotly sympathetic with Cuban demands for independence and would have accorded a precipitant recognition to the paper Cuban republic in 1869 had it not been for the restraining influence of Hamilton Fish, Secretary of State.

In addition, Grant's thinking was as nationalist and expansionist as that of the Democrats of 1854. Their program had been engulfed by the internal conflict; but the storm of the Civil War had in turn whipped up a fresh consciousness of national power. Moreover, the experience of the Navy and the leasing of the harbor of Mole St. Nicolas in Haiti during the war years had been a signpost pointing to the need for naval bases, the importance of the Caribbean as a key to our defenses. Chameleonlike, the Republican party in the postwar years was to take on the color of the earlier "Young America" movement.

Seward, Secretary of State under Lincoln and Johnson, was the first to revive the Pierce plan of empire. The familiar objectives—a commanding position in the Caribbean, a safeguarding of interoceanic communication, and the development of American influence in the Pacific—were only partially realized during his years in office. The purchase of Alaska and the acquisition of transit rights in Nicaragua were achieved. But Seward's plans for expansion in the Caribbean, his projects for the annexation of the Danish West Indies (now the Virgin Islands), for obtaining the Spanish islands of Culebra and Culebrita and the cession or lease of Samaná Bay from the Dominican Republic were not brought to completion.

It was this postwar program of Manifest Destiny that Grant inherited and sought to effectuate. Unfortunately it was a program that outran public interest and was politically tainted by its connection with Johnson's administration. In January 1869, before Grant's inauguration, a resolution to extend a protectorate over Haiti and Santo Domingo had been overwhelmingly defeated. In April the Senate deferred indefinitely action on Seward's treaty for the purchase of the Danish West Indies; Seward's policy seemed doomed to extinction. Grant's revival of the program, his singlehanded battle for the annexation of the Dominican Republic, became the pivotal political question of his first administration. Almost an irrelevancy at first, the question swelled into a political bomb. Its final detonations split the Republican party and left marks on Grant's later career.

Grant's negotiations for the annexation of the Dominican Republic were initiated shortly after his inauguration in 1869. Predisposed to expansion, various factors spurred him to the immediate and fateful crusade. The Cuban revolt kept the Caribbean uppermost in Grant's mind. The acquisition of Santo Domingo, he stated, would "settle the unhappy condition of Cuba and end an exterminating conflict." In addition, the project was related to Grant's design of building a canal across Nicaragua. Should the design be realized, naval bases would be indispensable. In this Grant anticipated the canal diplomacy of the twentieth century. Lastly, impetus to his general policy of expansion was given by a pressure group—a collection of speculators interested in dubious concessions. The President was dazzled by the picture which they drew of the future wealth to be drawn from the island. The negotiations for the annexation of Santo Domingo (lamentably entrusted to his secretary, General Babcock) were thus indelibly stamped with the impress of private influence and greed. The treaty, Grant's first venture in diplomacy, was touched with tar.

It was the opposition of Charles Sumner, chairman of the Senate Committee on Foreign Relations, to this treaty that caused the bitter quarrel between the President and the New England leader—a breach that was never healed and that had far-reaching results. Grant had consulted Sumner and believed that he had received a pledge of support. On March 15, 1870, however, Sumner turned the batteries of his oratory against the ratification of the treaty. One of the most powerful men in the Republican party, he was a deadly opponent, a merciless master of invective, inordinately proud of his powers. "These speeches are my life," he had remarked when discussing the publication of his works, a project financed at his own expense, "if this were done I should be ready to go." To Grant, Sumner's attitude was not only unexpected but treacherous, and faithlessness had

always aroused Grant's scorn and his fighting spirit. A titanic
battle raged for months.

The President's policy, Sumner lashed out, "commits Congress to a dance of blood," and the accusing phrase, "Naboth's
Vineyard," rang through the Senate hall. Grant, smarting under
the flick of Sumner's tongue, made of the treaty a touchstone
of personal loyalty. In an effort to marshal his forces, he exercised pressure on the senators and resorted to unworthy political expedients to secure his ends. When the treaty failed, Grant
grimly exacted political retribution—the recall of Sumner's
friend Motley, minister to England, and the removal of Sumner from his place on the Committee on Foreign Relations.
By these actions Grant incurred Sumner's everlasting enmity
and alienated many outstanding men in his party, such as Carl
Schurz—friends of Sumner, men armed with able tongues and
ready pens who joined the Liberal Republicans in 1872. Even
more regrettably, Grant turned in gratitude to those who had
sustained him—the Mortons, Butlers, and Conklings. The battle for Santo Domingo was Grant's greatest mistake; it left
him with his trust in these new friends and thus affected in-
directly the domestic issues of his administrations.

Curiously, the struggle had fortunate by-products. Throughout the episode, Hamilton Fish, Secretary of State, retained
Grant's confidence. As a result Fish was able to exercise a control over other vexing questions of foreign policy. Grant's hot-
headed sympathy for the Cuban revolt was curbed, the recognition of the "Republic" prevented, and the question deferred
for the attention of a later administration. Of greater importance was the relation of the Santo Domingo struggle to the
problem of our relations with England. Since the Civil War,
accumulations of irritations had caused bad feeling in both
countries. Americans had resented England's ready recognition
of the Confederate belligerent status and her failure to enforce
a strict neutrality during the war period. Depredations by the
Confederate raiders built in England had given rise to a widespread demand that England should pay dearly for her negli-
gence. It was Sumner, chairman of the Senate Committee on

Foreign Relations, who had blocked every effort to settle these questions. The British flag must be swept out of the Western Hemisphere, he declared, before our claims could be satisfied, and he had demanded that England pay for such "national claims" as the increased cost of the war due to the Confederates' success on the sea.

With Sumner's removal from his place of influence, early in 1871, the main stumbling block in the way of happier relations with England was set aside. As a result negotiations for settlement were renewed. In the summer of that year the great Treaty of Washington, providing for the arbitration of all outstanding questions (the Civil War claims, the fisheries dispute, and the northwest boundary), was confirmed and the road to Anglo-American amity cleared. Grant was to pay dearly for Sumner's enmity, but perhaps the price was not too high, set against this triumph of diplomacy.

One other aspect of Grant's expansionist policy was carried through successfully—the development of American interests in the Pacific. In 1875 our first reciprocity treaty was signed with Hawaii, a treaty that prohibited the leasing of any port or harbor of the islands to any other power. The march of empire to the Orient had begun. There is a touch of irony in the reflection that in 1898 we went to war to free Cuba, that in 1917 we bought the Virgin Islands and occupied the Dominican Republic and Haiti, and that the Hawaiian Islands, annexed in 1898, have become, in Secretary Fish's prophetic words, our "outpost fronting and commanding the whole of our possession in the Pacific Ocean."

"We thought because we had power we had wisdom"—this might have been written of Grant assuming office in 1869, flushed with the victory of election, facing his task without hesitation. Eight years of obstinate struggle to carry out his party's pledges to the freedman, eight years of following consistently a political philosophy that fell short of the needs of his day, stripped him of overconfidence, laid bare the essential humility of the man. Grant is the only President who left his office with an address to the American public that echoes with the dignity of the General Confession: "We have left undone those things which we ought to have done; and we have done those things which we ought not to have done. . . ." He began his last annual message to Congress:

It was my fortune, or misfortune, to be called to the office of Chief Executive without any previous political training. . . . Under such circumstances it is but reasonable to suppose that errors of judgment must have occurred. . . . Mistakes have been made, as all can see and I admit, but it seems to me oftener in the selections made of assistants—in nearly every case selected without a personal acquaintance with the appointee, but upon recommendations of representatives chosen directly by the people. . . . Failures have been errors of judgment, not of intent.

Had he acted more as the military commander in office, browbeaten his party, issued orders to the representatives of the people with his old authority, Grant would have risen to Henry Adams' expectations and would have justified Charles Sumner's bitter arraignment of the military despot. Guided by a different concept of the uses of power, Grant might have left a better fame as President. "Upon what meat doth this our Caesar feed that he should assume so much?" thundered Sumner in 1872. The words entranced his followers, but they ring emptily against the record of Grant's actions. Yet to this day it is not the record but the hot-tempered excoriations, the hyperbolic extravagances of press and political enemies that have fastened in the public mind a misshapen image of Grant the President. The people of the North and their representatives in Congress, having sowed the wind, were content that Grant should reap the whirlwind of regretted errors—

> The painful warrior famousèd for fight
> After a thousand victories once foiled
> Is from the book of honour razèd quite
> And all the rest forgot for which he toiled.

X

Generals Hayes, Garfield, and Benjamin Harrison

———— ◆ ————

FOR THE CITIZEN SOLDIER there can be few tales more poignant than the epic of Odysseus, the warrior who wanted to get home from his wars, and whom the gods kept wandering for years upon strange seas. To return and resume has always been the conscript's dream cherished regardless of the fact that neither he nor his world can be the same as when he fared forth. It is never a road back which he traverses, but a new way which he does not know. The stouthearted will make passage, but for most this will be a lonely time, and so they turn to their old comrades for reassurance and to their old commanders for guidance. The longer and bloodier a war, the more closely knit will be the fellowship of veterans and the more profoundly will it affect the community. Holding fast to the past, the veterans project it into the present, and by the very fact of association they wield a weapon of political assertion.

Long before the last battles of the Civil War had been fought, it was already apparent that the future course of public affairs in America was to be influenced by the men then fighting, and that the persons then exercising military leadership were by that fact to assume dominating roles. Some of these persons were experienced in the ways of politics before they joined the colors, and to this not a few of them owed rank and promotion. For anyone who had gained renown in the field or who had won the confidence of his men, the possibility of capitalizing upon his war service was obvious. Out of the small army of colonels, brigadiers, and major generals only a corporal's guard achieved a secure fame of national dimensions. But such repute, though useful, was dispensable for office in a scheme of governments like our own, or for preferment within a party. Then, as now, the national party was merely the aggregate of state organizations, and its strength and continuity depended upon the vigor and stability of party structure in each state. It is with the party in his state that a man must find his political fortune.

By a happy coincidence the principle of localism had prevailed in the organization of both Union and Confederate armies. The state regiment was the unit, recruited in the state and officered by local men. A volunteer officer might rise to command a brigade, a division, or a corps, but his identification with his state regiment was something indefeasible. In consequence the commander who distinguished himself was assured not only a local pre-eminence but the initial following for a sortie into the politics of his state.

The three bearded generals whose careers we are about to consider were typical of the new generation of soldier-politician bred by the Civil War. Each of them had made a small beginning in politics before taking the field; each of them fought with bravery and honor; each of them owed something to his military service for his rise to civil eminence. In another era all of them might well have remained obscure, but the war persisted as a factor in our national life, kept vital by the alarums of Reconstruction and by the veterans who would not let it be forgotten. It glared in campaign literature, it reverberated in speeches, and it helped these generals to the presidency.

I

Rutherford B. Hayes was a middle-aged lawyer practicing in Cincinnati when the news about Fort Sumter came clicking over the wires. He had not been greatly stirred over the mere secession of the southern states, but the outbreak of hostilities moved him profoundly. Less than a week after the first call for volunteers, Hayes joined a home-guard company to learn how to drill. The conviction growing upon him that this was a "holy war," he soon decided he would have to participate. As he wrote in his diary, "I would prefer to go into it if I knew I was to die or be killed in the course of it, than to live through and after it without taking any part in it."

In due course Hayes was commissioned major in the 23rd Ohio, the first regiment in that state not to elect its own field officers. His colonel was William S. Rosecrans, a West Pointer shortly to be promoted brigadier. Hayes was greatly concerned that an appointed officer be acceptable to the regiment, and he obviously bent much effort to secure the attachment of the men and officers under him. There is no doubt that he soon established firm ties of respect and affection. Hayes's diary is replete with evidence of his own kindness and courtesy to the privates and the men's reciprocation. In his day the relationship might have been compared to that of an ardent Sunday-school teacher and his class; the metaphor of the godless modern would be a football coach and his team. Hayes's own devotion to his regiment was strong to the point that in 1862 he passed by a promotion to be colonel in another regiment rather than leave his beloved 23rd.

After a few brief weeks of training, Hayes's regiment was sent to Clarksburg, West Virginia, to participate in the continuing campaign so auspiciously begun by General McClellan. In this theater of war Hayes was to remain until August 1862. The first weeks of campaigning were spent in much maneuvering in the foothills of the Alleghenies. Hayes was charmed by the scenery and stirred by the excitement and was imperturbable in the first brush with the enemy at Carnifex Ferry. Lawyerlike, he reported to his wife that his actual feeling was similar to that experienced before beginning an important trial.

General Rosecrans, who was in command, appointed Hayes judge advocate general on September 19, 1861, and the latter, alternately irked and stimulated, devoted weeks to this task— a most important one, considering the general state of discipline and the peculiar problems of the border zone. Promoted to be lieutenant colonel, Hayes rejoined his regiment and was occupied with minor skirmishes and operations against the bushwhackers.

During this winter, in the reshuffle of military districts the western Virginia region was incorporated into the short-lived "Mountain Department," and General Frémont was put in command. Plans for spring operations had already been submitted by General Rosecrans, and as these seemed to give promise of fulfilling Lincoln's cherished scheme of rescuing the East Tennessee loyalists, the new commander proceeded more or less along the lines suggested. In general, the design called for an advance to the Blue Ridge conducted by widely separated columns. The objective of the troops in the Kanawha Valley under the immediate command of General Jacob Cox was an offensive along the New River Valley with the ultimate purpose of cutting the East Tennessee-Virginia railroad. Its defect lay in the fact that it bore no relation to what other departments were about. In this respect it was typical of the aimless and unco-ordinated "up and at 'em" operations of this period in the conflict.

Early in May, Hayes's regiment, which had been pushed forward to Flat Top Mountain, was attacked by the rebels. The enemy was repulsed and Hayes followed the retreating Confederates with great vigor. Reinforcements were sent in, but Cox, a political general, hesitated to order a general advance. The Union forces penetrated as far as Pearisburg, but discovering that the enemy was concentrating in strength and no help being forthcoming, were compelled to retire. Hayes was proud of the manner in which he conducted the retreat, and he was complimented for his "energy and courage" by General Frémont.

In the weeks following this campaign bungled by Cox and Frémont, the summer days were frittered away while the lieutenant colonel read *Ivanhoe, Waverley,* and *The Bride of Lammermoor.* Hayes was irritated at the inaction, anxious to be in a more active theater of war. An occasional party was sent back of enemy lines, and late in July, Hayes wrung reluctant permission from his superior, Colonel Scammon, to head a rescue of a Union family in Monroe County—one of those romantic but senseless enterprises that peppered the history of this war. The coup was successfully executed—"a pretty jolly expedition," wrote Hayes. Ten days later, when the rebels staged a party of their own, Hayes set out to cut them off: "I sent the band to give them music and told the men: 'Fighting battles is like courting girls: those who make the most pretensions and are boldest usually win.'" The enemy made off, a Union officer having burned the ferry which had been the enemy objective.

In the midst of these summer diversions Hayes's regiment with others was ordered east and eventually took part in the campaign which culminated at Antietam. The lieutenant colonel was very discouraged about the second battle of Manassas, in which he did not participate, his regiment, with others of Cox's division, being ordered to cover Alexandria in the event Lee's whole army should interpose between the capital and General Pope's army. Hayes thought the eastern soldiers were inferior to the western troops and that rebel generalship was superior to the Federal. It is curious to read how intensely proud this stanch Unionist was of his state. When he heard how gallantly the Ohio men had behaved at Bull Run bridge, he wrote: "Good. Honor of Ohio sustained. Eastern correspondents fail to tell the facts." Hayes was chafing for battle. At South Mountain, near Turners Pass, the men of the 23rd Ohio got their chance to prove Hayes's belief in their mettle.

The action at South Mountain was the prelude to Antietam. Immediately upon the defeat of Pope at Manassas, General Lee had determined upon a thrust into northern territory in the hope of drawing the Union army away from Virginia and of precipitating sentiments favorable to Confederate peace proposals. The Potomac was crossed at Leesburg, and the rebel army advanced to Frederick, Maryland, where it was in position to threaten both Baltimore and Washington. Embraced in Lee's strategy was an incursion into Pennsylvania, and to this end the maintenance of a line of communication in the

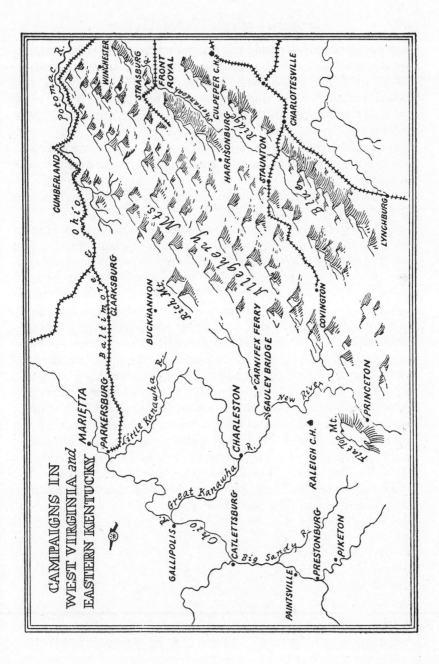

CAMPAIGNS IN WEST VIRGINIA and EASTERN KENTUCKY

Valley was essential. Stonewall Jackson was ordered to reduce
the Federal garrisons at Harpers Ferry and Martinsburg.
The rest of the Confederate army was withdrawn across South
Mountain, and by September 13 had, in part, reached Hagers-
town. Some of Stuart's cavalry guarded the South Mountain
passes.

In the meantime McClellan had been restored to command,
and although speed was of the essence the riposte against the
bold southern attack was conducted with his customary caution. Hayes's regiment had been sent out of Washington on
September 7 and moved into Frederick five days later, not
without considerable skirmishing. At that place a copy of Lee's
order fell into Union hands, but instead of instant advance to
save Harpers Ferry, twenty-four hours were dallied away.

On September 14 General Cox's division moved up South
Mountain with Hayes's brigade in advance. Hayes's regiment
was ordered to follow a mountain path and strike the enemy's
flank and take a battery on the crest. The 23rd moving
through the woods was not seen until it had passed over
the crest and had turned on the enemy's rear. There was a
sharp fight. Hayes ordered a charge, and the rebels gave way
but quickly re-formed. A second charge was ordered, and at
this moment Hayes was wounded in his left arm just above
the elbow. He continued to direct things until he was removed
back of the line. Prevented from seeing action at Antietam,
at which his regiment fought with honor, Hayes slowly re-
gained his old vigor. Years later the message sent from his
bed to Governor Tod was immortalized in a campaign ballad
(to the tune of "Auld Lang Syne"):

> "I'll be on hand again," said Hayes
> While bleeding on his bed,
> And proudly looked his wife her praise
> When "shortly" too he said.
> He'll shortly be "on hand again,"
> Columbia's well-tried son.
> His country ne'er called him in vain
> When work was to be done.

Promoted to be colonel of the 23rd, Hayes rejoined his regiment in West Virginia on November 30. The winter was spent near the falls of the Kanawha River, and here the command of a brigade devolved upon him. This was an interval almost idyllic. The regiments were snugly housed in log cabins; there was time for more novel reading, and things were peaceful enough for Mrs. Hayes to visit. In March, Hayes was ordered to garrison Charleston (West Virginia), where he established a camp opposite the town. Here life was scarcely more active than in the preceding months. There was an occasional raid to give the otherwise picnic existence a sort of Robin Hood flavor, but no operations of any consequence were undertaken. Then, in July 1863, came news of John Morgan's raid into Indiana and Ohio and an urgent request from General Cox in command of the Military District of Ohio to concentrate some troops at Gallipolis. General Scammon, Hayes's superior, had to be persuaded to co-operate, but finally two regiments, including a band, were embarked on steamers. It was, as Hayes wrote, the "liveliest and jolliest campaign we ever had." The steamers cruised the Ohio from point to point to be on hand to catch the raiders. Two hundred prisoners were captured. "It was nothing but fun"—except to the fifty Union casualties.

The river expedition was the last excitement for many months, for the fall and winter were spent in the monotony of garrison duty. Then, in the spring of 1864, Hayes participated in the West Virginia campaign which was part of Grant's grand strategy of simultaneous centered movement. The plan was for Sigel to move up the Shenandoah Valley while the West Virginia troops under General Crook advanced from the Kanawha, destroying railways and all useful military works. In this operation Hayes was in command of a brigade. Crook's army moved more or less according to schedule, but Grant's plan was thrown out of gear by the defeat of General Sigel. He was displaced by Hunter. The two armies joined at Staunton and, moving southward, reached Lynchburg. Here Hunter found it prudent to withdraw, and Crook's army returned to the Kanawha Valley.

After Early's famous raid which took him to the very gates of Washington, Grant decided to end incursions down the Valley and to destroy its value as a granary. On August 5, 1864, the pugnacious Sheridan took command. Hayes's brigade had reached the Valley in July at the time Early was retiring, and he had participated in a sharp action at Winchester, where the Federal troops were defeated.

For some weeks Sheridan moved with caution, as it was essential that any engagement be decisive, with the national elections in the offing. Finally, after consultation with Grant, the attack was made on September 19 at Opequon. Hayes's brigade took part in the attempt to turn Early's left, a movement which involved storming a strong position—the enemy was entrenched behind a stone wall, with his flank protected by a swamp. The operation was conducted successfully with a reckless daring.

In the next fight, at Fishers Hill, Crook's command again was set a task of turning the rebel left, on this occasion by climbing a mountain which Early had neglected to fortify. Upon Hayes's assurance that his men had been climbing mountains in West Virginia for three years and could climb anything, the turning tactics were decided upon. The victory had an amusing aftermath. Wrote Hayes:

There are five or six brigadier generals and one or two major generals sucking their thumbs in offices at Harpers Ferry and elsewhere who would like to get my command. One came out here yesterday to ask for it, but General Crook tells them he has all the commanders he wants and sends them back.

In the battle at Cedar Creek fought on October 19—an affair immortalized in the ballad, "Sheridan's Ride"—General Early, taking a leaf from the Union book, executed two brilliant flanking movements. Crook's division on the left received the first brunt of surprise, and in spite of all efforts to hold the troops the line gradually fell back. After a retreat of some four to five miles a stand was made. It was at this juncture that Sheridan arrived and with consummate skill turned defeat into victory. Hayes was badly thrown and stunned when his horse was shot. He was erroneously reported killed along with many other survivors. As Hayes remarked years later, "These reporters liked a good butcher's bill, you know."

Hayes's promotion to be brigadier general was made on the day after this battle. Crook's division was put into winter quarters at Cumberland, and the spring found Hayes back in West Virginia. A mountain expedition planned for him was made unnecessary by the capitulation at Appomattox, but on March 13, 1865, he was brevetted major general. His promotions had come slowly, but, as he wrote in 1886, he had never made any political efforts. This was a matter on which he displayed an integrity of character that was unusual. When he was nominated for Congress in 1864 he rebuffed attempts to draw him into electioneering with the gruff refusal, "Any officer fit for duty who at this crisis would abandon his post to electioneer for a seat in Congress ought to be scalped." His abstention from wire pulling to secure promotion was grounded as well on his aversion to office seeking as upon his consciousness that he lacked military education. Unlike so many of his contemporaries, he shrank from responsibilities for which he was not certain he was fitted lest the lives of his men should be imperiled if he should prove incapable. With engaging candor he wrote in his diary (1863), "I would rather be a good colonel than one of the poor generals."

Grant wrote of Hayes in his *Memoirs:* "His conduct on the field was marked by conspicuous gallantry as well as the display of qualities of a higher order than that of mere personal daring." Hayes's own estimate of his career was more modest. Greatly moved by Grant's commendation, he wrote (1886): "I may feel without undue personal vanity that although unknown as a general, I was one of the good colonels in the great army." We think Hayes was overmodest. As a good colonel he had so often commanded a brigade in action that he deserves as a brigadier general the credit he asked as colonel.

He lacked assertiveness, but he was a brave and doughty fighter. He was completely without nerves, and he never lost his head. Grant's estimate should stand.

II

There have been few Americans for whom opportunity knocked so often and in so many different guises as for James A. Garfield. When the Rebellion swept over the land, this son of Ohio was, at thirty, state senator; but he had already been successively schoolteacher, Campbellite preacher, principal of the Western Reserve Eclectic Academy, and, self-taught, had been admitted to the bar. Endowed with a vigorous, acquisitive intellect and a restless ambition, Garfield was a proponent of the American faith that out of books one can learn to do anything. Hence it was that on the day President Lincoln called for volunteers, the senator wrote his wife that he and Jacob Cox (later major general) "are spending all our leisure time reading military science and the campaigns of Napoleon and Wellington." Two days later he tendered his services to Governor Dennison for any position in the military organization of Ohio.

Garfield's friends thought he might at once be made brigadier, but the governor first sent him out recruiting and next to secure arms from the state of Illinois. The trip was fatal to his ambition to be elected colonel of the 7th Regiment. During his absence a rival, "by bargains and brandy," got an informal ballot by which he was elected, and triumphed again when the formal election took place upon Garfield's return. There is little doubt that Garfield sulked after this misadventure. Mere enlistment in the ranks by what he called men of character he regarded as demagogism, and as he nourished the conviction that he was qualified to be a staff officer, such a course would have been impossible. Indeed, his faith in his capacities was so firm that he declined a lieutenant colonelcy in June. Finally, however, in August, Garfield had a change of heart and accepted this rank in the 42nd Ohio. Within a few weeks he was commissioned colonel.

Except for tours spent recruiting, Garfield devoted four months to organizing, equipping, and drilling his regiment. These tasks he performed well, engaging the affections of his men. The 42nd was ordered into the field on December 14, 1861, as a part of General Buell's army and commanded to proceed to Prestonburg, in eastern Kentucky. A Confederate force had invaded the Big Sandy Valley and was entrenched at Paintsville, within striking distance of Ohio and interposing between the Union forces in central Kentucky and West Virginia. Buell proposed to push this force back and at the same time to send General Thomas against a larger rebel force to the west. The Eighteenth Brigade, organized for the Big Sandy expedition, was put under the command of Garfield.

It was characteristic of Garfield that after an interview with Buell he secured a map of the state and the census report and boned up on Kentucky. His problem well studied, he presented a plan. He proposed to move part of his force from central Kentucky toward the Valley and himself to proceed up the Big Sandy from Catlettsburg. Buell ordered Garfield to leave one regiment at Paris or Lexington to block the enemy and to take the main body of his force up the Big Sandy. Why Buell saw fit to entrust a brigade to a man whose military training consisted of four months' intermittent drill and whose adversary was a West Pointer with Mexican War experience, remains a mystery.

The campaign was a very minor affair, but, conducted in the dead of winter in difficult country with soldiers for the most part undisciplined, it presented its hardships. The Confederate general Marshall withdrew from his entrenchments to a stronger position. On January 10, 1862, the two forces engaged. Garfield relates that "for the sake of bravado" he ordered a battalion drill in the face of the enemy, but apparently he actually was compelled to throw forward several detachments to draw the enemy's fire in order to discover Marshall's exact position. Fortunately the Confederate troops were as green as the Federals. The ensuing action was typical of the amateur slugging matches which characterized the first year of the Rebellion. The two forces blazed away at each other for hours without inflicting many casualties, and finally at sunset the Confederates withdrew. Prestonburg was occupied, but Garfield, finding he could not supply his command, moved back to Paintsville. Subsequently on Buell's order he advanced to Piketon, and presently the Confederate force retreated out of the state.

Garfield exhibited vigor and personal bravery in his campaign, but he had acted with considerable recklessness. Years later he admitted lack of prudence, but at the moment he celebrated with a proclamation to his brigade in the style of Old Hickory's rodomontades. A great deal of praise came his way, including felicitations from General McClellan. The Ohio politicians, glued to the notion that Ohio must lead in the war, were able to conjure for him a promotion to a brigadier generalship.

On March 19, 1862, the Eighteenth Brigade was ordered out of the Big Sandy Valley and was turned over to General Morgan. Garfield was ordered to report to Buell at Nashville. He was given command of another brigade and within a few days was hurrying with the rest of Buell's army to reinforce General Grant. He arrived at Shiloh on the second day of the battle, but was not ordered to the extreme front until evening. By this time the battle was over. Garfield had tasted glory in the Big Sandy Valley, but at Shiloh, awaiting the call to action amid the carnage of hard combat, he was harrowed by the knowledge that renown has also a bitter, bloody cost.

There was further disillusionment in store for him. When Halleck took command and, fired by extraordinary caution, began a siegelike advance with pick and shovel, Garfield acquired a rage against professional soldiers and in particular a contempt for the strategic capacities of his commander. His duties were largely routine, and their execution was not rendered easy by the fact that he became ill of camp fever, so ill, indeed, that on July 30 he was relieved of his command

and given leave of absence to recuperate. It was during this fur-
lough that Garfield was nominated by his district for Congress
and was later elected. In September he left for Washington
in quest of a new military assignment.

This was an extraordinary interlude. In Washington he lived
at Secretary Chase's house for a space and with the help of
that talented politician probed the possibilities of future command. At this moment the professional soldiers were under a
cloud. Chase, Stanton, and other crossroads Clausewitzes were
cooking a variety of bizarre schemes, in at least one of which,
an expedition to Charleston, S. C., Garfield was promised a
part. In November, however, he was appointed to the court
of inquiry on General Fitz-John Porter, and when this was
reconstituted as a general court-martial, sat for long weeks
hearing testimony and arguments. To improve his leisure and
occupy his restless intellect, Garfield began a study of Frederick the Great's campaigns and set about to make a translation of the celebrated *Secret Instructions*. Finally, in January
1863, came an assignment to duty in the Army of the Cumberland under Major General Rosecrans.

When Garfield reached headquarters near Murfreesboro,
Tennessee, the army was recuperating from the bloody Stone
River campaign. Rosecrans was charmed with his new brigadier. He took him to his heart and for nights sat up into the
small hours debating religious problems. The war had few
moments more whimsical than this protracted debate between
the former Campbellite preacher and the devout convert to
Roman Catholicism who habitually purged his cursing of all
reference to the Deity. Much to Garfield's chagrin, this inti-
macy did not lead to the expected command of a division. Instead Rosecrans appointed him chief of staff. There were advantages in having a congressman-elect on hand who could
also give light should some ticklish question of Biblical exegesis
pop into the commander's head.

It seemed a happy chance that put Garfield on the staff, for
his study of Frederick must have given him a much better notion of what staff work consisted in than most citizen officers

possessed. Rosecrans has been rated one of the able strategists of the war, but earlier, at Iuka, he had bungled because of poor staff work, and with the problems he was presently facing it was essential that such errors be avoided. Garfield was worried that he would be only a sort of superior clerk, and he set himself the task of becoming Rosecrans' *alter ego.*

The practice during the Civil War was for the chief of staff to concern himself with matters pertaining to operations. But as Garfield discharged his office it appears that he also occupied himself with intelligence, although it is not clear exactly what his responsibilities were in this particular. He also collated reports from brigade and divisional commanders and managed the correspondence with Rosecrans' superiors. It does not appear that there was any apportionment of staff functions in the Army of the Cumberland, for on one occasion Garfield writes of having "the entire burden of getting up and fitting out the expedition of Col. Streight"—a raid against Confederate communications.

Rosecrans was an inveterate procrastinator, for, trained as an engineer, he was unwilling to move until there was grease in every cup. Although it was imperative that General Bragg, whose army Rosecrans was opposing, should not detach any troops to relieve beleaguered Vicksburg, the commander of the Army of the Cumberland did not budge. Early in June the situation at headquarters seems to have become tense, for Rosecrans resorted to the hallowed American questionnaire by which an opinion on the wisdom of an advance was sought from all corps, division, and cavalry commanders. The answer was a unanimous no. This did not suit the restless and chafing Garfield. He prepared a report collating and analyzing the generals' answers to the several questions, and proceeded to set out an estimate of the enemy's strength based upon the latest advices. The report concluded with a summary of the arguments, military, economic, and political, why instant action should be taken. This document possesses interest as an exhibit on Garfield's activity as chief of staff. It was later used by Whitelaw Reid as proof of his military flair. Whatever may have been Rosecrans' reaction, twelve days elapsed after he had received the report before "Old Rosy" finally succumbed to the pleas of the War Department and the Army of the Cumberland was set in motion.

The succeeding operations which drove Bragg out of central Tennessee consumed eleven days and are known as the Tullahoma campaign. The strategy consisted in feigning in the front and on the right of Bragg and moving with speed against his left. The plan of encirclement failed owing chiefly to inclement weather. Bragg withdrew out of Tullahoma and retreated over the Tennessee River at Bridgeport. The pursuit was ordered halted on July 4, the very day Vicksburg surrendered.

There ensued a second interval of dally. The defenders of Rosecrans have justified this course by reference to the urgency of rebuilding bridges and repairing the railroad to keep intact communications with Nashville, the main depot of the army, and to the necessity of carefully scouting the difficult mountainous terrain which barred the way to further advance. Communications were operating by July 18, and from then on Garfield bent every effort to energize his deliberate commander. The War Department was in a very sweat of impatience, fearing that Johnston would reinforce Bragg. On July 24 Halleck telegraphed Rosecrans to "push forward rapidly" and, for meat and forage, to live off the country. In view of the fact that the country ahead was poor and that the comb of the rebel army had just been run through it, the advice was ill-considered. Subsequent urgent communications indicate beyond a peradventure that Halleck was blissfully ignorant of what the mountain region was like.

While these pourparlers were in train, Garfield, unable to restrain his impatience, wrote to his friend Secretary Chase expressing his concern over the delays, intimating a lack of strength in Rosecrans, and stating, "I feel that the time has come when it [the War Department] should allow no plea to keep this army back from the most vigorous activity." Even if Garfield had not felt restrained by considerations of military discipline, the personal affection which he ardently professed and a sense of loyalty to his superior should have stayed his hand. It is a significant commentary on the desuetude of old virtues that years later Jacob D. Cox, himself a political general, found justification in Garfield's duty to the Administration as a congressman-elect.

On August 5 Halleck telegraphed that the orders for advance were peremptory, but it was not until August 16 that the general advance got under way. The strategy projected was roughly similar to that of the Tullahoma campaign, and for it Garfield claimed some credit. As he wrote his wife, "There is so much of myself in this campaign that I must help to realize my ideas." The plan called for vigorous demonstrations along the Tennessee River above Chattanooga, where Bragg was lodged, while the bulk of the army crossed at points ranging from twenty to forty miles below and then moved eastward and northeastward.

Bragg was completely deceived, for he analyzed the Union objective to be an attempt to catch him between Rosecrans and Burnside, whose army was moving on Knoxville. He evacuated Chattanooga on September 8 and withdrew toward Lafayette. Rosecrans, conceiving that the rebels had retreated to the east along the line of the railroad into Georgia, ordered a general pursuit, each of his three corps proceeding eastward along independent routes spread out over some sixty miles. The actual location of Bragg's army did not develop until Thomas' corps made contact. Bragg was then in a position to strike at will and to defeat Rosecrans' army in detail. Unfortunately for him he was perplexed by the dispersion of the Union forces and, as Confederate General D. H. Hill put it, "bewildered by 'the popping out of the rats from so many holes.'"

For the Army of the Cumberland, unaware of Bragg's irresolution, the situation was fraught with peril. It became, as Rosecrans reported, a matter of life and death to effect a concentration. This was accomplished, but at the cost of having better than a third of the troops exhausted with marching before the enemy was engaged. It is difficult to disagree with

General W. F. Smith that the battle at Chickamauga was brought about by Bragg's "forcing a concentration at an unexpected time and place and was not the result of a legitimate campaign conducted on proper military principles."

From the start Rosecrans conceived of the impending engagement as a defensive battle. His concentration had been effected south of Chattanooga on the west side of Chickamauga Creek. At the back of the Union army lay Missionary Ridge. The valley was hilly, forested, and relieved by only a few rough clearings. General Gordon Granger was posted with the reserve at Rossville Gap, through which the state road ran to Chattanooga. The main body of the army lay some eleven miles south of that city when Bragg launched his main attack on September 19. During this first day of battle the struggle continued without advantage, and by nightfall the tactical situation was substantially unaltered. Rosecrans improved the hours of darkness to settle on a readjustment of his lines, arranging them so as to cover the road to Rossville and the Dry Valley Road, which led through a gap in the ridge immediately in his rear. The Union divisions established from left to right were Baird, Johnson, Palmer, Reynolds, Brannan, Negley, Davis, and Sheridan. Van Cleve and Wood were in general reserve near the center.

Early on the morning of September 20 General Thomas, in command on the Union left, where the brunt of Confederate attack was expected, requested support from General Negley's division. This was ordered, and General McCook was directed to fill the space left by this shift, "if practicable." McCook ignored the order, and Negley, not being relieved, failed to move.

As had been anticipated, a terrific attack fell upon Thomas, who had taken the precaution of putting up some rude works of rails and logs. It was discovered that Negley had not moved, but by this time Rosecrans permitted only one of his brigades to leave. Subsequently the rest of Negley's division was sent to the left, but, confused by the topography, finally took position to the rear and right of Thomas, where they could do

no good. General Thomas, concerned at the failure of reinforcement, repeated his requests. Two aides arrived at headquarters in close succession and were assured that Negley had
been sent, that General Brannan's reserve brigade was available, and that Van Cleve would also be sent. Then, shortly
before eleven o'clock, another of Thomas' aides arrived with
news that he was hard pressed, and adding that Brannan was
out of line and Reynolds exposed. This was incorrect. General
Wood, who had taken Negley's place in line, was ordered to
fill a non-existent gap, and in executing this unnecessary order
himself left a gap between the Union center and right, of
which Longstreet took instant and terrible advantage. The
Union right was broken and, after desperate efforts to reorganize, Rosecrans and his staff, unable to make through to
Thomas, rode off for Chattanooga on the Dry Valley Road.

The events of this ride have been disputed. There is reliable
testimony that Rosecrans wished to rejoin Thomas and send
Garfield into the city to attend to its defense, but that the
latter was unwilling to assume this responsibility. It was finally
agreed that Garfield should attempt to reach Thomas via the
Rossville road and direct him to retire to Rossville at night.

In the meantime and at about the moment of crisis, General
Granger, "great in battle" and reputedly of an insubordinate
temper, had become anxious. In despite of his orders, he set
forth with Steedman's command and at one o'clock came up
with Thomas. There, on a spur of Missionary Ridge where
the Union lines had been reformed, the battle raged on with
unabated fury. There Garfield arrived to find the remnant of
the Army of the Cumberland holding their own against the
overwhelming force of rebels closing in for the kill. There
Thomas with his valiant men fought out the drama of blood
and death and made the "Rock of Chickamauga" a name immortal among warriors.

At nightfall, obedient to an order from Rosecrans that
Thomas held to be mandatory, the indomitable and shattered
regiments withdrew. Their ammunition was spent, but the last
guns to roar into the night were the guns of the Union.

There was no battle more sanguinary in this war, and none over which dispute has raged more hotly among the survivors on both sides. The orders of that fateful September 20 and the records of the courts of inquiry leave one in little doubt that staff organization was faulty. This is apparent not only from the confusion of orders, but from the miserable liaison between headquarters and the corps commanders. Thomas wanted a division on his left, and he kept repeating his request. Headquarters kept dispatching brigade after brigade, weakening the Union right, and so ignorant of what had happened to the reinforcements that Rosecrans apparently concluded that Bragg was interposing between Thomas' left and Chattanooga. In a most difficult terrain unfamiliar to the divisional and brigade commanders, certain vital orders lacked directional explicitness. When Longstreet attacked, the disorganization and panic was increased because it fell upon divisions in the process of moving toward Thomas' left. As chief of staff, Garfield must bear some responsibility for the fact that he had not perfected the machinery of transmitting and checking orders. But the blame cannot all be his. Clearly, too, Rosecrans under the stress of excitement acted without reference to his chief of staff. The fatal order to General Wood, Rosecrans dictated to his own aide, and the explanation which would have left Wood some discretion was called out verbally by Garfield when it should have been written. Wood naturally took the order to be peremptory.

Garfield remained at Chattanooga until October 10, when he was relieved of duty. He proceeded to Washington and received there his final military honor—major general of Volunteers. Shortly thereafter he resigned to enter upon his duties in Congress.

It is not easy to gauge exactly Garfield's merits as a general officer. Of his bravery and assiduity there is no doubt; of his capacity for command the evidence is limited to the excursion in the Big Sandy Valley. What can be written to his credit during the months he served as Rosecrans' chief of staff is conjectural, for there is no means of determining Garfield's share in the shower of orders which bear his signature. He was disposed to an optimistic estimate of his contribution, but in the end it was the experienced Rosecrans who took the blame and he did not off-shoulder it to his chief of staff.

The ultimate and indispensable resource of the good officer, the quality of steadfastness, Garfield did not possess. This defect he disclosed by his act in writing to Secretary Chase about the shortcomings of Rosecrans, a deed far from true-hearted. He exhibited this trait again when he resigned his commission to enter Congress. This was a moment when the Union needed soldiers and not speakers.

III

The adventurous humor which coursed in the veins of the Harrisons brought the first of them to Virginia, made a Revolutionary patriot of another, and carried William Henry to the wilds of the Northwest Territory, was still warm in the blood of the grandson of Old Tippecanoe. Born in 1833 at North Bend, Ohio, Benjamin Harrison, while yet a student in a law office, married at twenty. Within six months the couple moved to Indianapolis, where Harrison began the practice of the law. His total capital is reported to have been eight hundred dollars, and his single acquaintance in the Indiana capital was the clerk of the United States District Court. On this slight foundation, from which the cosseted youth of today would shrink with foreboding, Benjamin Harrison built himself a career.

By 1860 Harrison had so far advanced in his profession and political affiliations that he was nominated as Republican candidate for reporter of the Supreme Court, and he triumphed with the rest of the party ticket in Indiana. Harrison does not appear to have had the "holy war" fever, and it was not until the summer of 1862, after Lincoln had requested additional troops from the loyal states, that he acted. A raid of the Confederate, John H. Morgan, into Kentucky had quickened both the interest and anxiety of the Indianians. Morgan had only a small force, but he moved swiftly and effectively, taking post after post on the Louisville & Nashville Railroad. His boast that he was the advance guard of a large army struck terror on both banks of the Ohio. In the midst of this raid, on July 12, 1862, a monster patriotic meeting was held in Indianapolis at which Harrison spoke. He had previously offered his services to Governor Morton and on this occasion made dramatic his call for troops by publicly volunteering as a private. Shortly thereafter Morton commissioned him second lieutenant. Harrison devoted great energy to recruiting, and when the 70th Indiana Regiment was finally complete he was commissioned colonel.

Throughout his adult life Harrison was pre-eminently the lawyer. As he knew nothing about matters military, it was characteristic that he should engage a drillmaster, exactly as if he were retaining co-counsel in a case on a branch of the law in which he was not expert. When the regiment marched off for Kentucky, on August 13, 1862, the Indianapolis *Journal* was to comment favorably: "The marching was admirably performed for a regiment scarcely ten days old, and if it can have a week or two of instruction before engaging actively in the field it will have acquired a proficiency in drill that will have prepared it for almost any emergency." Colonel Harrison was to take these words to heart.

Meantime the situation across the Ohio River was moving toward a crisis. The Confederate generals Bragg and Kirby Smith had concerted a strategy for the reduction of Kentucky. The former was to clear middle Tennessee and move toward the heart of Kentucky while Kirby Smith was to march from Knoxville through a region where no opposition could be expected. On the day the 70th Indiana set out for war Kirby Smith began his march. In this emergency Harrison's sketchily trained regiment was dispatched to Bowling Green, Kentucky, and was stationed there and along the line of the Louisville & Nashville Railroad, so vital to Union communications. Unexpectedly Bragg, sweeping up from Chattanooga, by-passed Nashville and Bowling Green and reached Bardstown, a bare

fifty miles from the Ohio. It was at this juncture that the 70th
Indiana, in the backwater at Bowling Green, had its first experience with fighting. A raid was made upon near-by Rus-
sellville, where a small force of rebels was encamped. This
assignment, which involved repairing a railroad bridge, was
briskly executed. Fifty rebels were killed or wounded and ten
prisoners taken. The expedition next went to Glasgow and
captured ten more prisoners.

The threat to Kentucky was terminated by Bragg's defeat
at Perryville on October 8. Five days later he was in full retreat. Harrison's regiment spent the winter guarding the
Louisville & Nashville Railroad between Nashville and Galla-
tin. This tour of duty was enlivened by repelling raids and
chasing bushwhackers, and dulled by constant drill. Harrison
is said to have incurred dislike because of his emphasis upon
proper training, and later his campaign biographers were at
pains to collect statements proving the attachment of the
privates to their colonel. The fact remains that he produced
a well-disciplined military instrument that earned the praise
of no less a soldier than Fighting Joe Hooker. Harrison was
equally intent upon instructing himself in the military art.
The most amusing and characteristic tale of this winter concerns the evening "chalk-talks" held by Colonel Harrison, at
which he sought to teach and test his officers in the mysteries
of tactics. This was one war where the lawyer, trained to
careful preparation for trial, gave the lie to the chaffers who
doubt his military usefulness.

Harrison's regiment, which had been brigaded with one
Ohio and three Illinois regiments under the command of
General W. T. Ward, was next attached to Granger's corps,
which constituted Rosecrans' reserve in the Army of the Cumberland. When the march on Chattanooga was begun that
terminated so dismally at Chickamauga, this brigade was sent
to Nashville and detailed to the protection of the trains carrying supplies from this base. This was a dangerous and exciting
duty, for that incomparable railroad wrecker, Forrest, with
his awesome cavalry, was operating with Bragg's army. But

the hazards were cheerfully described by one of Harrison's men: "We take frequent excursions at reduced rates over the Chattanooga Railroad, occupying the upper berth on the out- side to keep the brakemen from getting lonely."

It was not until the opening of the year 1864 that Ward's command was called to the front. In the course of the organi- zation of the great force for Sherman's campaign into Georgia, embracing the three armies—Cumberland, Tennessee, and Ohio—Ward's brigade was incorporated in the Twentieth Corps of the Army of the Cumberland. This corps was com- manded by General Hooker.

General Grant had communicated his plans to Sherman in early April, and the movement against Joseph Johnston's army, which was concentrated at Dalton, Georgia, began on May 5. Sherman opened the campaign with 100,000 men; Johnston had an army variously estimated at from 43,000 to 60,000. The theater of operations was a very difficult one, mountainous, virtually unmapped, and strongly favoring the defense. The plan was for Thomas in the center and Schofield on the left to hold Johnston to his fortification while McPher- son was to move through Snake Creek Gap and cut behind the rebel army, hitting Resaca, on the railroad fifteen miles south of Dalton.

McPherson found the Gap undefended, but moved with such caution against Resaca that Johnston had time to send in three divisions. Two days passed with no movement of consequence. Finally Sherman pushed his main forces through Snake Creek Gap. Simultaneously Johnston evacuated Dalton and moved into Resaca. Here the position chosen was strong—a creek and swamp in front and fortified hills north and west of the town. During the first day of battle, on May 14, 1864, the Twentieth Corps remained in reserve, except for one brigade. But on the next morning orders contemplated that the principal attack should be made by the Twentieth against the entrench- ments in the hills on the enemy right. The assault was carried out through thick woods. The first line of works was carried, but it was commanded by a hill overlooking that already captured. Colonel Harrison's troops finally gained a position so that an entrenched battery of the enemy was silenced by his sharpshooters.

Harrison exhibited great personal bravery and coolness under fire. He had acted with resolution, and his troops were the only ones of the brigade to gain their objective. That day General Ward was wounded, and the command of the brigade devolved upon Harrison.

Johnston succeeded in effecting a complete and miraculous withdrawal during the night, and thenceforward ensued the slow retreat of the Confederates along the line of the railroad, ably flanked out of every position by Sherman, with Johnston no less skillfully extricating himself from each threatened envelopment. Week after week the struggle continued. The incessant nature of the combat is indicated by the fact that the average daily expenditure of munitions by the Army of the Cumberland alone during May and June was two hundred thousand rounds of musketry and twelve hundred cannon shot. The difficulties of movement can be imagined from the fact that in June there were nineteen days of almost unceasing rain. Harrison participated in the fights at Cassville, New Hope Church, and Golgotha, and in all of them he acquitted himself well.

Johnston withdrew from his position on Kenesaw Mountain, which Sherman recklessly and vainly attempted to carry by assault. The Confederate plans to make a stand on the Chattahoochie River were abandoned when the Army of the Tennessee effected an undisputed crossing, and consequently a new line was selected on the high ground south of Peach Tree Creek on the outskirts of Atlanta. Johnston, who now commanded about seventy thousand men, states that he was planning to attack Sherman. But on July 17 he was relieved and command given to General Hood. Two days later Sherman moved five divisions over the Creek, and on July 21 Hood attacked. Four divisions of the Army of the Cumberland received the onslaught of two corps. Colonel Harrison seized a hill considerably in advance of the main line just as the enemy

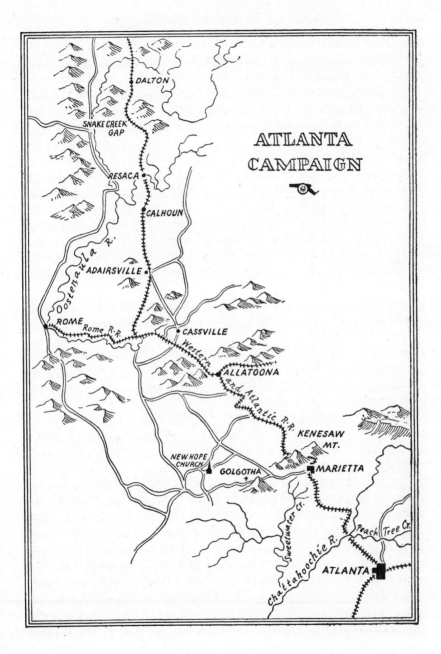

ATLANTA
CAMPAIGN

began to advance. This move broke up the consecutiveness of the rebel assault, and from this salient was made the final charge as the Confederates began their retreat. Harrison's boldness did not pass unnoticed. The story is told that Hooker swore, "By God, I'll make you a brigadier general for this fight." But months were to elapse before the promotion was finally made.

During the siege of Atlanta, Harrison's brigade was ordered to hold the bridgeheads on the Chattahoochie River, and it was stationed there when the city fell September 2, 1865. Three days later Secretary Stanton telegraphed General Sherman suggesting that in view of the armed organization against the Union in Indiana, it was expedient that Harrison and certain other Indiana officers be sent home. This had reference to the treasonable activities of the "Sons of Liberty," at that moment convulsing the state. Since prominent Democrats were implicated and since the state elections were only a month away, Governor Morton had pleaded that Indiana troops be given furloughs to come home. The politicians had broached this matter early in August. At that time Sherman had bluntly refused any furloughs and characteristically had suggested to Schuyler Colfax that if the President used the conscription law freely, "he can checkmate the Copperheads who are not in favor of being governed by Jeff Davis but are afraid to go to war." With the surrender of Atlanta, Sherman's mood softened. Logan was released to Illinois, Blair to Missouri, and Harrison to Indiana.

Harrison remained in Indiana until after the national election in November. He was unable to rejoin his brigade, for when Sherman cut loose from his communications on his march across Georgia the railroads fell into Confederate hands. In consequence Colonel Harrison was put in command of a brigade in the so-called Provisional Division of General Thomas' army defending Tennessee against Hood. Harrison began organizing this force on November 20 at Chattanooga. It was composed of veterans recovering from wounds and some recruits. Harrison reported that he had about a thousand men under him, a large number of whom were foreigners who could not speak English. This "brigade" was ordered to Nashville on November 29 and when it reached there was occupied chiefly in the work of making entrenchments. It formed part of the reserve in the battle of Nashville (December 4), at which Hood's army was smashed.

Although Harrison's force did not get into the fighting on December 4, it saw plenty of service during the next weeks in the pursuit of the shattered Confederate host. Specifically, the brigade was engaged in maneuvers to trap Lyon's troops in northern Alabama. The report of these operations gives a vivid picture of their miseries. Harrison concluded his account:

> The campaign though not characterized by much fighting was one of unusual severity and hardship, and considering the character of the men composing the command certainly much more was accomplished and endured by it than could in reason have been expected. The officers were utterly without baggage and often without blankets and several times without rations.

Fifty-one winters earlier, Jackson had campaigned in these environs to make the land safe for the white man. The ghosts of the old Creek prophets must have grinned sardonically at the chase in their old hunting grounds.

After the recall of the Union column Harrison was ordered to join Sherman at Savannah. Unfortunately he contracted scarlet fever, and it was not until April that he finally again took command of his old brigade at Goldsboro, North Carolina. The well-deserved promotion to brevet brigadier general had come in February 1865. General Cruft had recommended Harrison with others on the ground that he had been a brigade commander of experience and reputation in the Army. The finest encomium had already been written months before by Major General Hooker:

> My attention was first attracted to this young officer by the superior excellence of his brigade in discipline and instruction, the result of his labor, skill and devotion. With more foresight than I have witnessed in any officer of his experience he seemed to act upon the principle

that success depended upon the thorough preparation in the discipline and esprit of his command for conflict more than any influence that could be exerted on the field itself, and when the collision came his command vindicated his wisdom as much as his valor.

The record bears out these words of praise. Harrison had proved that he possessed his grandfather's courage, and he demonstrated that he was fundamentally a better soldier, for he possessed a talent for discipline, a care for detail, and an imperviousness to political advantage that the hero of Tippecanoe never achieved. His grasp of tactics was exhibited at Resaca and Peach Tree Creek, and likewise a capacity to make bold decisions. If his assignments had carried him sooner into the larger combat area, he might have attained a greater military fame.

From a story told in the regimental history of the 70th Indiana we catch some insight into the nature of this man. Harrison's lieutenant colonel, James Burgess, was as easygoing as the colonel was strict. The men resolved to purchase a sword for Burgess and by one stroke compliment their favorite and score off the martinet. At the presentation ceremony Burgess' embarrassment was such that he was unable to utter a word. The soldiers, who loved a speech "better than pie," shouted for Harrison. Colonel Harrison, fully aware of what the men had been up to, arose and delivered a thrilling oration on the war and the soldier's duty. It was always the cause which captivated Harrison. When he dedicated himself to a task, he became indifferent to opinion. The righteous doing of a righteous deed was sufficient.

IV

The close of Grant's administrations marked the end of an era. The inauguration of his successor, Rutherford B. Hayes, signalized the advent of a new America striding on to the future. The clamor over new problems—monopolies, labor agitation, and agrarian unrest—was to mute the cacophony of the Civil War and Reconstruction. The Republican party was still to "wave the bloody shirt," generals were still to be chosen as candidates, and the fading glory of bygone battles was still to garnish the civil record. Old hatreds were too useful a weapon to be cast aside when a campaign was to be won, but the fervors of past idealisms were no longer to dominate party councils. Captains of industry were to take the lead and new faiths to supplant the old. The gospel of wealth was spreading, and the gaudy extravagances of a decade of hyperbole were to pale with passing years into the soberer preoccupations of a rich respectability. It is no coincidence that the philosophy of pragmatism had its origin in the post-Centennial period, the bridge from the days of Reconstruction to modern industrial America.

In the years 1876–88, three Union generals were elected to the presidency. Unlike Grant, these men were citizen soldiers, and to civilian life they returned at the close of the war. Nor was any one of these men swept to the presidency by a spontaneous wave of popular enthusiasm for a hero. Other considerations dictated their selection. If they rose on the shoulders of the past, they faced forward; as the years passed, the military title retained significance chiefly as a badge of patriotism, a riband on the coat of a political career, but to veterans it remained unfaded and it still possessed its appeal.

First of these men was Major General Rutherford B. Hayes, Republican candidate in the disputed election of 1876. Following the Civil War, Hayes had served two terms as a member of Congress and had rapidly become a leading figure in Ohio politics. Reputedly a man of personal integrity, he had made an excellent record as governor of Ohio, an office to which he had been elected three times in the decade following Appomattox. Victor at the Republican convention in 1876 over the "plumed knight" James G. Blaine, his nomination was both a compromise between the Blaine and Conkling factions and a concession to the public's disgust with the prevalent political corruption. As governor, Hayes had shown adminis-

trative ability and political courage, and—*mirabile dictu*—in
the year 1876 his name was unsmirched by even a hint of
scandal.

His candidacy was, therefore, acclaimed by the liberals
while his record as a regular party man, faithful to Grant in
1872, made him not too unpalatable to Senator Conkling,
leader of the Stalwarts. Carl Schurz, one of the prime movers
in the Liberal Republican split four years before, returned to
the party fold and rallied the reformers to Hayes's support;
while old Zachariah Chandler, unregenerate believer in the
efficacy of a judicious distribution of campaign funds, served
as chairman of the Republican National Committee and directed the campaign. The discords of 1872 were thus happily
dissolved. "His chief excellence," wrote one of Hayes's supporters, "is in his intuitive perception of what at the moment
is practicably attainable." It was a quality that was to be
severely tested.

The Democratic nominee, Samuel Tilden, ex-governor of
New York, was a lawyer of intellectual pre-eminence, and in
his early career he had shown himself a master of practical
politics. He was justly renowned for his work first against
Boss Tweed in New York City and his later attack upon the
"canal ring" of his state. The Democratic campaign was
focused on the scandals of the Grant administration and on the
radical southern policy. The Republicans, as was to be expected,
endorsed Grant's stand on Reconstruction, sound money, and
the tariff, and as a sop to the Liberal Republican dissenters of
1872 made much of the platform's civil-service-reform plank.
The familiar charges against the Democrats as the party of
treason and rebellion were reiterated; of the validity of this
issue, Hayes, the ex-general, was firmly convinced. In fact the
campaign followed the well-marked grooves of orthodox
issues, orthodox methods. Only the outcome was unprecedented.

The story of the disputed election of 1876 is too well known
to need recapitulation. As a result of the vote cast on November 7, the electoral returns showed 184 votes for Tilden,
163 for Hayes, with four states in the balance—Florida,

South Carolina, Louisiana, and Oregon. The Oregon vote hinged on a technicality and was rightfully Republican; but in each of the southern states the validity of the returns was dependent upon the legality of a carpetbagger regime. Not even the presence of Federal troops had prevented fraud and violence in the elections. In South Carolina and Louisiana rival groups, Republican and Democrat, claimed the state elections and concomitantly the presidential electoral vote.

For weeks tension rose as the two parties battled over the problem of the disputed returns; civil war even was feared. Compromise was essential and compromise was found. The Electoral Commission, set up by a distracted Congress, validated the Republican claim to the twenty-two contested votes. As a *douceur* realistic Republican politicians gave "assurances" regarding the restoration of the state governments to the s uthern whites. With a narrow margin of one electoral vote, Hayes was peacefully inaugurated; in April 1877 all Federal troops were withdrawn from the South. Home rule was won, and the Solid South rose from the ruins of the carpetbagger empire. Contemporaries and posterity alike were to puzzle over the vagaries of the southerners, who had, presumably, voted a Republican President in and simultaneously voted Republican state administrations out, but the peace of the country was secured. The election, having brought the country to the verge of crisis, had acted as a catalytic agent on public opinion. Hayes was committed to a policy of conciliation toward the South; congressional reconstruction was tacitly abandoned.

It was symbolic of the coming era that, three months after the withdrawal of the troops from the southern states, the Army was to be employed to protect property and preserve order threatened by the great railroad strikes of 1877. In July of that year Federal troops were poured into Maryland, West Virginia, Pennsylvania, and the Middle West, where railroad workers, infuriated by a ten per cent wage cut, had seized roundhouses and railroad stations, paralyzing all freight traffic. "The whirligig of Time brings its revenges"; years

were to pass before the Federal Government would again
challenge state infringement of the freedman's franchise.

Hayes's administration was a troubled period of party and
factional conflict. Within his own party he soon faced a bitter
opposition that verged on open rebellion. "He serves his party
best who serves the country best," he declared in his inaugural
address, and the phrase, if sententious, was significant. Although the President was a zealous Republican, he was to display considerable independence and on many points refuse to
subordinate policy to party. In the selection of his Cabinet he
failed to consult or show favor either to James G. Blaine or to
Roscoe Conkling, the two acknowledged leaders of the party.
The inclusion of David M. Key, an ex-Confederate soldier
and Democrat, as Postmaster General added to the wrath of
old Radicals, resentful of his declared policy of conciliation
toward the South. Hayes's championship of civil-service reform was bound to alienate the Stalwarts, and the appointment of Carl Schurz as Secretary of the Interior was a bitter
pill to the spoilsmen. In June 1877 the President's executive
orders forbidding the assessment of Federal employees for
campaign funds and prohibiting party work by officeholders
shocked stanch party men. Reform, Conkling had sneered,
paraphrasing Samuel Johnson, "is the last refuge of the scoundrel." The confidence of even the moderates was shaken. "I
am inclined to believe that his election has been an almost fatal
blow to the party," wrote James Garfield sadly within a year
of Hayes's inauguration.

In the fall of 1877 Hayes opened battle against senatorial
control of the patronage. Without warning, Senator Roscoe
Conkling's lieutenant, Chester Arthur, collector of the Port
of New York, and Lorenzo Cornell, naval officer of the New
York customhouse, were asked to resign and new nominations
sent to the Senate. The administration of the New York customhouse had been notoriously corrupt, but Hayes's action was in
direct contravention of the principle of senatorial courtesy and
was an open defiance of the New York machine. Defeated in
this move by the Senate's refusal to confirm his own nominees

to these offices, Hayes bided his time. ". . . The end is not yet," he wrote in his diary. "I am right, and shall not give up the contest." Nor did he. Following further investigation of the customhouse that clinched the charges of corruption, in the summer of 1878 the President suspended the two officers in question. The following January he sent a strong message to the Senate in justification of his action. This time Hayes won. His nominees were confirmed, despite the fury of the New York senators. It was Hayes's most significant victory for the cause of reform.

At the same time the President's support of the civil-service movement fell short of the expectations of the liberals. The forty-three loyal Republican members of the notorious Louisiana Returning Board who had given their votes for Hayes (and two months later, as a result of the withdrawal of the Federal troops, been deprived of their state perquisites) were almost all appointed to Federal offices and safely lodged under the Republican umbrella. The Treasury under John Sherman and the Post Office (guided by First Assistant Postmaster Tyner) remained two strongholds of party patronage. The executive orders against party levies were admittedly not enforced and, despite the drama of the conflict with Conkling, congressional control of the spoils was not ended. J. D. Cox lamented in 1878 that ". . . the President had utterly failed to accomplish anything in the way of civil service reform," and the New York *Nation,* self-appointed keeper of the people's conscience, excoriated Hayes's concessions to the politicians. "Only one battle can be fought at a time," Hayes wrote in later years in extenuation of his lack of a thorough reform policy. The "burning question" of his administration, he affirmed, had been the financial problem, a revival of the inflation movement. To win victory on this front he had sacrificed principle. In his compromise between the demands of spoilsmen and reformers he had pursued a practicable policy.

In addition to the opposition of Republican factions, Hayes was harried by Democratic obstructionists. Southern Democrats had been partially appeased by the President's conciliation policy. Northern Democrats (men "invincible in peace and invisible in war," as a southern colleague remarked) remained unreconciled to the election of 1876. Mocking at "His Fraudulency," the Democrats made an abortive attempt to investigate the election and invalidate Hayes's title to office. After the Democratic tidal wave of the congressional elections of 1878, Hayes was confronted by a hostile majority in both houses of Congress. The result was two years of long-drawn-out struggle between the executive and legislative branches of government. Throughout this conflict Hayes stood firm against what he deemed a misuse of congressional power and against open attack on the powers of the national government. During the spring of 1879 the Democrats repeatedly attempted to wipe out the Enforcement Acts of 1870 and 1871, authorizing Federal supervision of congressional elections and the use of the Army at the polls, by attaching riders to appropriation bills. Hayes, refusing to be bludgeoned by these tactics, vetoed each bill, even in the face of an adjournment of Congress that left the Federal marshals without salaries for six months. In this he showed courage and common sense, for such a use of the rider would have constituted, in Hayes's opinion, coercion of the executive and would have set a dangerous precedent. His attitude on the Enforcement Acts was typical. In theory he upheld the power of the Federal Government to regulate congressional elections; in practice, he abandoned the earlier Republican policy.

More significant than factional and party wrangling was the inflation controversy, an issue that cut across party lines. The Resumption Act of 1875 had checked but not defeated the cheap-money forces. In the Middle West farmers continued to agitate for more currency as a lever to higher prices; scarcity of money was held responsible by labor for poverty, unemployment, and wage cuts such as had precipitated the railroad strikes of 1877. Social discontent shattered party lines; in 1878 men of all parties, Republicans, Democrats, and Greenbackers, opened a new crusade. To the old demand for greenbacks was added the fresh vigor of the Free Silver cry. Silver miner and farmer, worker and debtor, rose in fury against the "Crime of 1873," the currency act that had demonitized silver.

The new battle of the West against the East opened in October 1877. Bills to repeal the Resumption Act and to provide for free coinage of silver were swept through the House by votes of more than three to one. In modified form providing for the coinage of not less than $2,000,000 nor more than $4,000,000 worth of silver per month, the Free Silver bill passed the Senate and was presented to Hayes. "In view of the strong public sentiment in favor of the free coinage of the silver dollar," wrote the politically cautious John Sherman, "I thought it better to make no objections to the passage of the bill." Not so Hayes. "I feel the importance and responsibility of my action. But I have no misgiving," he confided to his diary. On February 28, 1878, he sent his veto message. Although the Bland-Allison bill was passed over his veto, his stand contributed to the strength of the sound-money forces. Hayes was repudiated by western Republicans, but on January 1, 1879, specie payment was resumed. With returning prosperity, the greenback movement died down and the soundness of government credit was made patent.

But the victory had not been achieved without political maneuverings. Inflation, wrote Hayes candidly in 1891, ". . . *was prevented,* and by the influence of the Administration with unfriendly senators and representatives. The history of the *how* has not been written. Very few know it. There was nothing questionable done. The *truth* brought home to a few minds did it. But I could not fight both battles [i.e., inflation and the civil-service reform] at the same time with equal vigor and success," he added naïvely. It was a practical policy and, by Hayes's own standards, a justifiable one.

In his foreign policy the President showed himself at his best. During his administration he followed the line of Americanism and yet eschewed a screaming-eagle attitude. Like his predecessor, Hayes accepted the dream of Manifest Destiny and even expected that ultimately the United States would absorb Canada and expand southward. He was not, however, "in favor of artificial stimulants to this tendency." Of more immediate interest, he felt, was the establishment of American control over any transisthmian projects in Central America. Interoceanic communication—whether by canal or by railroad —in his opinion involved paramount interests of the United States. Not only the Monroe Doctrine but considerations of national defense, national prosperity, made American control imperative. Early in 1880 the attempt of De Lesseps, a French entrepreneur, to organize a company for the construction of a canal across the Panama Isthmus, under the aegis of French promoters and with the aid of French capital, called forth a statement of the President's views. "The policy of this country is a canal under American control. The United States cannot consent to the surrender of this control to any European power, or to any combination of European powers," he declared firmly in a special message to the Senate on March 8, 1880, and indicated that the Clayton-Bulwer treaty of 1850 should be abrogated in order to give the United States a free hand. The problem did not come to an issue in his time, but, like Grant, Hayes paved the way for the later predominance of the United States in the Isthmus.

On the other hand, he refused to countenance congressional strictures on Chinese immigration to this country. When the Chinese Exclusion bill of 1878 was laid before him, he vetoed it as a direct violation of the Burlingame treaty of 1868, which had guaranteed freedom of movement to the peoples of both countries. Owing to his stand, a more diplomatic policy was evolved. A special mission was dispatched to China; the treaty of 1880, by which the exclusion of Chinese workers was achieved, was the fruit of Hayes's policy. A nationalist at heart, he was not insensible to fine shades of international honor, nor was he willing to take the easy and popular stand at the expense of principle.

"Success is the final test of public men and public measures," runs the record of Hayes's diary ten months after he left the presidency. ". . . I can say with truth 'I left this great country prosperous and happy and the party of my choice strong, victorious and united.' In serving the country I served the party. . . ." Contemporaries would have denied, and historians have challenged, these conclusions. Yet Hayes had some grounds for his self-complacency. Neither as general nor as President had he shown himself self-seeking or ambitious of personal ends. If his administration was lacking in brilliance, it was distinguished by practicality. If to many his personality seemed lacking in warmth, to others his rectitude and old-fashioned sense of duty was comforting. European diplomats might raise their eyebrows at the innovations introduced at the White House by President and Mrs. Hayes; but thousands of Americans read with approval of the "strictly temperance banquets" or the simple Sunday evening gatherings given over to the singing of old familiar hymns. "Why he was just as common as any man I ever met," declared a Michigan farmer of this well-to-do and well-read President. It was this quality of plain Americanism that brought Hayes the esteem if not the warm love of the people. Perhaps as an officer he had gained an appreciation of the perils of recklessness rather than a zest for glory tipped with the flame of danger. "Let me try to live during my remaining years a useful life," he wrote October 5, 1879, after his fifty-seventh birthday. "To make others happy and to make men and women better to the extent of my power —this must be my aim." As a President he pictured himself as a soldier of the Lord rather than as a military hero. And with that picture he was content.

V

Despite Hayes's happy certainties, the Republican party in 1880 (as James G. Blaine pointed out instructively to President-elect Garfield) was divided into three groups. The Stalwarts (Grant men, unreconciled Radicals, Southern Republicans, and spoilsmen) were still marshaled by Senator Roscoe Conkling; at the other extremity were the "unco guids," the reformers and advocates of "snivel service," Conkling's favorite jibe. The rest of the party (modestly claimed by Blaine) was composed of the Half-Breeds, faithful to the standard of the Plumed Knight. In the Republican convention at Chicago, June 2, 1880, the relative strength of the factions was clearly shown. President Hayes had neither anticipated nor desired a second term; his name was not even brought before the convention. Six names were put into nomination; the first ballot was an index of factional strength. General Ulysses S. Grant, his popularity resurgent after his triumphal tour around the world, received the 306 votes of the Conkling men. Blaine, former Speaker of the House and senator from Maine during Hayes's administration, claimed 284. John Sherman, nominated by his political protégé, Garfield of Ohio, garnered 93 votes. Senator George F. Edmunds of Vermont, candidate of the reformers, reaped a total of 34, and scattered votes were cast for two other minor figures. The rank and file of the Republican voters might fall into three groups; clearly, the politicians were more nearly divided into two camps.

The result was a deadlock, a not unfamiliar political circumstance, and a resultant compromise. On the thirty-sixth ballot the Grant men still stood firm, casting their final 306 votes for the old leader, but the other delegates, following the example of the Blaine men, stampeded for James A. Garfield, John Sherman's floor manager and supporter. As the hesitating Garfield failed to withdraw his name, the nomination was made unanimous; Chester A. Arthur of New York, a bone thrown from "sheer sympathy" to Conkling, was added to the ticket.

Although Garfield's nomination was unexpected, it aroused a good deal of enthusiasm. Of the younger men in the party, he was an outstanding figure. From 1863 until 1879 he had represented Ohio in Congress and during Hayes's administration had risen to the position of party leader in the House of Representatives. Member of the Ways and Means Committee, chairman of the Committee on Currency and Banking and chairman of the Committee on Appropriations in turn, he had shown skill and even brilliance in dealing with financial problems and had gained considerable reputation as an exponent of sound money. If his views on the tariff and the civil service were less unequivocal, this but made him more available. As a lawyer he had attained some prominence and had appeared before the Supreme Court in important cases. His activities as co-counsel for the petitioners in the notorious case *Ex parte Milligan,* where the military trials of the Indiana "Sons of Liberty" were held unconstitutional, had been a dramatic exhibition of his courage and forensic abilities. Moreover, his reputation had been reinforced by his skill in debate, his power as an orator, and even more by the charm of his personality. Five months prior to the Republican national convention he had been elected United States senator, a position he owed in part to John Sherman's anxiety to sidetrack him as a presidential possibility. Despite the murmurings of the Sherman men and mutterings of the Stalwarts, Garfield seemed to be a happy choice. The virtue of the old maxim, "United we stand, divided we fall," was well appreciated. With a surface party unity the campaign got under way.

The Republican strategy was a curious mixture of new and old. Since the destinies of the Democratic party in the South were in the hands of the ex-rebel leaders, the "Confederate Brigadiers" who had led their people out of bondage, it was prudent to keep alive the old memories of war as a means of discrediting the Democrats. At the same time, and with real political acumen, it was not Garfield's military service which was made the chief theme, but his civil record. Cleverly gauging the psyche of the new and rising generation of civilians, the Republican leaders presented Garfield as the self-made American, the man who had pulled himself up by his bootstraps. Urged the outgoing President Hayes:

We must neglect no element of success. There is a great deal of strength in Garfield's life and struggles as a self-made man. Let it be thoroughly presented—in facts and incidents, in poetry and tales, in pictures, on banners, in representations, in processions, in watchwords and nicknames.

How from poverty and obscurity, by labor at all avocations, he became a great scholar, a statesman, a major general, a Senator, a Presidential candidate. Give the amplest details—a schoolteacher, a laborer on the canal—the name of his boat. The truth is, no man ever started so low that accomplished so much, in all our history. Not Franklin or Lincoln even. . . . He is the ideal candidate because he is the ideal self-made man.

Hayes may have waxed overlyrical on Garfield's attainments, but he correctly divined the quality of Garfield's appeal which Horatio Alger was to capitalize in his *From Canal Boy to President.* Garfield honestly exemplified the American tradition of individualism, self-improvement, and success; his was a record bound to strike a responsive chord in the minds of his contemporaries. In speeches, newspaper articles, and pamphlets alike, this was made the central theme of the campaign. *American Pluck or General James A. Garfield at College* ran one stirring title—an allusion to Garfield's phrasing "A pound of pluck is worth a ton of luck"—the central theme of his oration on "Elements of Success" delivered in 1869. Much was made of his long years in civil office as a suitable preparation for the position of chief executive, and his military service as the citizen soldier was cleverly contrasted with the record of the Democratic nominee, Major General Winfield Scott Hancock, educated at West Point, hero at Gettysburg and still an officer in the Regular Army.

"The 'soldier dodge' will not win," said the New York *Tribune* blandly. "Hancock is not a soldier in the sense that Grant was a soldier. He represents the regular army and West Point alone. Grant was of the people, for he entered the Army at the beginning of the war from civil life." The tactics the Democrats had so successfully employed against General Winfield Scott in 1852 were now turned against their own candidate, Scott's namesake. Even Hancock's heroism was deprecated; in his military service he had only done his duty, it was stated. "How much more credit is due to the man who leaves his home, his family and his friends at the first call of duty to fight and perhaps to die, for his country," declared one orator. And Carl Schurz in an impassioned speech warned, "You may spoil an excellent General in making a poor President," a phrase that was quickly turned into the caption of a campaign publication entitled *The Nail Hit on the Head— Don't Spoil a Good General to Make a Poor President.*

As in previous elections, gibes of rebellion and disunion were leveled at the Democrats. Now that the war was long over and the country at peace, the Democratic party was coming to the front of battle, frantically waving the "bloody shirt," charged Republican General Charles Albright. "Hancock is the candidate of the mass of men who were disloyal during the war. General Garfield is the candidate of the party which saved the Union." The old controversy over Hancock's conduct during the days of Reconstruction when, by President Johnson's order, he had supplanted Grant's favorite, General Phil Sheridan, in command at New Orleans was revived. Hancock's famous instruction at that date, "The military law must be subordinate to the civil power," and the mildness of his rule were cited as proof that he had favored the South and had helped Johnson defeat Reconstruction. "We see the rebel army comes first and following it the Copperheads of the North" when Hancock reviews the army, declared Senator Logan sardonically.

Throughout the summer months old issues stemming from the Civil War and the days of Reconstruction were fought over. Efforts were made to excite the fear that a Democratic victory would result in the payment of southern war claims, compensation for the slaves, and the payment of pensions to Confederate soldiers. The Democrats, in turn, revived the charges linking Garfield with the *Crédit Mobilier* and the De Golyer pavement scandals and reiterated the charge that the Republicans had stolen the election of 1876.

The Republican offensive tactics included a new and plausible argument and one which was later to serve them well—the claim that theirs was the party of prosperity. By 1880 the country had recovered from the aftermath of the panic of 1873 and was well on its way to a new high-water mark of affluence. For this the Republicans claimed credit. "High Tariff, High Wages and a High Old Time," ran one slogan. "Hancock, Free Trade and Lawlessness," read another political banner.

With some justification the Republicans accused their opponents of hedging on the tariff and money issues. Petroleum V. Nasby ("hungrin and thirstin") ridiculed at length General Hancock's guarded and meaningless statements and his futile efforts to reconcile the discordant views of different sections of his party:

After his various utterances wat kin any Dimekrat find in him that they don't want. . . . He hez an extensive assortment uv prinsiples, and everybody kin be sootid. . . . Wat ever may be his noshens on tariffs and sich, I know he is sound on post offis, and that is the grate prinsiple we are strugglin for.

On October 11 the badgered general, in an interview in the *Daily Guardian,* a Democratic paper published at Paterson, New Jersey, incautiously stated that there would be as much protection for American industry under a Democratic as under a Republican administration. "The tariff question is a local question," he stated, and indicated that it was a problem of little concern to the Federal Government. For the Republicans this was a happy phrase. From that date until election day Hancock's words were ceaselessly kept before the public as proof positive of his ignorance of the economic conditions of the day and of his incapacity for civil office. The Republicans began to face forward.

As the campaign developed, Republican strategy seemed on the surface aimed more and more at the past; Republican tactics, however, were reflective of the business ethics, business methods of the day. For behind the fanfare of speeches, organization of "Boys in Blue" clubs, torchlight processions, and parades lay the solid work of the party leaders. Strenuous efforts had been made to bind all party factions together and to win over the disgruntled "306" Grant-Conkling men. In August, Garfield had journeyed to New York for a conference with the eastern leaders, and if the old Fifth Avenue Hotel was not a Canossa, it was at least the scene of a party concordat. Although Garfield always averred that he had on that occasion given no pledges concerning the patronage to Conkling's lieutenants, the New York machine from that date rallied to his support, and further encouraged by "the Treaty of Mentor," Conkling's return visit to the candidate's home town, was later to raise bitter charges of broken promises.

Republican organization was further distinguished by a callous pressure for campaign funds. Federal employees, despite Hayes's well-known order, were assessed the regular ten per cent. Garfield was perfectly cognizant of the practice and had, indeed, regarded Hayes's prohibitions as impractical if not almost politically frivolous.

"My dear Hubbell," he wrote during the campaign, "Please say to Brady that I hope he will give us all the assistance he can. I think he can help effectually. Please tell me how the Dept's generally are doing."

As Brady was Second Assistant Postmaster, the implications of the letter were obvious. In addition to the government service, financial and business interests were tapped. The secretary of the National Republican Committee, General Stephen Dorsey, ex-carpetbagger senator from Arkansas, had no nonsensical reservations as to the expediency or usefulness of a large campaign chest. A close associate of Brady, he was with the latter soon to achieve notoriety in the "Star Route" postal frauds; both men worked industriously for the party in the months before the election. Levi P. Morton, influential New York banker, Jay Gould (of earlier "Black Friday" fame), and "Mr. Rockafeller of Cleveland" were spurred to generosity. One hundred thousand dollars was collected in New York whereby the doubtful state of Indiana was made safe, a coup indiscreetly revealed by Vice-President Arthur at a dinner held at Delmonico's on February 11, 1881, in tribute to General Dorsey. Despite the efforts of the Democrats to discredit the records both of Republican candidate and Republican party, the Republican strategy and tactics proved successful. On November 2, 1880, Garfield and Arthur were elected.

Like Lincoln, Garfield was to be assassinated in office; like William Henry Harrison, he was to die so soon after his inauguration that we possess the merest premonitory shadow of what record he might have made had he served his full term.

Between the election and Garfield's death on September 19, 1881, certain trends in the character of his presidency had been delineated. James G. Blaine, brilliant and magnetic figure, had achieved and would have held a dominating position. "Your Father and I have picked out Garfield's Cabinet for him, and have devoted to him for two mornings our waking, but not risen, hours," wrote Mrs. James G. Blaine gaily three days after the election, exulting that "there is no danger that any of the tomfoolery of the Hayes policy will be tried." To some extent, the Blaines' speculations were realized, for within a few weeks Blaine was selected for the office of Secretary of State. In the months that followed, as friend and political counselor, he exercised a growing influence over Garfield. "I shall never *urge* a man upon you for the cabinet; but I will not hesitate to protest vigorously many men," he wrote Garfield; but he seldom confined himself to these bounds.

Garfield's ambition was to conciliate all party factions and, in particular, to appease Conkling, whose resentment and suspicions flared up anew when news of Blaine's appointment leaked out. Weeks were consumed in conferences and cabinet juggling as the President-elect sought to placate the party leaders. As late as January 31, 1881, Garfield even considered the inclusion of Conkling in the Cabinet, a solution which Blaine quashed with the comment that Conkling's "appointment would act like strychnine upon your administration—first, bring contortions and then be followed by death." Conscious of his political indebtedness to Blaine, soberly aware of Conkling's following, Garfield strove to hold the two factions in equilibrium. His Cabinet was ultimately a compromise slate and included both Half-Breeds and Stalwarts, but the perilous balance was soon to be upset.

Garfield's inauguration took place within three days of the one hundredth anniversary of the adoption of the Articles of Confederation, a circumstance which furnished the central theme of his inaugural address. At some length he reviewed the "century of growth" and the benefits which the years had brought to the country—the territorial expansion, the increase of population, the supremacy of the Union, and "liberty throughout the land to all the inhabitants thereof."

On the policy toward the South he spoke temperately, urging an end to "all those bitter controversies concerning things which have been irrevocably settled; and the further discussion of which can only stir up strife and delay the onward march." Like Grant, he commended an acceptance of the *fait accompli* —the emancipation of the Negro and his endowment with full rights of citizenship. The "free enjoyment of equal suffrage" must be preserved, he declared, assailing the southerner's reputed violations of the Negro's political rights. He stated:

. . . there was no middle ground for the negro race between slavery and equal citizenship . . . to violate the freedom and sanctities of the suffrage is more than an evil. It is a crime which, if persisted in, will destroy the Government itself. . . . It should be said with the utmost emphasis that this question of the suffrage will never give repose or safety to the States or to the nation until each, within its own jurisdiction, makes and keeps the ballot free and pure by the strong sanctions of the law.

Recognizing the dangers arising from an ignorant electorate, however, Garfield preached the remedy of universal education. "In this beneficent work [education] sections and races should be forgotten and partisanship should be unknown." And he added in the sentimental vein of a *Friendship's Album,* "Let our people find a new meaning in the divine oracle which declares that 'a little child shall lead them,' for our own little children will soon control the destinies of the Republic."

The rest of his address was devoted to optimistic anticipation of the future progress of the United States, premised upon the current prosperity. A sound-money policy, aid to the farmers, encouragement to industry and transportation, an American canal policy—in his advocacy of these matters Garfield was prophetic of the future of his party. To civil-service reform he pledged adherence and called for congressional measures against polygamy and the political power of the Mormon Church. Lastly, mindful of his predecessor's record, he gave a pledge of executive co-operation. "I shall greatly rely upon the

wisdom and patriotism of Congress and of those who may share
with me the responsibilities and duties of administration. . . ."
The inaugural was politically reassuring, but it must have come
as a bitter disappointment to those who had gathered to enjoy
the President's oratory. For Garfield was a speaker of de-
servedly great repute, and some of his efforts, the moving
eulogy of General Thomas, the incandescent appeal to the
young Democrats, "Don't Pitch Your Camp Among the Dead,"
rank with the best of contemporary orations.

Within a few weeks of the inauguration, the weight of
Blaine's influence was felt. For it was the Secretary of State who
nerved Garfield to an open break with Conkling. As in the case
of the Hayes-Conkling struggle, the battle was fought over the
position of collector of the port, the prize of the New York
patronage. Unlike his predecessor, Garfield lacked the motiva-
tion of civil-service reform; indeed, the President had even
shifted the competent and honest E. A. Merritt (Hayes's appointee) to the diplomatic service in order to make his office
available. Garfield's bland nomination of Judge William H.
Robertson, a marked Blaine adherent, to the collectorship was
therefore not only a surprise but a deliberate affront to the
New York senators. The Stalwarts were convulsed with anger.
It was not an honest fight of the executive against the principle
of senatorial courtesy; it was, in essence, a question of Blaine
versus Conkling. "You must be firm and resolute as if you were
fighting Chickamauga over again," Blaine exhorted the President. Ultimately Robertson was confirmed by the Senate;
Conkling and his colleague "Me Too" Platt went down in
ignominious defeat; Garfield (and Blaine) triumphed. For
both men it was to prove a Pyrrhic victory.

Despite the defeat of the New York machine, Garfield's
action was severely criticized. An avalanche of hungry office
seekers flooded the capital, and as Garfield's appointments were
announced, the hopes of the independents for civil-service reform faded. The disclosure of the "Star Route" frauds further
discouraged the "unco guids." Garfield was not responsible for
this condition; indeed, it was his new Postmaster General,
Thomas L. James, who uncovered the corrupt practices whereby

extra appropriations of almost two million dollars a year had been granted to certain back-country postal routes in the West and South on the pretext of "expediting" the service. But the managers of Garfield's campaign chest—General Dorsey and Second Assistant Postmaster Brady—were the leading figures involved in the scandal. This circumstance, coupled with Brady's spiteful publication of Garfield's "My dear Hubbell" letter, raised a buzz of suspicion and inevitably threw a shadow on the President's reputation.

On July 2, 1881, Garfield was shot by a crazed office seeker, a Stalwart hopeful of Arthur's accession; on September 19, the anniversary of Chickamauga, he died. During the brief months of his presidency, Blaine's star had been rising steadily. Had Garfield lived, the Administration's foreign policy would have been Blaine's, the "spirited" defense of American interests, expansion of American influence. And in domestic affairs Blaine's hand would have directed a business administration shorn of the fads and frills of reform. Garfield's months in office had not been happy. Harried by party faction, his days had been frittered away in the apportionment of spoils. "Four years of this kind of intellectual dissipation may cripple me for the remainder of my life," he wrote a few months before his death. The presidency brought him little glory and great grief. Possessed of a rapid intelligence, a vivid and emotional nature, and the incalculable quality of charm, he was at the end belittled by his outstanding virtues. "I think it is a valuable trait in any man's judgment of affairs to be able to know when he is beaten," he had written in his diary. He did not believe in "continuing a fight merely for the sake of a fight." Here lay the tragedy of Garfield's career. Overanxious to please, overingratiating, he lacked the iron of resoluteness. He died the aide rather than the commander.

VI

"Individuals are ephemeral. . . . But party is like a rope of many strands, wherein the strength of one adds to the

strength of the whole. Party is a past with a record. It is
the present and the future. . . . It is an institution, and from
its traditions and faith it speaks." So Uncle Joe Cannon was
to pontificate out of the wisdom garnered in his long career. In
the mid-1880s only the past was clear. Garfield had died, and
Arthur had taken his place; the election of 1884 had come and
gone, and for the first time since 1860 the Republican party
had gone down in defeat. But the present and future of the
major parties remained obscure during Cleveland's administration. On the rising issues of the day—silver, trusts and monopolies, railway regulation, labor agitation, and farmer discontent
—there was no clear-cut definition of party stand. Sectional
rather than party interest governed senators and representatives and determined their votes on legislative proposals; the
label "Republican" or "Democrat" had validity largely in
terms of past action, past tradition. The Republicans still
boasted of their record as the party of the Union. In June
1887 Cleveland's attempt to return to the southern states the
Confederate flags captured in battle stirred anew the sediment
of old loyalties, old hatreds, and from Kansas to the eastern
seaboard Republican generals, political leaders, and editors
shrilled their protests, reviving the old taunt that the Democrats were a "wing of the Confederate army." But on the
problems troubling the voters, party oracles remained dumb.
The election of 1888 was to be the turning point. Political principle was to replace tradition, present and future jostle aside
the petrifying past.

It was Cleveland's annual message of December 1887 that
ended the period of political shadow-boxing and gave new life
to party distinctions. During his term of office the surplus in
the Federal Treasury had mounted from $17,000,000 to $140,-
000,000. Troubled by this excess of income over expenditures,
Cleveland broke all precedent by devoting his entire message
in December 1887 to tax reform. "It is a condition that con-
fronts us, not a theory," he stated incisively. The solution he
proposed was starkly simple—tariff reduction. At once the
Republicans rallied to the standard of protection. The message,

declared James G. Blaine, defeated candidate of 1884, was a "free trade manifesto." Blaine's cabled interview, known as the "Paris letter," galvanized the Republican party. "You have given us our platform for next year," wrote John Hay jubilantly; the parties at last acknowledged the future.

When the Republicans assembled at Chicago in June 1888, therefore, their battle cry only needed to be spelled out. The usual salute to the past was given in a plank endorsing "the supreme and sovereign right of every lawful citizen . . . white or black to cast one free ballot in public elections"; but the clarion call was the defense "of the American system of protection." No such unanimity marked the choice of a candidate. Blaine, defeated in 1884, had withdrawn his name from the contest; the convention, lacking a single outstanding leader, milled erratically around the standards of a dozen favorite sons. John Sherman, Elder Statesman of the old days, led the field, but Sherman could not command the Blaine votes. "The nomination was ours to give, certainly it was ours to keep," Mrs. Blaine had boasted some months earlier. Like Henry Clay, Blaine missed the presidency but played the Warwick. On the eighth ballot political lightning struck Benjamin Harrison of Indiana.

Harrison was only a middling figure in Republican councils, but he was one of the most zealous adherents of party tenets. As he told the old veterans who had voted for his grandfather in 1840, he had come naturally by the Whig doctrines of a "reverent devotion to the Constitution and the flag, and a firm faith in the benefits of a protective tariff." He had turned to the Republican party at the moment of its founding; his experiences in the field and even more the perilous struggle waged on the home front in Indiana during the Civil War between peace Democrat and Republican had bred in his mind a conviction that the preservation of the Union was the especial trust of the Republican party. In that conviction he never wavered.

Although Harrison's record of public office was meager (two terms as reporter of the Supreme Court of Indiana during the 1860s and one term as United States senator [1881–

87]), he was noted for his ability as a public speaker. It brought him fame at the bar; it made him a valuable asset to his party. Since the election of 1856, when, at the age of twenty-three, he had stumped the state for Frémont, he had campaigned for every Republican candidate for the presidency. Representative of the Indiana state organization at the party conventions of 1880 and 1884, he had been offered and refused a position in Garfield's Cabinet.

His pre-nomination record was thus less distinguished than that of Hayes, less outstanding than Garfield's, but as an expositor of Republican principles Harrison surpassed them both. On his mind the campfires of the Rebellion still cast their light and shadow. To the end of his life "the broad and deep grave at the foot of Resaca hill," the "falling tents and wet and weary marches" of the Atlanta campaign were to retain hegemony over his spirit. This feeling colored his belief in the Republican party and transfused his speeches with a moving, even poetic quality. The Republican platform was a confession of faith to this political Puritan, and it was a faith held rigidly, inflexibly. Theodore Roosevelt regarded him as a "first-rate man," and his nomination was received with general satisfaction. If the figure of the distinguished lawyer and Presbyterian elder seemed deficient in popular appeal, his family name was linked to the traditions of the country and could be counted upon to evoke the warmth of old memories.

"I congratulate you most heartily upon the work of the national convention," cabled Blaine on June 26. "Your candidacy will recall the triumphant enthusiasm and assure the victorious conclusion which followed your grandfather's nomination in 1840." It was a felicitous circumstance and was not neglected by the Republican managers. General Lew Wallace, nationally famous as the author of *Ben Hur,* hurriedly turned out a campaign life incorporating a review of President William Henry Harrison's career and his deeds for the West and the Union. Again log cabins and coonskins decorated political banners, and the magic of 1840 was invoked. Democrats might sneer and cartoonists delight in "the Man in his Grandfather's

Hat." Republicans rallied to the watchword, "Old Tippecanoe and Young Tippecanoe."

Nor was Harrison's attraction as a Civil War veteran overlooked. By the year 1888 the old-soldier vote had assumed a real political importance. Early in the 1880s the Grand Army of the Republic, with a membership of 450,000, had set up a lobby in Washington for the purpose of securing more liberal pensions for Civil War veterans. This effort was ably abetted by pension attorneys, outstanding among whom was George E. Lemon, editor of the *National Tribune,* a paper with a circulation of over one hundred thousand. President Cleveland had incurred the open hostility of the G.A.R. by his wholesale vetoes of private pension bills and of the Dependent Pension bill of 1887. As the party of the Union, the Republicans claimed the old soldiers' attachment; this pretension was buttressed by a pledge of future generosity. "The gratitude of the nation to the defenders of the Union cannot be measured by laws," the Republican platform stated, in preface to a promise that the treasury surplus should be used for the care of indigent veterans. Since the close of the Civil War, Benjamin Harrison had uniformly supported the soldiers' cause. "I pledge myself, and I am sure I can pledge the Republican party, to be faithful, generous and liberal to the soldiers that survive, to care for them and to honor them until the last veteran sleeps his last sleep," he had stated in 1886. It was a pledge that expressed a deep conviction, that was to win him votes in the election, and that was to be generously fulfilled.

The real issue of the campaign, however, was the tariff. Throughout the hot summer months, while Congress wrangled over the tariff bills framed for campaign purposes, the Republican managers cajoled big business to a solid defense of the protective tariff and the Republican party. Matthew Quay, boss of Pennsylvania and chairman of the National Republican Committee, was busily engaged in what he called "frying the fat" from manufacturers, while John Wanamaker, retail merchant, zealously organized an auxiliary committee of businessmen in order to swell the campaign chest. Tariff reduction, it was claimed, would prostrate American industries and injure American labor. The "full dinner pail" argument was expounded in speeches and pamphlets, and manufacturers grimly enforced the appeal to the workers by threats of shutdowns and layoffs in the event of Democratic victory. Americanism and protection against foreign competition were presented as synonymous.

Harrison had stated in a speech some months before his nomination:

I believe the Republican party is pledged and ought to be pledged to the doctrine of the protection of American industries and American labor. . . . I am one of those uninstructed political economists that have an impression that some things may be too cheap; that I cannot find myself in full sympathy with this demand for cheaper coats, which seems to me necessarily to involve a cheaper man and woman under the coat. I believe it is true today that we have many things in this country that are too cheap, because whenever it is proved that a man or woman who produces any article cannot get a decent living out of it, then it is too cheap.

It was a theme frequently repeated by the candidate in the innumerable addresses he made, day in, day out, before the election.

The reproach of "pro-British" was flung at Cleveland. His championship of a tariff for revenue, his effort to settle the northeastern fisheries dispute, were alike pictured as the American eagle bowing before the British lion. Cleveland had "made the mistake of mistaking the flashlight of some British lighthouse for the light of day," remarked Harrison. By a scurvy trick the British minister, L. S. Sackville West, was trapped into the fatal blunder of a written endorsement of the Democrats as the party favorable to British interests, a letter which led to the unfortunate minister's recall and swelled the Republican vote. With the triple appeal of patriotism, protection, and profit, the Republicans carried the day. "Providence has given us victory," wrote Harrison thankfully to Wanamaker. Perhaps Matthew Quay's cynical comment, "He ought to know Providence hadn't a damn thing to do with it," was more accurate.

The victory owed something to the old party tradition but more to new methods.

Success at the polls in 1888 gave the Republicans control of both houses of Congress as well as of the presidency; the admission of the new states of the Far West in 1889 and in 1890 was further to increase their political power. This spelled a golden opportunity for the realization of the party program, provided that party unity could be preserved and party dissensions averted. It is this circumstance which furnishes the key to Harrison's cabinet making and distribution of the patronage. Harrison wrote:

It was best I thought to select the whole Cabinet before offering a place to anyone and as the responsibility was mine, and the failure would be mine if failure ensued, to let it be understood at once that I was hospitable to suggestion but that I could keep my own counsel and act upon my own judgment.

It is clear, however, that his judgment was frequently governed by the political formula for party unity—satisfaction of the claims of party leaders, recognition of the sensibilities of diverse geographical sections. It was a task for which he was temperamentally unsuited and which he performed with little success.

As a result, the announcement of the Cabinet produced a good deal of dissatisfaction. James G. Blaine, still popular albeit his armor had grown a little tarnished, could not be passed over. Despite his own reservations and the opposition of anti-Blaine men, Harrison tendered him the position of Secretary of State, but after a delay so protracted as to be almost a humiliation to Blaine. "But I did not think it well to name him at once as my Secy of State," Harrison wrote candidly in a private memorandum. "The Administration could not be a success unless each member of it, from the head down, was all that his position implied and no more." The Treasury Department was assigned to Windom of Minnesota, a selection made in deference to western interests. An attempt was made to propitiate Boss Platt of New York (who had marked the Treasury for his own) by the choice of Benjamin Tracy, a member of Platt's "Sunday school," as Secretary of the Navy. John Wanamaker was rewarded with the office of Postmaster General, an appointment that caused a furor and was not particularly pleasing to the Pennsylvania machine. Harrison's old law partner, Miller, was made Attorney General, and the other posts distributed largely in terms of geographical representation. No interest had been neglected; no faction was completely satisfied. This was to be characteristic of the Administration.

The same mixture of independence and party conciliation characterized Harrison's lesser appointments. Whitelaw Reid, owner and editor of the New York *Tribune,* was the most outstanding in a group of Republican editors rewarded by assignments to the diplomatic service. Boss Platt of New York was offered—and refused—the position of minister to the court of Spain. Fred D. Grant, son of Ulysses S. Grant, was sent to Austria (a tidbit for the Stalwarts), while Andrew D. White, noted educator, was made minister to Russia. "I had but two personal enemies in Maine and one of them Harrison pardoned out of the penitentiary and the other he appointed collector of Portland," declared "Czar" Reed, Speaker of the House of Representatives, caustically. Harrison also mortally offended James G. Blaine by a refusal to make Walker Blaine First Assistant Secretary of State. "The idea apparently is that having given Blaine the head of the table, no distinctively personal friend shall also have a seat," wrote Mrs. Blaine indignantly. And a month later she commented:

It is all interesting, though Harrison is of such a nature that you do not feel at all at liberty to enjoy yourself. For instance, he objected to Jacky as First Assistant Secretary of State. . . . All first propositions are rejected. It is a most uncomfortable twist in the make-up of a man.

Yet Harrison himself was charged with nepotism, and a merry cartoon of the President sheltering a large number of relatives under the umbrella of the Administration publicized the criticism.

In spite of pre-election pledges, once more the civil-service reformers were doomed to disappointment. Theodore Roosevelt was appointed Civil Service Commissioner, but within a short time his confidence in Harrison was shaken. "Platt seems to have a ring in the President's nose as regards New York," Roosevelt had commented only a month after Harrison's inauguration. By April 1892 two thirds of the consular force had been replaced by Harrison appointees; Platt's province, New York, carried off the lion's share. The Post Office was frankly utilized for the reward of party workers. Ex-President Cleveland's order extending civil-service rules to the railway mail service was suspended until over two thousand of the five thousand clerks had been removed. Within a year of First Assistant Postmaster Clarkson's appointment to office, seven thousand postmasters had been removed and fifteen thousand had resigned. "Oh Heaven, if the President had a little backbone, and if the Senators did not have flannel legs," lamented Roosevelt. Indeed, by the close of the Administration the Civil Service Commissioner had despaired of the President's "half-and-half, boneless policy" and had publicly damned Postmaster General Wanamaker. Harrison paid lip service to civil-service reform, but loyalty to the party governed his conduct.

On other policies Harrison's performance was more consistent with his campaign pledges. This was particularly true of questions stemming from the Civil War. Harrison could not have been unaware of the political aspects of the pension question, but his championship of the old soldier was emotionally bound up with his memories of the Civil War, his devotion to the Union. For that cause the soldier had fought; in his old age the "veteran of time" should not be neglected. He declared:

Can it be possible that, while the survivors of this great struggle are still with us, while they walk our streets, a generation has come on forgetful of their great achievements? Has the moth of avarice, the canker of greed, so eaten into the hearts of this generation that they are unmindful of these men?

These sentiments had earlier colored Harrison's speeches
even before his candidacy and were never abandoned. When
with a more muted undertone of emotion he put the question to
his first Congress, the Republicans, rejoicing in the surplus,
gave a generous answer.

"God help the surplus," Corporal Tanner, a leader in the
G.A.R. and newly appointed Commissioner of Pensions, is reported to have said; during his six months in office the gates
of the Treasury were opened wide. In 1890 Congress passed a
new pension law, a measure favored by the President. The
restrictions of the old General Law system were now relaxed.
Under the new law, any soldier (or his dependents) who had
served in the Union army for ninety days during the Civil War
and was, by 1890, incapacitated for physical labor, was eligible
for a pension, no matter when or how the disability had been
incurred. As a result the pension lists swelled in number from
223,417 in 1878 (more than a decade after the war) to 846,-
751 in 1892. Costs leaped correspondingly. From 1789 until
1860 the total pension bill of the United States for all its wars
had been $90,000,000; in 1890 alone, $106,000,000 was expended, and the operation of the new law entailed yearly
increases. The veterans were never to be dislodged from the
redoubts gained in 1890.

One other issue—the freedman's vote—reawakened the
dying echoes of the Civil War. The passage of the Thirteenth
Amendment had necessarily increased the congressional representation of the southern states. Since 1877 the curtailment
of the freedman's vote by a variety of openly admitted though
unofficial expedients had inevitably given the southern whites
(and thus the Democratic party) a political strength disproportionate to their numbers. This was a by-product of the Civil
War that northern Republicans had not anticipated, nor did
they relish the situation. The Republican platform of 1888
had reaffirmed the right of the Negro to vote; in his speeches
Harrison had frequently denounced the southerners' interference with the freedman's franchise as illegal. He had stated:

Our controversy is not one of the past; it is of the present. . . . What is it we ask? Simply that the South live up to the terms of the surrender at Appomattox . . . that they shall cease to use this recovered citizenship which they had forfeited by rebellion to oppress and disfranchise those who equally with themselves under the Constitution are entitled to vote—that and nothing more.

In 1890 the Republicans made a last effort to redeem their old pledge and reinvigorate the Fifteenth Amendment. A Force bill, endorsed by the President, was introduced in Congress by Henry Cabot Lodge of Massachusetts. Designed to safeguard the southern Negro, it provided for a stringent supervision of Federal elections. Hardheaded party chieftains viewed the bill with alarm; it passed the House but failed in the Senate. Republican senators from the newly admitted western silver states frankly traded their votes in return for southern Democratic support of the pending Sherman Silver bill. It was the final attempt to revive Grant's policy. Within a decade the alarmed southerners had fortified their position. Grandfather clauses and literacy tests had put a coat of constitutional whitewash on the limitation of the Negro vote. The Republican party had snapped a link with its past.

Harrison's administration was to be remembered as a business administration. For the first time since 1874 the President had a working majority in both branches of the legislature. Moreover, Harrison welcomed congressional government. Like Grant, he believed that the President's function was the execution of the will of the people as expressed by Congress. He had stated in his inaugural address:

It is the duty of the executive to administer and enforce in the methods and by the instrumentalities pointed out and provided by the Constitution all the laws enacted by Congress. . . . As a citizen may not elect what laws he will obey, neither may the executive elect which he will enforce.

The philosophy is reminiscent of Grant's; in practice, Harrison followed John Sherman's advice to "touch elbows with Congress."

Congress, therefore, not Harrison, molded the Administration's course; "Czar" Reed, not the President, cracked the party whip. Despite the profound personal antagonism that existed between the two men, they were at one in their solicitude for Republican measures. An enormous amount of legislation was enacted. The Sherman Anti-Trust Act, the Sherman Silver Purchase Act, the McKinley Tariff Act were all passed in the summer of 1890. A new day was dawning. The Sherman Act was an acknowledgment of the public's mutiny against trusts and monopolies; the Silver Act was a concession to the new western fury for inflation; the McKinley tariff was the party's underwriting of big business. In the same session the bigger naval program was pushed by a bill authorizing the construction of three battleships. It was a policy Harrison had favored as senator; it was a policy related to expansionist aims, accentuated by a growing awareness of international rivalries and ambitions.

"The Old Flag and Appropriations" was the Republican slogan. Under the onslaughts of the "Billion Dollar" Congress, the surplus melted. River and harbor bills, pension and navy appropriations were swept through. By the close of Harrison's administration the public could take cold comfort in an empty Treasury, and Republican leaders had been chilled by party reverses in the congressional elections of 1890. The rumble of agrarian and labor discontent was growing louder, the shadow of the Populist revolt was darkening the political sky. Imperturbable, oblivious, Harrison's faith in the Republican program remained unshaken. Restricting his vetoes to individual pork-barrel items and one or two bills for the reorganization of the Federal judiciary, he clung to his role of the administrator, executor of the congressional will.

In foreign affairs the President played a more notable part. Publicly, Blaine, Secretary of State, held the spotlight, but in fact Harrison shared the direction of our foreign relations to an unsuspected degree. Never congenial with Blaine the man, Harrison was in general accord with the ideas of the Secretary of State. Nationalists, expansionists, both men furthered the program sketched out so many years before. The Pan-American policy was peculiarly Blaine's, and to him belongs the credit for the Pan-American Congress of 1890 and the reciprocity clauses in the McKinley tariff alike designed to bind together the republics of the Western Hemisphere. But the final settlement of the Bering Sea controversy with Great Britain owed much to Harrison, and it was the President rather than the Secretary of State who boldly denounced the Chilean Government for its virtual condonation of the *Baltimore* affair of October 1891 and vigorously pressed for reparations. Both men agreed on a strong defense of American interests in Samoa, for some years a storm center of imperialist ambitions, and thus paved the way for the acquisition of Tutuila with its valuable harbor of Pago Pago in 1899. Exponent of a large navy, in 1891 Harrison was impressed with the necessity of securing coaling stations for the Navy, considering leasing Samaná Bay in Santo Domingo and Chimbote in Peru for that purpose, and even contemplating the purchase of the Danish West Indies. Indeed, in this respect, the President exceeded his Secretary of State in enthusiasm.

To the actual administration of the State Department Harrison gave close attention, conferring with Blaine on appointments, scanning and revising the dispatches. To this work he gave the lawyer's assiduous attention to detail and scrupulous regard for the implications of a phrase. During the last year of Blaine's service, Harrison shouldered a large part of his Secretary's work, for Blaine, harried by grief over the deaths of his two eldest children and by declining health, grew careless of the minutiae of his office. In the spring of 1891 a serious illness incapacitated the Secretary of State for months. Wrote the President:

It would be very gratifying to have you here and very helpful to have your suggestions, but I do not want to retard your recovery by giving you any worry about business—all that I will gladly carry myself as long as it may promote your comfort and hasten your convalescence.

It was a generous letter, yet tension in the relations between the two men—and their wives—increased. The Blaines could not forgive Harrison's aloofness, his refusal to promote Blaine's children. Harrison, in turn, found the Blaines lacking in gratitude. The President is quoted as saying that he was ". . . perfectly willing to carry a soldier's knapsack, when the soldier is sore of foot and tired, and all that he wanted in return was acknowledgment of the act and a show of appreciation." In May 1892 Blaine was mortally offended by a newspaper report of comments attributed to "Prince" Russell, the President's son and secretary. Blaine's ill health, according to the New York *World's* story, put him out of the running for the coming presidential election. "He cannot remember the simplest things, and all the work of the State Department has been on my father's shoulders for over two years. It is simply absurd to talk of nominating Mr. Blaine," the President's son was reported as saying. Although the story was denied within a few days, the breach was irreparable. A month later, on June 4, on the eve of the Republican convention, Blaine resigned; in less than an hour and without demur, Harrison accepted the resignation.

If Blaine's action was designed to forestall Harrison's renomination, it failed. If it was intended to injure the President's chances of re-election, it succeeded. Three days after Blaine's resignation the Republicans, assembled at Minneapolis, named Harrison their candidate on the first ballot. Blaine's name had evoked only an echo of earlier enthusiasm, and a boom for McKinley of Ohio died stillborn. Administration men dominated the "Postmaster's Convention," yet theirs was an empty victory. The convention was dispirited, the campaign listless. Blaine men and party bosses were resentful, the rank and file apathetic. Public opinion set against the party responsible for the McKinley tariff and the extravagances of the past four years. Labor was inflamed by the Homestead, the Coeur d'Alene, and the railway strikes of 1892; the western farmer turned in bitterness to the new "People's Party." The Civil War issues were dead and forgotten; the people were concerned with their present and future. In November, Cleveland and the Democratic party returned to power.

During the last months of his presidency, Harrison remained titular head but, in fact, discredited leader of his party. It was under these circumstances that he attempted the consummation of a project he had long favored—the annexation of Hawaii. The policy of establishing American dominance in the Pacific dated back to Pierce and had been supported by the pronouncements of successive administrations and by the growth of economic interests since the Civil War. Grant's reciprocity treaty of 1875 had been supplemented in 1887 by the concession to the United States of exclusive rights to Pearl Harbor. With Harrison's inauguration in 1889, plans for a more sweeping recognition of American ascendancy had been agitated. The accession of the fiercely nativist Queen Liliuokalani to the throne in January 1891 had created unexpected difficulties, and Harrison had been filled with uneasiness. "I feel sure that American interests there [i.e., Hawaii] are in jeopardy," he wrote Blaine in September of that year, "but just how far we can go and what action we can take to thwart the schemes of those who are seeking to bring the islands under the control of European powers I do not yet see."

In January 1893 a revolution cleared the road. A provisional government representative of the American party was set up; on February 1 a temporary American protectorate was announced by Stevens, the overeager United States minister, and commissioners were hurried to Washington to secure annexation. "The Hawaiian pear is now fully ripe, and this is the golden hour to pluck it," wrote Stevens. On February 15, 1893, Harrison submitted the desired annexation treaty to the Senate with a message urging immediate ratification. "The influence and interest of the United States in the islands must be increased and not diminished," he stated. ". . . It is essential that none of the other great powers shall secure these islands. . . . Prompt action upon this treaty is very desirable."

It is a commentary on Harrison's leadership that the treaty remained unconfirmed and was withdrawn by President Cleveland shortly after his inauguration in March. The annexation of Hawaii was to be deferred another five years, until the fever

of the Spanish-American War swept the country. McKinley
and his successors were to reap the fruits of the expansion
policy envisaged by Harrison.

The lonely outgoing President had done his best, but he had
failed. His avowed policy of party harmony had not produced
party unity. He had apportioned the party patronage and given
party leaders their share, but he had given grudgingly, almost
disdainfully, and he had withheld himself in the giving. A
fundamental reserve, a kind of aristocratic contempt for the
men with whom he had perforce to deal, had defeated the
President's purpose. The cause, not the individual, stirred his
ardor. "He was like a great fire sweeping over the prairie,"
wrote a fellow lawyer of Harrison at the bar. Yet the man
who could thus set a jury aflame could freeze a congressman
seeking patronage. Politicians tagged him "the White House
iceberg"; talking to the President was like "talking to a hitch-
ing post." "Kid-gloved" Harrison he remained, never the
warmhearted hail fellow well met. As President he performed
his duties conscientiously, laboriously; as party chieftain he
fulfilled his political obligations with a cold scrupulosity, but he
failed to achieve popularity.

Harrison's term of office marked the end of the first century
of union. In his administration, more truly than ten years later,
came the *fin de siècle*. The closing of the frontier in the West
with the opening of the old Indian Territory to settlement, the
suppression of the last desperate outbreak of the Indians inspired by the Ghost Dance religion, the winding up of the controversies which had torn and threatened the Union's existence,
spelled the completion of the period of the nation's youth. New
issues would rise, party and faction continue, sectional antag-
onisms persist, but the Union would stand. For this Harrison
the general had fought. It was this conviction that illuminated
his political motives, his adherence to party tenets.

On April 30, 1789, Washington had taken the oath of office
as first President of the United States in New York. One hundred years later, at the commemorative celebration in the
same city on April 30, 1889, Harrison voiced the political faith

that the century had engendered. To the toast, "The United States of America," he replied:

> . . . I prefer to substitute for the official title which is upon the programme the familiar and fireside expression 'Our Country.' . . . Have we not learned that no stocks and bonds, nor land, is our country? It is a spiritual thought that is in our minds—it is the flag and what it stands for; it is the fireside and the home; it is the thoughts that are in our hearts, born of the inspiration which comes with the story of the flag, of martyrs to liberty. It is the graveyard into which a common country has gathered the unconscious deeds of those who died that the thing might live which we love and call our country. . . .

Last of the General-Presidents, he expressed their faith.

XI

Conclusion

———◆———

SHOULD ALLEGORICAL PAINTING again come into favor, one can imagine, under the title "Prejudice Yielding to Pride," a colorful representation of the events we have related. The conflict of the two elements in popular fancy was least obtrusive in the post-Civil War elections. Better than four million Americans had borne arms, and until glory faded there was a good following for the commanders who strode the path from military to civil leadership. Yet even in this interval the proud figures of warrior politicians appear like the portraits of El Greco against a background stabbed with the sharp lights of bias. Men of the North railed at the "Confederate Brigadiers" who represented the South in Senate and House. Nowhere in the land was a soldier candidate immune from taunts of waving the bloody shirt unless his opponent had also served. Irrepressibly civilian in outlook, America was ready for taps to sound next following retreat.

It is obvious from the record that, in spite of our mislike of soldiers, no political presumptions and, still less, norms of political action can be based upon it. Nothing could be more unstable than the climate of voters' opinion, yet there have been astute political weathercocks who have assumed the army camp to be among the unlikely directions from which a storm might rise. When the erratic wind of circumstance has quartered on them, the puffs of public fancy have sometimes misled them into a course which proved they were right in the first place. How wrong the Whigs who thought they could win with Scott because they had won with Taylor; how deluded the Democrats who ran Hancock the Superb in false reliance on a public taste for generals. If there is anything proved by the campaigns in which soldiers figured, it is the absence of any factors of predictability common to them all.

But it is the business of the molders of party destiny to make forecasts, and every nomination is an exercise in the art of prophecy. Popular reaction is anticipated by selecting candidates with reference to prevailing tastes and prejudices. In the case of the presidency there must be some reckoning with the popular expectation that the man who aspires to this office should be distinguished by some outstanding excellence. It is not enough, as De Tocqueville suggested, that a candidate be put forward as the symbol and personification of party principle. Even the sound party voter nourishes a higher ideal than this of the presidential office. The intractable independent, upon whose judgment so many contests have turned, needs persuasion as well of personalities as of principle. There are no better exhibits on this than the campaign handbooks themselves.

To a greater or less extent every general who became President owed something to public anxiety that the place be filled by a personage. The election of Washington established the precedent. When the original design of a deliberate choice by the electoral college of an individual "pre-eminent for ability and virtue" was altered by the growth of political parties and party mechanisms, the tradition of distinction remained unbroken until well into the nineteenth century. Yet with the change in the process of nominating and electing a President, and the obvious corollary that a candidate could win only as a partisan, and as a partisan succeeded or failed in the presidential office, the tradition presently suffered impairment. The quest for ability being confined to workers in the party vineyard, the range of choice was narrowed. In the conflict of individual claims for recognition the plebeian doctrine of availability emerged supreme. In the normal course of events it is only after a decision in these terms has been reached that the necessity presents itself of establishing compliance with the tradition of pre-eminence. To this the vulpine energies of party managers have been bent. A Polk or a Pierce must be given the stature of Andrew Jackson; the achievements of his ancestors may exalt the person of Benjamin Harrison.

The artifices used to enhance the merits of presidential candidates are only a piece of the complex pattern of principle, persuasion, and promise that constitutes election tactics. But they are a crucial piece whenever personalities overshadow issues of policy. Moreover, these representations of quality cannot bear repetition without occasionally possessing real substance. Just as the people cannot forever be put off with unfulfilled promises, they cannot forever be made to believe the false encomium.

One may weary of thrusting greatness upon mediocrity and yet not properly bestir oneself for a remedy. Even if party discipline were no obstacle, the time for action is mistakenly believed to be upon election day; yet by then the party managers, those plausible leeches who minister to political ills, have prepared the quadrennial potion. The initiative can never wholly be wrested from them, but well-timed popular clamor has sometimes forced an otherwise unlikely choice. In revolt against party maneuverings the public voice has turned to military chieftains because they have possessed reputation and have given promise of ideals beyond mere party. The enthusiasm on these occasions may not have flared up with complete spontaneity, but unlike the artificial shouting for the "Businessman as Hero" or the "Engineer as Hero" (if one may spin out the classifications of Carlyle), acclaim of the general is for something achieved in which the citizens have had a share. By valor and sacrifice, by hardship and victory, the soldier may engage the patriot emotion as political career men can never do. In the face of enduring prejudice against the profession of arms the gage of virtue in civil office has been found in the belief that the general's service has been not for party but for country and thus for the people themselves.

That sentiments of this sort have from time to time been entertained is certain, but whether they would have possessed political potency without some direction is doubtful. When John C. Calhoun wrote Jackson in 1824, "Your country's fame and yours are one," he was merely voicing what a great many people felt. But when the theme was expanded in the nominating resolution of the Tennessee legislature, "The welfare of a country may be safely entrusted to the hands of him who has experienced every privation and encountered every danger to promote its safety, its honor and its glory," it is apparent that sagacious leaders were exploiting this feeling. Similarly, the exuberance over Taylor's Mexican successes that first found expression in public illuminations was adroitly sluiced into a party flume by meetings and resolutions. The Whigs had earlier succeeded in reviving faded laurels by the non-partisan appeal. For Harrison, whose deeds were nearly forgotten, *The Contrast*, a political pamphlet, argued: "General Harrison will be the President of the People instead of the mere agent of a party . . . because he is opposed to party violence and in favor of Union and harmony among the people." The fine showmanship that made the battles of Tippecanoe and the Thames the prodigies of only yesterday gave validity to the assurance of another pamphlet that "every act and event of General Harrison's life prove him to have been the faithful and self-sacrificing servant of his country."

In the case of General Grant, the lapse of three years after Appomattox had little weakened his hold upon popular imagination, and if there is small evidence of a spontaneous popular demand for his nomination, the Democrats were as anxious to claim him as the Republicans. Badeau tells us that Grant himself believed he was a people's candidate, and the campaign books certainly promoted him as such. Much was made of Grant's protest over Sheridan's removal, "This is a Republic where the Will of the People is the law of the land. I beg that their voice may be heard." This was the motto on the pamphlet *Speeches of General U. S. Grant*, a collection of the general's salty sayings. In another opus this dictum was used to bottom the assertion that "General Grant is not a prejudiced partisan nor versed in the crooked ways of politicians." *The Record* of the Union League announced solemnly: "His was not the nomination of a caucus or a convention but the choice of the loyal people."

In none of the elections where generals have been promoted as people's candidates has the popular vote furnished evidence of an appeal so overwhelming that party lines did more than bend. Nevertheless, the margin of victory, slight though it has often been, seems in some cases to be attributable to no other cause. This was certainly the case in the two Whig victories, and although Grant's majority is commonly attributed to the newly enfranchised vote in the South, one may properly wonder how well the Republican party would have done in certain northern states without the formidable sentiment evoked by Grant's prestige.

The interval between convention and election has always been fraught with peril. No matter how strong or widespread the popular enthusiasm may seem before and immediately following a nomination, this has been a difficult thing to sustain. Nor must it be forgotten how trenchantly the opposition, running a civilian candidate, has ever wielded the bayonet of prejudice, whether this be in the general terms of anti-militarism or the more specific insinuation of unfitness of professional soldiers. The vote-cutting power of such persuasion, reviving as it does the primordial American unease, has been effective and sometimes devastating.

Although the arguments leveled at soldier candidates have frequently been mere rabble-rousing devices like the coffin handbills, they have also purported to appeal to the intelligence. In this form they have either fastened upon some vulnerable episode in the general's career, like the polemics of Scott or Hancock's administration of New Orleans, to impeach the individual's capacity, or they have invoked the experience of mankind with the power complex of soldiers. The "military chieftain" argument is in essence an appeal to prejudice, but it has the appearance of an appeal to reason, for it has consistently been cast in terms of principle. The proposition that liberty is endangered if civil government be entrusted to a military leader has the very flavor of a maxim, a conclusion of reason so sure as to be incontrovertible. When it has seemed desirable to point up this principle of politics by dire example, it was not our own General-Presidents who were the object lessons, but the ever terrible figures of Caesar, Cromwell, and Napoleon.

It has not been the relatively innocuous records of the generals in the presidency that has spared them from being coupled with the bad precedents when the issue of voting for another soldier has come up anew. Long before the professors undertook to teach politicians how to suck eggs, the art of perverting history for party ends had been developed and might have been usefully employed to implement the argument against military chieftains. The reason American experience has not been harped upon has been due to circumstance. Every major American party has raised an estoppel because every one of them has dallied with military heroes. Furthermore, when general has been running against general, the argument itself has been taboo, or has taken the form of disparaging the professional at the expense of the citizen soldier. As a consequence, the voter curious to find evidence of Caesarism in the administrations of ex-generals must draft his own bill of particulars.

The materials for such a bill have been set forth in the preceding pages, and it remains only to direct our attention briefly to the two phases of presidential activity which relate immediately to the chief ingredients of national prejudice—the fear of a large army and the suspicion that, given an army, a soldier will want to use it.

The policy with regard to our military establishment pursued by the General-Presidents has been remarkably conservative. The recommendations of Washington for the standing army were modest, not only because he shared the anxieties of his countrymen but because he cherished the plan of a well-regulated militia posited upon the duty of universal service, trained sufficiently for defense but not with an intensity to give rise to a militaristic spirit. It is true that there was opposition to both branches of the scheme, and Senator Maclay saw the Regular Army as a first step toward a sinister goal. He charged that the militia bill was sacrificed to assure the passage of the army bill, but as he also conceived that the Indian uprising in Ohio was a war precipitated by the Administration without the necessary declaration by Congress, his comments may be discounted as the jaundiced views of a partisan. The fact that subsequently Washington appears to have refrained from pressure to secure enactment of the militia plan in the form desired by himself and his advisers and that the eventual law, although quite inadequate, received his signature, is the best evidence of the temperance of his military policy.

The fire-breathing Jackson announced his opposition to standing armies in his inaugural and reiterated his sentiments in two separate annual messages. He requested legislation for the regulation of the militia, and, another time, for a strengthening of the corps of engineers because of the peacetime activities of this body. The only significant permanent addition to the Army during his administration was an authorization for a regiment of dragoons. Years later Zachary Taylor, faced with the problems of policing a vast territorial acquisition, recommended "an increase of our Army at our distant Western posts." Congressional response consisted of a statute permitting an extension of the period of enlistment to five years and sanctioning the recruiting of each existing company up to a maximum of seventy-four men, a possible total numerical increase of less than forty-five hundred.

Franklin Pierce, with modest reference to his own martial experience, imitated Jackson's inaugural declaration against standing armies. Nevertheless he saw fit in his first annual message to request an expansion and was the one General-President who received a substantial increase. The Congress added four regiments, two of infantry and two of cavalry, raising the total authorized strength to a little over 17,500 men. The actual strength was considerably less. And it may be observed that there persisted a difference between the troops authorized and the number for which appropriations were available.

During the presidencies of the four Civil War generals the Congress chanted an incessant *Nunc Dimittis,* and the Army still refers to these years as its dark ages. Grant's messages disclose his active interest in the internal administration of the

Army, but he did not press for an expansion. Hayes, who was compelled to call an extra session of Congress in 1877 because no appropriations for military service had been made, subsequently requested a slight increase and recommended that something be done about the militia. Harrison's interest was mainly in the Navy, and the extension of coastal defense works was the only phase of army activity that particularly engaged his attention. When it is recalled that throughout this period the Army was almost constantly involved in suppressing Indian troubles—in other words, that a limited war was being waged —the forbearance of the soldier-Presidents is remarkable. True, this was the era of congressional predominance; nevertheless, if the taint of Caesarism had existed, the executive could have exerted pressures which in other matters were sometimes not spared.

Although in our system of government the President can indulge his fancies with respect to the size of the military establishment only if he is blessed with a most complaisant Congress, his prerogatives with respect to military enterprise are less hampered. In the early days of the Republic, as we have seen, a chief concern of the liberal-minded was the reckless use of the Army to abridge the people's liberties, an anxiety latterly experienced by labor groups. The domestic disturbance suggests itself as the most obvious temptation to the military mind, and yet the roster of such occasions upon which Federal troops have been employed discloses the honors to be evenly divided between civilian and soldier executives. Even Mr. Jefferson, who inveighed against the military suppression of the Whisky Rebellion as a deed done to "strengthen the government," himself did not forbear to use troops to enforce the Embargo Act.

What the Cassandras of these early years did not clearly envisage were the hazards involved in the connection between the President's authority over the armed forces and his powers in the field of foreign relations. No student of foreign affairs can be unaware of the potentialities of our constitutional setup which has committed to the executive the management of diplomatic relations, safeguarded only by the Senate's authority in treaty-making and the Congress' power over the purse and over declarations of war. In the magisterial words of Mr. Justice Sutherland, "In this vast external realm with its important complicated and manifold problems the President alone has the power to speak or listen as a representative of the nation." Equally, the student cannot be impervious to the fact that by usage the so-called executive agreement has emasculated the limitations upon the treaty-making power, and the fact that negotiations can be manipulated to the point where the declaration of war may be a mere ceremony. If there be any doubts that the President's functions as commander in chief are not a precious adjunct, that the Army and Navy may be counters to expedite the play at the green table, let not the invasion of Florida be forgotten, nor the sagacious disposition of Taylor's army in 1846, nor the ships at Vera Cruz in 1914. The conduct of our foreign relations during the presidencies of former generals seems, in consequence, the most crucial test of the dangers of the military mind in civil office, and this is why so much attention has been devoted to the subject in this study.

However one may choose to divide the credit between a President and his Secretary of State for the good achieved or the perils avoided in the conduct of foreign relations, there is no doubt that the responsibility is the President's and is entered by the people in his political ledger. The fact that the message to the Congress or to the Senate has been the medium whereby the intentions, the explanations, or the accomplishments of the Administration are announced, fixes this responsibility for the purpose of domestic politics. At the same time this practice possesses also a function in foreign affairs, since the message has the power of giving a particular color to a negotiation or to the general state of a relationship with another country. Here the President, irrespective of who may have assisted in composing his speech, stands alone; the public interpretation and summation of the flat and artful language of diplomatic interchange is his.

The means at a President's command being what they are,

the manner in which these have been employed in foreign relations is no less significant than the concrete results. With the generals, since they once lived by the sword, one turns immediately to the record of their use of armed forces as an incident of negotiation. The show of force and actual landings or intrusions upon foreign soil to protect American interests are scattered episodes during the first century of Federal union. Many of these occurrences were the result of decisions made on the spot by a naval or military officer, but the necessity of ultimate sanction or disavowal has rested upon the President. A count of these various affairs discloses that they were not more frequent during the incumbency of a soldier than a civilian, and that the ex-generals were not especially prone to ratify the acts of subordinates. Jackson, for example, approved the violent dispersion of an Argentine colony on the Falklands by the U.S.S. *Lexington,* but despite his own earlier contempt for borders, refused to sanction the march of General Gaines into Texas.

All of the former generals were imbued with a strong feeling of nationalism, to which no doubt their military service contributed. This affected as well their posture in particular negotiations as their broader designs of policy. As to the former, the sobriety displayed at all critical junctures must have astonished contemporaries plagued with doubts about the risks of committing diplomacy to military commanders. Even Pierce, the brummagem brigadier who conformed least to type, for all his stirring about, avoided the violent path toward which the Ostend Manifesto beckoned. It was unusual for any of these soldiers to indulge in truculent pronouncements with reference to delicate issues under negotiation. Jackson's harsh message on the French spoliation claims and Benjamin Harrison's on the murder of American seamen at Valparaiso were uncharacteristic of the whole of their diplomacy, yet these messages were scarcely more intemperate than Jefferson's repeated denunciation of depredations upon our commerce, Tyler's references to Mexico, or Polk's discussion of the Oregon question. There was a lot of spirited Americanism in nineteenth-century presidential addresses, but it carried no general beyond the limits of prudence. It was not the generals who moved us into our wars, and there is no better testimony of their conciliatory spirit than the four pacificatory landmarks in our relations with Britain—the Jay Treaty, the settlement of the West Indies trade controversy by Jackson, the Clayton-Bulwer Treaty, and the Treaty of Washington by which the claims arising out of the Civil War were submitted to arbitration. If like the Caesars the generals dreamed of empire, in their lack of aggressiveness they could say with Scipio Africanus, "My mother bore me a general, not a warrior."

With so long a tradition of electing soldiers to the presidency, it would be marvelous, indeed, if this should not again occur. The changes in modern warfare have moved commanding generals out of the Olympian retreats where in the last great conflict they were free to plan and contrive, aloof from the human contact with their men that is the first condition of hero worship. If mystical bonds such as attached the soldiers to Washington, to Jackson, and to Grant should again be welded, the political sequel may be similar. There will be those who will still believe that if a man has burned powder he must forever smell of brimstone. But the remembrance of valor will be with us once more; once more Americans may cast their prejudices to the winds and, heeding the Biblical word, apply their hearts to know wisdom, and to see the business that is done upon the earth.